How to Win the Job You Really Want

JANICE WEINBERG

How to Win the Job You Really Want

An Owl Book

HENRY HOLT AND COMPANY

NEW YORK

Copyright © 1989 by Janice Weinberg
All rights reserved, including the right to reproduce
this book or portions thereof in any form.
Published by Henry Holt and Company, Inc.,
115 West 18th Street, New York, New York 10011.
Published in Canada by Fitzhenry & Whiteside Limited,
195 Allstate Parkway, Markham, Ontario L3R 4T8.

Library of Congress Cataloging-in-Publication Data
Weinberg, Janice.
How to win the job you really want.
"An Owl Book."
Bibliography: p.
Includes index.
1. Job hunting. 2. Career development.
3. Vocational guidance. I. Title.
HF5382.7.W435   1988   650.1'4   88-12805
ISBN 0-8050-0587-0 (pbk.)

Henry Holt books are available at special discounts for
bulk purchases for sales promotions, premiums, fund-raising,
or educational use. Special editions or book excerpts can
also be created to specification.

For details contact:

Special Sales Director
Henry Holt and Company, Inc.
115 West 18th Street
New York, New York 10011

First Edition

Printed in the United States of America
1 3 5 7 9 10 8 6 4 2

Contents

Acknowledgments

The following people offered generous advice and encouragement during the writing of the book: Sarah Burns, Dorothy Cotton, Geri Coughlin, Tom Litwack, Robert Ritchie, Henry Shove, Lawrence Walker, Arthur Wallace, and my father, Joseph Weinberg.

I also wish to express my appreciation to the following individuals who provided me with valuable information:

Marge Baxter, Senior Research Associate for Handy Associates
Jeff Blumenfeld, President of Blumenfeld & Associates, Inc.
Jerry Buegler, Staffing Manager for 3M Corporation
William Byrnes, President of TeleSearch, Inc.
David Cheifetz, President of Conference Management Corporation
Sean Hallinan, Vice President of College Relations for Spencer Sports Media, Inc.
Sara Johnson, Language and Speech Pathologist, CCC
Lorna Joselson, Employee Relations Manager—Retail Packaging Division, Champion International Corporation
Howard Lehrman, Executive Recruiter
Maurine Pyle, Administrator, Certification Reciprocity Consortium/ Alcohol and Other Drugs of Abuse
John Trost, President of Trost Associates
George "Bud" Wassell, CEAP, EAP Director for Meriden-Wallingford Hospital.

Preface

This is a big book and you may be wondering whether the time you'll invest in reading it will be worth it. I assure you that it will.

My knowledge of the work world is not founded solely on theory and book learning, like that of many career consultants, but also on my own well-rounded and successful fourteen-year corporate career. During that time I held positions in programming and information systems, sales, marketing, and strategic planning while employed by IBM, General Electric, and other companies. I also consulted to many *Fortune* 500 and smaller firms representing a cross-section of American business, and, as an adjunct faculty member of General Electric's Management Development Institute (Crotonville), taught management practices.

In 1979, equipped with this practical experience, I founded Career Solutions of Westport, Connecticut, a company providing personalized career planning and job-search assistance to individuals, as well as outplacement services to corporations. Since then I have helped thousands of men and women develop individualized job-search and career-change plans, enabling them to achieve their goals primarily through their own efforts.

In my successful method—followed closely in this book—

- I provide career changers with a clear understanding of the work world and its substructures so that they can select those career options consistent with their interests and abilities;
- I teach my clients to put themselves in the employer's shoes, so that they can develop a strategy that addresses the perspective of those who have the authority to hire for the positions they want;
- I provide step-by-step guidance in the management of a job campaign, along with clear explanations of the logic behind the advice; and
- I give my clients valuable information and novel ideas they can use to favorably distinguish themselves from other job hunters.

The process of selecting a career book should be as discriminating as that of selecting a career consultant for yourself, since that is essentially what the author will be. And, whether you are an executive forced out by a merger or a recent graduate disenchanted with your career choice, you'll be rewarded amply for choosing my book. Turn to the road map on page 3 and see why.

Janice Weinberg
Westport, Connecticut
October 29, 1988

How to
Win the Job
You Really
Want

1

Road Map to
Your Career Strategy

A CAREER STRATEGY—
WHAT IT IS AND WHY YOU NEED ONE

Not since the industrial revolution have changes as disruptive as the ones we are seeing today occurred in the workplace. The introduction of the computer has both eliminated many jobs and created new ones. The shifting of our economy from a manufacturing to a services orientation has similarly made many jobs obsolete while creating major new industries. The dramatic employment gains made by women and minorities have resulted in greater competition for professional positions. The cost competition from Japan and other countries has resulted in a constant fear of recession on the part of business today, reflected in numerous mergers—and in companies operating with much leaner staffs than was common twenty and more years ago. And the emphasis on personal growth and fulfillment has made many people come to the conclusion that "there's got to be a better way to make a living."

Thus, to say that skillful career-changing and job-hunting techniques have become extremely important is an understatement. I find it lamentable—and puzzling—that, while as students we spend many years studying material we will apply *on* the job, we spend relatively little time learning the *process* by which we will gain the opportunity to apply these skills. Yet wisely selecting our careers and searching—and negotiating—for our jobs can make the difference between a lifetime of happiness and a life sentence of misery.

In a society characterized by keen competition for limited employment opportunities, those who will succeed are those who control their career selection and job-hunting activities, as opposed to being manipulated by external factors. And the best way for you to exercise control over your situation is to develop a formal, detailed career strategy consisting of

1

- identification of your near- and long-term career goals;
- formulation of a plan by which these goals can be attained, and knowing how to implement it;
- acquisition of specialized education and work experiences required to enter and/or advance in your chosen field; and
- development of the skills and tools for getting and succeeding in your jobs—for example, writing and public-speaking skills, job-hunting documentation (résumé, cover letter)—so that you can implement your career strategy successfully.

Having a formal, detailed strategy offers these advantages:

- It forces you to *think today* about your expectations for the future. Thinking in advance about possible future outcomes enhances the probability that you can influence events, since you can foresee possible negative outcomes and develop contingency plans to prevent them from occurring.
- Establishing a strategy with a plan of implementation provides you with a *benchmark* against which to compare your results. If your plan calls for advancement to the next higher step in your career path within two years after you assume a new job and it doesn't happen on schedule, you'll be motivated to explore the reasons for the delay and implement timely corrective action.
- With a career strategy, it's much less likely that you'll procrastinate.
- Having a career strategy means that you're *taking charge*—that your actions will be deliberate, rather than being reactions to external factors—and, if you succeed, you'll get more satisfaction, since *you* accomplished it.
- And most important: you'll be able to *compete* more successfully in a job market characterized by limited employment opportunities.

All job hunters should keep this fact in mind: *there is always a place for those who can convince an employer that they can contribute to the organization's productivity and profitability.* I know of many companies that, in the midst of layoff campaigns, have hired new employees who convinced the management of their usefulness. For this reason you will find a very strong emphasis in this book on how to convince an employer of your value.

EVALUATE YOUR PRESENT ABILITY TO SUCCEED IN YOUR CAREER PROJECT

Give yourself a rating from one to ten (with ten equaling the highest confidence level) on each question below:

1. (For career changers only) How confident am I that I can find a rewarding new career that draws upon skills I already possess? _____

2. How able am I today to conduct a search for prospective employers solely through my own efforts, using advertisements minimally or not at all? _____

3. How would I evaluate my ability to prepare a résumé and cover letter that will make me a highly attractive candidate to prospective employers? _____

4. How capable am I of negotiating interview appointments over the telephone with some executives I will be contacting during my job hunt?
_____

5. How confident am I of my ability to convince a prospective employer during an interview that I am a strong candidate for the position in question? _____

6. How prepared am I to write a thank-you letter after an interview that will enhance my impact on a prospective employer? _____

7. How confident am I about my ability to negotiate a higher salary than the one offered? _____

8. How able am I to make the wisest decision when choosing from one or more offers (or to evaluate an offer against my current position)?
_____

ROAD MAP TO THIS BOOK

Like most authors, I secretly hope that you will read my book from cover to cover. However, I realize that, for efficiency's sake, you might want to tailor the book to your particular situation, so I have prepared the table that follows. Find those items in the left column that apply to your situation and find appropriate page references in the right column.

If Your Problem Is:	*To Find the Solution Read:*
You need guidance in writing a great *résumé* and *cover letter*.	⟶ pages 97–153
You seek a career in the business world but *lack* a clear *understanding* of how a business organization functions.	⟶ pages 208–213
You want to be sure that you are well prepared for any job *interview*.	⟶ pages 165–189
You know that making *phone calls* to prospective employers is *better* than conducting mail campaigns, but you do not feel confident about your ability in that area.	⟶ pages 159–164

You have been making *phone* calls to try to get *interview* appointments, but you can never get past the secretary. $\longrightarrow$ page 158

You have identified one or two *industries* as offering excellent job opportunities, but you are at a loss as to how to *find* specific companies in these industries. $\longrightarrow$ pages 82–87

You have gotten a dismal response to your *letter-writing* campaign to obtain a *new job*, and you wonder why—and what you can do about it. $\longrightarrow$ pages 154–164

You are seeking a *more gratifying* career and *need direction* as to which *field* would be *best* for you. $\longrightarrow$ pages 6–71

You have been *fired* from your current job and would like to find a better position in another organization. $\longrightarrow$ pages 259–262

You are satisfied with the kind of work you do, but feel you are in a *dead end* in your *current* place of employment. $\longrightarrow$ pages 72–96

You do not know what a *career strategy* is or why it's *important*. $\longrightarrow$ pages 1–2

You are looking for a job during an economic *recession*. $\longrightarrow$ pages 257–259

You are *new to the professional workplace* and are uncertain as to how to *identify* optimum career *options* and conduct a successful *job-hunting* campaign. $\longrightarrow$ the whole book

You would like guidance in *screening* firms that provide *career planning* and *job-hunting* services. $\longrightarrow$ pages 73–76

You are *not a college graduate* and wonder how to deal with this in an *interview*. $\longrightarrow$ page 174

You would like to *negotiate* a better *salary* than that included in a job offer. $\longrightarrow$ pages 195–197

You already have one or more *job offers* and need guidance as to whether to *accept* one or to stay in your present job. —————→ pages 197–200

You are a member of a *special group*; specifically,
* you are over 50; —————→ pages 273–275

* you are a woman; and/or —————→ pages 266–269
* you are a member of a minority group. —————→ pages 269–273

You are in a special situation; specifically,
* you need advice on improving your physical appearance; —————→ pages 251–254
* you would like to improve your speech; —————→ pages 249–251
* you believe you have been discriminated against with respect to employment; and/or —————→ pages 254–257
* you are a teacher, social worker, or counselor seeking a career change. —————→ pages 262–265

You are *new* to the *business* world and would like to know more about how it *functions*. —————→ pages 205–217

Now turn to the proper page to get started on the road to more fulfilling work.

2

For Career Changers: Find a Better Way to Make a Living

WHY ARE PEOPLE UNHAPPY IN THEIR CAREERS?

If you are not satisfied with your present work, you have a lot of company. And if you were to poll a hundred people who do enjoy their work, a fairly large percentage of them would probably tell you that they started in another career. Let's explore the reasons why so many people change careers at least once in their lives.

Through word of mouth and through the media the public has come to regard certain kinds of work as having qualities that contrast with the realities of working in these fields. Lawyers in television programs seem to behave more like detectives than lawyers. And isn't it strange that you never see a lawyer on television filling out a time sheet logging his hours for clients, or laboriously poring over a contract for errors? Television programs that glamorize the field of medicine project an image of the life-and-death decision-making power of the physician, and his or her deep emotional involvement in the patient's case. While these may be valid aspects of the physician's job, so, too, are being awakened in the middle of the night with a patient's problem, filling out voluminous insurance reports, and dealing with an increasing number of malpractice suits.

Many people who choose a field based on a romanticized notion of the work soon come to the conclusion that the reality is unacceptable to them. In addition to romanticization, several other factors influence people to undertake particular careers. For example:

- A friend or relative was involved in the career and suggested it. Since we are impressionable during the years when we begin to think about our vocational choices, we tend to rely on the opinions of adults. Thus, a father who is very happy as an accountant will communicate his enthusiasm for his profession to his child, and the child will mistakenly assume that his or her involvement in the same kind of work will necessarily bring similar satisfaction. It may, of course, but the enthusiasm of others for their work should not be a reason for choosing yours, since you are a different person and, therefore, may have very different needs.

• The particular vocation requires a skill in which the individual excels, and so he chooses that field assuming that he will be successful in it, frequently finding that there are other aspects of it that are unpleasant. Examples of this type of situation include: a teacher who enjoyed presenting ideas to students and motivating them to learn, yet resented having to discipline unruly class members, and an actor who became one because of his love of performing, but for whom the unpredictability of finding work became too nerve-racking.

The practical aspects of work are either unknown or largely ignored when we embark on a career. What seems to attract most people to their careers is the amount of compensation they can earn and their ability to perform the work. What I call the "fine print of careers"—analogous to the fine print in a contract that's often glossed over—is extremely important to study, for it can hold significant implications for one's decision to pursue a specific career . . . as you probably know from personal experience.

In many instances a career choice made ten or fifteen years ago was the best decision at the time. In these situations, here are the most common reasons for which people seek a change:

• The person changed and so did his or her needs. The mere act of living creates changes in our lives, with a consequent change in our needs. Also, as we develop as individuals we may gain more self-esteem and acquire the confidence to embark on a more challenging career.
• The work became boring. Repetition, by its very nature, produces boredom. The length of time it takes for someone's work to become dull and unstimulating will vary from person to person, but the fact is that very few careers offer the degree of variety needed to hold one's attention over the span of a lifetime.
• Some fundamental changes in the profession occurred, either in the process or the environment, that made it less appealing (e.g., new technologies, or more competition).

If the choice of your present career was the wrong decision at the time you embarked upon it, the likelihood is that you will avoid repeating that mistake because you will be making your decision based on a more mature approach, augmented by the methods explained step by step in this book. And since your new career will be more suited to your abilities and personality, the chances are that you will be more successful in it than you were in the field you are leaving.

WHY WOULD ANYONE WANT ME, A CAREER CHANGER?

One of the problems people face in making the decision to change careers is their belief that it will be an impossible task, that no executive in a new field will want them. After all, everybody knows that there is a lot of stiff competition for professional jobs—what chance would you have against people with M.B.A.s or other advanced degrees qualifying them for jobs in fields you might want to target? The reality of competition is a legitimate concern, but I would like to assure you that there are also valid reasons why an employer would be receptive to hiring you:

• People with advanced degrees gravitate to certain types of organizations. You could focus your efforts on other types of organizations that offer opportunities in the same line of work. For example, most people with M.B.A.s in marketing would prefer to work within a large corporate environment, since their sights are usually set on product-management or general-management careers. Thus, if you seek a market research job, you are likely to find the competition for this type of position—which can be a stepping-stone to product management—very keen in an end-user company (for an explanation of "end user," refer to page 215). On the other hand, getting a job in a market research consulting firm might be easier for you.

• The person you approach may be a career changer. If so, he or she will probably be very empathic toward your situation.

• Highly intelligent, secure people appreciate the transferability of skills. The fact that you demonstrate intelligence in your conversation with a prospective employer, that you speak in a well-educated tone, that you describe your current work in a manner that communicates that you have performed at a high level—all of these will help convince him or her that you can do the job.

• Almost every organization has some employees who perform poorly. If you approach an executive at a time when he or she has a problem employee, you may get the opportunity merely because you appeared at the right moment.

While I know you can achieve your goal of making a successful change, I also don't want to convey to you an unrealistic expectation of the process of making that change. When you approach people in your targeted field, some of them are going to make you feel that you have no right to expect that you can make the transition. Others will be receptive. Those who fall into the former category are mostly insecure people who, in order to maintain a sense of self-importance, must emphasize the gap between themselves and you. To justify all the years they spent getting to their present level, they may ascribe much more importance to extensive experience than the situation really requires. You must realize that since many people in this world are insecure— and since you'll be meeting a representative sample of the population—you will always encounter some naysayers. Don't let them deter you! You're taking a tremendous step. If you didn't have some self-doubt, you wouldn't be human. However, if you follow my advice you will be building yourself an arsenal of career and job-hunting skills and tools that will enable you to make this important transition within a reasonable period of time . . . and with the financial rewards you are seeking as the trophy.

As the person for whom the outcome of this important endeavor means the most, you can accept the opinions of others to whatever extent you wish, but bear in mind that the results are largely up to *you*. Most outcomes in life are self-fulfilling prophecies, i.e., if you believe that there will be a certain outcome to an event you will behave in a way that contributes to that result. While it's true that people in your targeted profession may know more about the requirements of the field than you do, the fact is that an individual's *preparation* and *perseverance* are usually the deciding factors for achieving success in a new field. I am not saying that you should ignore the opinions of those you consult, but if you truly believe that you can contribute to the field you are targeting, then concentrate all your energy on attaining your goal and *you will achieve it*.

Most people will judge you by the way you value yourself. Act as though you are worthless and people will surely treat you that way. Act timidly and people will think of you as timid. Therefore, it's in your best interest to display poise and self-assurance, to project the impression that you have the utmost confidence in your ability to do an outstanding job in your chosen field. It may be an act, but once you carry it off, people will regard you as a self-assured person; they will want to get to know you better and develop their relationship with you. In addition, the most wonderful consequence of this whole effort is that *because* people will be treating you as a confident, valuable person, you will actually begin to feel that way. Or, in other words, *you will not have to act anymore*.

Exhibiting an air of confidence is critical when changing careers, since, if you're not coming across as confident about your ability to perform in a new career, how can you expect the employer to feel confident in hiring you? Between you and me, of course you may feel unsure about your abilities, but the Catch-22 is that unless you pretend that you have the confidence, you won't get the opportunity you need to gain the experience and the resulting confidence in the new field.

COMMON MISCONCEPTIONS ABOUT
THE WORK WORLD

A number of my clients have mistaken beliefs about various aspects of careers and job hunting.

Avoid Glutted Fields?

We've both seen a lot of publicity about certain fields having too many practitioners in them—for example, teaching, the law, even the computer field. The interesting thing about gluts is that, because everybody hears about them, a lot of people are deterred from entering the glutted field, thinking they will have a tough time getting a job. As a consequence, within anywhere from three to six years later, we learn that there are not enough people in the field to satisfy the demand.

Such a situation happened during the recession in the early 1970s when a lot of engineers lost their jobs. Young people who might have aspired to an engineering career heard of their relatives and parents' friends losing engineering jobs and changed their vocational goals to fields that promised greater security. Because a lot of students were discouraged from studying engineering, this country had a shortage of engineers a few years later, resulting in new graduates getting very high salary offers for entry-level jobs.

The implication of all this? Don't be deterred from pursuing a particular career by talk of a glut in the field. Instead, research those specialties within it that hold promise for the future.

People in Business Are Smarter Than You Are?

This misconception is usually verbalized by people in the not-for-profit sector who are interested in business careers but have strong doubts about their ability to perform the required work. The fact is that people in business organizations make many mistakes, most of which do not receive publicity. Remember Coca-Cola Company's attempt to replace its long-standing Coca-Cola formula with what it believed was one with a more appealing taste? It failed miserably, despite extensive market research that indicated that it would be very successful against Coca-Cola's chief competitor, Pepsi.

There are many other examples of products and services that were commercial failures, and it's important for you to realize that everybody makes mistakes. Don't be intimidated by what you perceive as a higher level of intelligence on the part of business people. On the other hand, those who do make mistakes should not be scorned. The only way to avoid mistakes is not to take risks . . . which means that no progress would ever be made.

Management Is a Specific Job?

When I ask clients without business experience who seek careers in business if there are any jobs they would like to discuss, I frequently hear them say *only* that they think they'd like to be in "management," as though management is a specific type of work—like computer programming, teaching, and accounting. In fact, at the highest levels in organizations, there are individuals often called executives—rather than managers—directing managers who supervise functional areas. At those high levels, management as a specific function does exist. However, most people cannot avoid selecting a specific functional area at the outset of their careers, such as engineering, sales, or purchasing. They must become specialists in their chosen area first before being considered for a first-level managerial position.

Furthermore, while being a manager may be a desirable objective, there are many extremely well-paid nonmanagerial contributors at considerably higher levels than a first-level manager. This is especially true in high-technology organizations where a premium is placed on technical capabilities, and where compensation plans are developed to reward technical experts sufficiently so that they are not tempted to become managers for the money only. In many of these instances, technical experts are given the title "Manager" for prestige, although they do not have supervisory responsibilities.

THE STEPS IN CHANGING ONE'S CAREER

Four steps are necessary to accomplish a successful career change:

- You must know your talents and shortcomings, and understand which fields are compatible with your abilities and interests.
- You must formulate other criteria, beyond compatibility with your strengths and interests, to use in evaluating career options.
- You must evaluate the relative attractiveness of one or more new career options and your present work, and make a decision.
- If the decision is made to change, you will need a plan of implementation.

The last three steps will be relatively simple to complete and we will get to them in time. But now your efforts should be concentrated in accomplishing the first step: knowing your capabilities and finding work environments consistent with them.

Step One: Find Fields That
Draw Upon Your Capabilities and Interests

It should be simple for us to know ourselves, but the fact is that from the time we are children our self-assessments are constantly shaped by the authority figures in our lives. Our parents tell us we would be good at something, and the something may be a kind of work that they would like us to do (sometimes because they do it). A teacher may tell us we are not good at something, when in fact we may be very good at it but the teacher may be too busy or unqualified to recognize it.

If we're lucky, by the time we reach adulthood we're able to be objective about ourselves and our capabilities, without being affected by the opinions of those around us. And this has been borne out in my experience working with many adult clients. I have found that most people have a very good idea of their capabilities—they know whether they're good in math or writing, if they are at ease working with a lot of people or prefer solo work, if they work well under pressure or require a more relaxed work environment. For these people the "know thyself" requirement of the career-selection process is satisfied, and they're ready to move on to gathering information about the requirements of the many careers available.

Using Your Interests to Identify Career Options

I always ask my clients who are seeking new careers to describe their interests, since these frequently provide me with insight into the kind of work they'd enjoy. My experience working with large numbers of career changers has made me aware that people who have certain interests are often well-suited to particular kinds of work. The left-hand column that follows contains a list of interests, some of which you may be involved in. Adjacent to each interest are one or more vocations that draw upon the abilities suggested by these interests. I discuss the italicized fields in this chapter. Most of the other fields are described in the *Occupational Outlook Handbook* (see page 64). The remaining fields can be researched by locating associations serving practitioners in them in the *Encyclopedia of Associations* (see Appendix, page 278).

Fine arts and design	Interior designer; graphic designer
Designing and building things	Industrial designer; architect
Creative writing	*Advertising/sales promotion specialist*; *copywriter*; TV scriptwriter
Expository writing	*Public relations writer*; journalist; *technical writer*
Cryptograms; logical puzzles; chess	*Computer programmer*; *systems analyst*
Finance	Financial planner; financial analyst; credit analyst; commercial lending officer; *property manager*

Psychology; sociology	Psychologist; *market researcher*
Organizing community activities	*Meetings planner*
Persuading people	*Salesperson*; fund-raiser
Teaching; coaching	Teacher/professor; *training and development specialist*
Sports	*Sports marketing account executive*

ANALYZING THE RANGE OF CAREER POSSIBILITIES ASSOCI-ATED WITH YOUR INTERESTS: One way to help determine what kind of work would satisfy you is to list activities that relate to your interests and identify jobs that involve them. For example, someone with a love of the *fine arts* could develop a list like this:

Activity	*Career Possibility*
Conducting research	For a magazine catering to the art field; for a museum; for an author writing a fine arts book
Appraising it	For an auction house or insurance company
Restoring it	As a self-employed art conservator, or on the staff of a museum
Producing it	As a painter or sculptor
Marketing/selling it	For a gallery, or as an artist's representative
Buying it	As a curator for a company with its own art collection, or for a museum
Writing about it	For a publisher of fine arts books; for a magazine or newspaper as a reviewer
Teaching it	As a college professor/instructor or a high school teacher

While you probably know what activities you would enjoy, you may not be familiar with the jobs that involve them. If so, you could refer to the *Encyclopedia of Associations* (see Appendix, page 278), using your general category as a starting point to find organizations that can provide information about job possibilities.

Vocational Testing as an Aid

If you are unsure of your abilities, vocational aptitude tests can help by identifying them and linking them with careers that draw upon them. Vocational interest tests measure the degree to which your interests are compatible with specific careers. Although there is often a strong positive correlation between aptitudes and interests, this is not always the case.

Many private and not-for-profit organizations offer aptitude and interest tests. A national organization, with branches in about fifteen cities, that offers extensive aptitude testing is the Johnson O'Connor Research Foundation. For information on their services and the location of the branch closest to you, contact: Johnson O'Connor Research Foundation, 11 East 62nd Street, New York, NY 10021, 212/838–0550.

A widely used self-administered interest test, "The Self-Directed Search," was designed by John L. Holland and can be found in his book *Making Vocational Choices: A Theory of Careers* (Prentice-Hall). Dr. Holland's theory, fully explained in the book, is that people are happiest and most successful in work environments compatible with their interests and values. He has analyzed the requirements of over 500 occupations and determined the degree to which they conform with six personality types: realistic, investigative, artistic, social, enterprising, and conventional. Based on your answers to "The Self-Directed Search" questions, a personality profile can be developed and appropriate careers suggested.

Using Professional Career Services

I believe that adults seeking new careers should do most of the work toward identifying these options on their own. The process of researching information is not unlike a scavenger hunt, i.e., a piece of information gained from reading one source will lead you to another, and so on, resulting in your finding options that you didn't know existed. Sometimes, however, it helps to have an objective outsider review your preliminary conclusions and provide continued direction.

For this reason you might benefit from working with a career-consulting professional. Try to get a referral to someone who has worked with a friend or relative. If you do, however, remember that, since your needs are probably different from the person who waxed ecstatic about a particular consultant, you may have a different reaction. But the referral source is still the best way to begin your search. If you cannot get one, find professionals through your local Yellow Pages under a heading beginning with either "Career" or "Vocational," and try to obtain references of former clients in situations similar to your own.

You'll probably find that every company offers something a little different. For example, some will offer extensive testing with little or no job-hunting guidance, and vice versa. Unfortunately, as in any field that does not require licensing, you may encounter consultants whose competence is limited. To help you determine which service is best for you, refer to page 73 in Chapter 3 for a checklist of qualifications to look for in a firm providing career services.

The "Best Bet" Fields for Career Changers

When working with someone seeking an alternative care
one question early in our discussion; namely: would you be able ￿
formal education in order to prepare for the new career we would cu￿
for you? Ninety-nine percent of my clients have responded that they could
not afford to go to school on a full-time basis, since they have families or
other financial obligations that preclude temporary loss of their income, let
alone their being able to afford full-time tuition costs. And in most of these
cases they have not wanted to go on for further schooling, although they
would not rule out part-time study while working in a new field if they felt
it would advance their careers.

The overwhelming need of people changing careers to find alternatives that
do not entail specialized education led me to develop the "Best Bets" list of
careers, since I sought options that drew upon *general* skills—communication,
negotiating, analytical/creative, and project-management ability—that everyone develops through the process of general schooling and through work in
many fields, as opposed to technical skills, which require specialized training.
If you look at the functions in a typical business organization (see page 208
in Chapter 8), you can immediately eliminate a number of areas that require
formal training and are therefore out of the immediate reach of a career
changer—engineering, manufacturing (one area within this function is an
exception), law, finance, accounting, and strategic (corporate) planning are
the primary ones.

What's left? Marketing, sales, human resources, public relations, and purchasing, which in a manufacturing company will usually be in the manufacturing department. And I will describe a number of positions within these
areas that offer good opportunities for career changers. If you are very familiar
with how a business organization functions, you already know what working
within these areas entails. But if you are new to the business world—or would
like a refresher course—it's important that you read Chapter 8 before you
proceed from here.

A FEW WORDS OF CAUTION: What follows is an analysis of the specific
applications of creative/analytical, communication, project management, and
negotiating skills in jobs within marketing, sales, human resources, public
relations, and purchasing. While my emphasis will be on these functions as
they operate within a business organization, bear in mind that public relations,
human resources, and purchasing departments exist in organizations within
the public and not-for-profit sectors as well. Many not-for-profit and private
hospitals are increasingly establishing formal marketing functions. And while
most not-for-profit organizations other than hospitals do not engage in marketing and sales in the same sense as do businesses, they do get involved
heavily in fund-raising and membership drives, for which they need people
with marketing and sales abilities.

There is no job I know of that doesn't entail some routine, boring aspects, and those described in the following pages are no exceptions. Therefore, although I have limited my discussion to the more complex tasks and activities, be prepared in any of these jobs to complete repetitious reports for management, collate material for reports/proposals when the secretary is unavailable, and make six phone calls to track down a small piece of information you need to do your job.

The positions described are for individual contributor jobs, i.e., those performed by someone with no one reporting to him or her. Managerial jobs in all these occupations entail, in addition, the hiring, training, and supervision of individual contributors. Establishing and administering budgets are important managerial responsibilities, as are negotiating resource commitments from other managers, and delivering presentations to upper management. Those who have had managerial experience in the fields they wish to leave may qualify for a managerial position as the first one in a new field, depending on the conceptual similarities between the two jobs. And to the extent that a career changer below the managerial level can convince an employer in a targeted field of the similarities between the desired job and one's former employment, he or she may be able to negotiate a job higher than entry-level.

You will note that I refer to "end user," and "supplier" in the following pages. For an explanation of these terms, see Chapter 8, page 215.

Salaries for any one position described on the following pages vary considerably depending on geographical location, industry, and company. Use all of the following sources to formulate a probable salary range for the position you target:

- newspaper advertisements in your locality for the position
- salary surveys, which are often conducted by professional associations and trade publications serving the field (these are listed under "Information Sources" in the section pertaining to the particular field)
- people who are employed in the field

MARKETING: The three marketing areas I will review are Product Management (also called "Product Planning" and "Brand Management"), Market Research (sometimes called "Marketing Research"), and Advertising and Sales Promotion. Following are the tasks of entry-level positions in each function, and job strategies and career paths associated with these positions.

PRODUCT MANAGEMENT: The entry-level position within the product-management function is that of product planner. Marketing consulting firms are sometimes hired by end users to assist in their product-planning activities, but obtaining such a position in a consulting firm usually requires an M.B.A.

in marketing and/or end-user marketing experience. The product-planning process is discussed in considerable detail in Chapter 9, starting on page 219.

Tasks of the Product Planner

Creative/Analytical	• Conceives of ideas for new products/services and for new features to existing ones • Analyzes costs associated with proposed new product programs to determine whether they are consistent with the company's requirements • Analyzes results of market research studies to determine if they point to favorable reception of products/services in the marketplace • Analyzes existing products/services for potential cost improvements and assesses their probable impact on sales • Analyzes sales trends of products or services offered by the company and its competitors • Analyzes causes of quality problems and works with technical personnel (e.g., engineering, manufacturing) to develop cost-effective solutions
Oral Communication	• Delivers presentations on proposed new product programs to management • Represents the Marketing Department at meetings reviewing the design and safety of engineered products • Represents the company at trade shows by explaining new products/services to buyers visiting the exhibit
Written Communication	• Prepares a document, typically 10–40 pages, proposing allocation of company funds to support new product programs • Writes a design guide, a document detailing specifications of a proposed new product or service • Writes copy for promotional materials associated with products or services, e.g., package copy, catalog copy • Writes/edits questionnaires used in market research studies

Negotiating	• Negotiates schedule and work commitments from engineering and manufacturing personnel to ensure the on-time production of new products • Negotiates support of headquarters sales personnel in getting feedback from customers regarding proposed new products/services and new features for existing ones • Negotiates support of market research and advertising/sales promotion personnel in establishing schedules and resource requirements
Project Management	• Leads teams of representatives from various company departments who cooperate to develop new products or services • Leads technical staff in developing solutions to quality or service problems

Job Strategies: Product management is a wonderful field, but it might require a little more perseverance to penetrate than those described on the following pages. The reason is that the M.B.A.s grab these jobs first, since they lead to top marketing management and general management positions. Someone who is interested in this field but who does not have an M.B.A. might consider a market research or advertising and sales promotion position in an end-user company, since these positions are stepping-stones to product management.

Individuals without marketing experience are sometimes able to get a product-planning job as a first marketing position. A skill valued by product managers in hiring for product-planning positions is the ability to manage projects under time-critical deadlines, with an emphasis on leading technical and nontechnical personnel to meet schedule and task objectives. Financial knowledge is also desirable since product planners must continually monitor the profitability of their product lines, as well as analyze the financial soundness of proposed new product programs. An electronics or mechanical/electrical engineering background would be a strong asset in obtaining a product-planning job in a company marketing products using these technologies.

Someone without a technical background who aims for a product-planning job should focus his or her efforts on low-technology consumer products manufacturers—for example, automotive aftermarket, health and beauty aids, stationery supplies, simple appliances—since these products do not require mastery of complex technical concepts associated with their use.

Career Path

Product Planner—Responsible for one or two product lines, e.g., all food processors and skillets for a manufacturer of household appliances; conceives of new products to add to lines and of new features for existing products; coordinates market research studies and prepares requests for funds to support new-product programs; establishes and monitors product-development schedule, working closely with representatives of various company departments

Associate (Assistant) Product Manager—Provides support to the Product Manager in the areas of budgeting, planning and implementing marketing programs

Product (Brand) Manager—In charge of a number of product lines logically grouped together; for example, in a diversified household appliance manufacturer there would be a product manager for all food preparation appliances, and one for all personal care appliances (hair dryers, manicure sets, etc.); also develops and administers departmental budgets; may have several product planners reporting to him or her

Vice President (Director) of Marketing—Oversees the product management, market research, and advertising and sales promotion functions; develops and administers marketing budgets; contributes to major policy decisions governing the operation of the business

MARKET RESEARCH: Detailed here are responsibilities of a Project Leader—sometimes called a "Study Manager" or "Project Director"—in a market research firm (usually referred to as a "supplier"). In some companies this is an entry-level professional position; in others, one would begin as an Assistant Project Leader. Some of the responsibilities listed below may also be part of a market research analyst's job in the end-user environment. A more extensive discussion of market research is presented in Chapter 9, beginning on page 223.

Tasks of the Market Research Project Leader

Creative/Analytical	• Analyzes objectives of market research studies to determine best methodologies, e.g., simulated sales test, focus group, one-on-one interviews
	• Estimates time and costs associated with each component of the proposed method, e.g., preparing questionnaire, training interviewers, conducting interviews, writing final report

- Analyzes and interprets data generated by market research studies; formulates recommendations regarding proceeding with or terminating product programs
- Develops novel market research methodologies

Oral Communication

- Delivers presentations on market research study results to client personnel
- Moderates focus groups
- Conducts private, in-depth interviews of consumers to obtain opinions on proposed new products or services

Written Communication

- Writes proposals detailing recommended research approach, schedules, and estimated costs for submittal to clients
- Writes questionnaires to be used in studies
- Writes instructions to guide interviewers in questioning study participants
- Writes reports on study findings

Negotiating

- Negotiates fees and schedules with client market research personnel
- Negotiates fees and schedules with survey companies and other suppliers of services

Project Management

- Monitors project schedules to ensure on-time completion of each activity
- Coordinates shipment of products and study materials to survey sites, working closely with client personnel

Job Strategies: The New York Chapter of the American Marketing Association publishes an annual directory of market research companies throughout the United States, categorizing them according to geographical region and type of research conducted; it also provides the names of company principals. Many public libraries have this directory. You can purchase it from the publisher (see Information Sources on page 25). Another approach is to research companies through your local telephone company's Yellow Pages, looking under "Market Research and Analysis" or a similar heading.

Project-management experience, writing ability, and mathematical and statistical knowledge are the most easily transferable skills to the market research function. In addition, some market research suppliers place a premium on a behavioral science background. Because suppliers use computers to analyze data and issue reports—with some developing sophisticated computer models—computer skills would provide a further advantage.

Career Path

The easiest way to break into this field is by gaining employment with a market research supplier, which provides services to end-user companies. Making a transition later to an end-user company is fairly easy, since the exposure one gets to clients through these positions often results in unsolicited offers.

In a supplier company:

Assistant Project Leader—Assists the Project Leader in all of his or her duties.

Project Leader (Project Director, Study Manager)—Has full responsibility for the successful implementation of client studies, including design of the study methodology; establishment of the schedule; determination of human resource requirements and costs; hiring, training, and supervision of free-lance interviewers and other personnel; preparation of proposal to get the contract for the project; preparation of final report; presentation of findings and recommendations to the client

Vice President or Partner—Plays an important role in planning the company's business direction, budgeting, soliciting new business, and hiring professional staff; usually receives a percentage of the firm's profits, in addition to a salary

Other career opportunities and lateral paths include:

In a supplier firm:

Field Director—Works with project leaders to outline logisitical requirements of studies; plans and coordinates surveys, e.g., researches, evaluates, and hires survey companies, traveling to them as necessary; trains telephone interviewers to question survey participants

In an end-user company:

Junior Market Research Analyst—Assists senior personnel on projects, e.g., questionnaire development, supplier interface, product-planner liaison

Research Analyst—Manages one or more projects, acting as interface between product-management personnel and suppliers; reviews proposals; develops questionnaires; coordinates final report and presentations

Senior Research Analyst—Performs all Research Analyst duties, and may also contribute to the design of novel study methodologies

Manager of Market Research—Supervises entire market research staff; develops and administers budgets; negotiates schedule and resource commitments with product managers; has final say on selecting market research suppliers; oversees the design of novel market research methodologies

ADVERTISING AND SALES PROMOTION: The best entry point into this field is as an advertising and sales promotion specialist in an end-user company. I will present the tasks of this position here; those with an (A) at the end are also performed within an advertising or sales promotion agency. However, in a large agency they're much more specialized—for example, a creative director will conceive of the creative approach; a copywriter will write the copy; a media planner will analyze the costs and benefits of various advertising media. If you would like a more detailed explanation of advertising and sales promotion, turn to page 225 in Chapter 9.

Tasks of the Advertising and Sales Promotion Specialist

Creative/Analytical	• Evaluates competitive advertising agencies' presentations aimed at "stealing" the company's advertising from its present agency
	• Analyzes costs and benefits associated with various media (e.g., TV, radio, print) in planning how to allocate the advertising budget (A)
	• Studies data pertaining to competitive advertising and market shares (A)
	• Studies data pertaining to demographic composition of markets where advertising is planned (A)
	• Analyzes costs associated with promotional programs, and develops budgets for these projects (A)
	• Conceives of advertising campaign concepts, radio/TV commercial ideas, graphic approaches (A)
	• Analyzes statistics pertaining to advertising campaign effectiveness (A)
	• Creates promotional programs using coupons, sweepstakes, gift-with-purchase, etc. (A)
	• Designs catalogs, trade show exhibits, point-of-purchase displays, etc. (A)
Oral Communication	• Delivers presentations to marketing personnel on recommendations for promotional strategies for new product/service introductions (A)

Written Communication	• Writes copy for brochures, coupons, contests, specification sheets (highlighting specific products and their features), etc. (A)
	• Writes proposals detailing advertising and sales promotion program strategies and costs (A)
Negotiating	• Negotiates prices and terms with free-lance photographers, graphic designers, typesetters, printers, exhibit houses, etc. (A)
	• Negotiates completion dates of advertising and sales promotion projects with product-management personnel
Project Management	• Plans and manages a large advertising campaign, with responsibility for budgeting, and for scheduling and hiring of outside contractors (A)
	• Monitors work performed by in-house and/or free-lance personnel on promotional programs to ensure timely, successful completion (A)
	• Plans and manages the company's participation in a trade show, e.g., establishes schedule for creative and production aspects; supervises on-site activities
	• Designs and implements creative presentations for national sales meetings, and for executives' meetings that may or may not be related to specific product programs

Job Strategies: Job security in an advertising or sales promotion agency is often unpredictable due to the highly competitive nature of the business, the occasional fickleness of consumers, and the fact that the loss of an account often means the loss of jobs for people associated with it. Furthermore, the inherent instability of the business has been aggravated in recent years by a spate of mergers, resulting in staff duplication, the loss of business through the acquisition of competing accounts, and consequent layoffs. Because of this, I recommend that individuals interested in this field focus on end-user companies—specifically, consumer products manufacturers with sales in the $75–$200 million range.

A skill frequently sought by executives in this field is the ability to manage projects involving the contributions of many people, since that's largely the kind of work this function performs. Experience in negotiating terms with outside contractors and in supervising their work is also an asset, since this type of job often entails dealing with free-lance artists, typographers, printers, etc. Copywriting or artistic ability might be useful, too, and applicants aspiring to these areas should be prepared to show writing or artwork samples to prospective employers who seek these skills. Once someone gained experience in an end-user company, it would be feasible to obtain a position within an agency, should that environment be appealing.

Career Path

In an end-user company:

Advertising and Sales Promotion Specialist—Assists manager in planning and coordinating ad campaigns, trade show exhibits, product catalogs, coupon programs; acts as liaison to advertising and sales promotion agencies in communicating product/service information and company objectives; interfaces with in-house creative and production personnel, as well as with typesetters, free-lance designers, audiovisual production houses, etc.

Advertising and Sales Promotion Manager—Manages one or more specialists, as well as (in a medium-to-large-size company) in-house creative director and staff (e.g., artists, photographers, writers); hires and negotiates terms with agencies providing creative services; provides direction to product-management personnel in formulating budgets for ad campaigns and promotional projects; develops and administers departmental budget

In an agency:

Junior Account Executive—Entry-level position; assists with administrative aspects of account; expedites creative and production work; acts as liaison to client in communicating advertising program status and changes

Account Executive—Contributes to the development of advertising program schedules, as well as coordinates and expedites agency activities to support each component of the program; acts as liaison to clients on scheduling, budgeting, creative and production aspects of projects

Account Supervisor—Supervises one or more account executives in devising and implementing clients' advertising programs; negotiates internal resources and scheduling commitments from agency's creative and production management; supervises overall development of advertising programs to ensure that objectives are met

Management Supervisor—Directs several groups of account personnel working for various clients, with responsibility for managing the relationship with the client; provides direction on advertising program strategies; assigns personnel to projects; develops and administers departmental budget

Other career opportunities and lateral paths in an agency:

Copywriter—Writes ads for TV, radio, and print ad campaigns

Media Planner—Evaluates costs/benefits of various media in terms of their potential for meeting ad campaign objectives

Media Buyer—Analyzes the costs/benefits of placing ads during alternative time periods (e.g., holiday, evening), and decides what size the ads should be; also negotiates fees and terms with media suppliers

Information Sources for Marketing

Journal of Marketing (quarterly), 250 South Wacker Drive, Chicago, IL 60606, 312/648–0536.

Journal of Marketing Research (quarterly), 250 South Wacker Drive, Chicago, IL 60606, 312/648–0536.

Ovid Riso, *Sales Promotion Handbook*. 7th ed. Chicago: The Dartnell Corporation, 1979. Contains sales promotion plans successfully used by companies. Provides guidance on how to get the most impact from promotional tools, e.g., displays, exhibits, contests. Advice is also given on dealing with new product introductions, upgrading sales territory performance, and budgeting.

William M. Weilbacher, *Advertising*. 2nd ed., New York: Macmillan Publishing Company, 1984. This book presents an overview of advertising, focusing on its definition, socioeconomic aspects, relation to marketing and to society, and the future of the industry.

Advertising Age (weekly), 740 N. Rush Street, Chicago, IL 60611, 312/649–5200.

Adweek/National Marketing Edition (weekly), 820 Second Avenue, New York, NY 10017, 212/661–8080.

Creative Black Book, Creative Black Book, Inc., 401 Park Avenue South, New York, NY 10016. This two-volume directory, published annually, provides the names and addresses of vendors/suppliers categorized by type of business, including advertising agencies, TV production and postproduction companies, and design, illustration, and creative services.

Standard Directory of Advertising Agencies, National Register Publishing Company, 3004 Glenview Road, Wilmette, IL 60091. This directory is published three times yearly and provides information on mergers, acquisitions, and key personnel. Agency data can be accessed by location and by targeted markets (e.g., medical, financial, resort/travel). Information is also provided on personnel, clients, and agencies for accounts billing more than $75,000 annually.

Standard Directory of Advertisers, National Register Publishing Company, 3004 Glenview Road, Wilmette, IL 60091. Lists 17,000 corporations that advertise regionally or nationally. Companies can be accessed by SIC code. Information is provided about the companies' key executives, sales, advertising budgets, advertising agency, and type of media used.

Greenbook—International Directory of Marketing Research Houses and Services, New York Chapter, Inc., American Marketing Association, 420 Lexington Avenue, New York, NY 10170. Categorizes market research suppliers alphabetically, geographically, by principal personnel, type of research, computer programs available from these companies and the functions they perform, and by various types of marketing research services.

The Direct Marketing Market Place, Hilary House Publishers, Inc., 1033 Channel Drive, Hewlett Harbor, NY 11557. This annual publication contains information on over 16,000 key executives and their organizations, including descriptions of the companies' business activities, revenue data, and profiles of advertising and direct-marketing usage and expenditures.

American Marketing Association, 250 South Wacker Drive, Chicago, IL 60606, 312/648–0536. This organization has published a pamphlet entitled "Careers in Marketing," which is available for a nominal price. A marketing bibliography is free.

Marketing Research Association, 111 E. Wacker Drive, Suite 600, Chicago, IL 60601, 312/644–6610. Offers a free bibliography.

American Association of Advertising Agencies, 666 Third Avenue, 13th Floor, New York, NY 10017, 212/682–2500. Offers two pamphlets: "A Guide to Careers in Advertising" and "Advertising Agencies: What They Are, What They Do, and How They Do It."

Direct Marketing Association, 6 East 43rd Street, New York, NY 10017, 212/ 689–4977.

PURCHASING: Although the majority of purchasing jobs are found within manufacturing companies, many other types of organizations have purchasing functions, including service companies, educational institutions, hospitals, and government organizations. Background information on the field of purchasing is presented in Chapter 9, beginning on page 228.

THE PURCHASING AGENT: Detailed below is an analysis, by skill category, of the tasks of a purchasing agent in a manufacturing company. Purchasing positions in nonmanufacturing organizations will entail similar duties.

Tasks of the Purchasing Agent

Creative/Analytical	• Conceives of ways to obtain needed materials, components, products, and services more cheaply; for example, a manufacturer that uses the same knob for two radio models will be able to buy greater quantities, thereby obtaining a more favorable unit cost • Works with Engineering and Manufacturing to develop ideas for cost improvements to existing products • Analyzes vendor price quotations to determine optimum quality at lowest cost • Analyzes results of tests performed by Engineering and Manufacturing to determine quality level of vendors' materials and products
Oral Communication	• Delivers presentations on recommendations for purchases of products and/or services
Written Communication	• Prepares written specifications of needed products and/or services
Negotiating	• Negotiates prices, terms, and delivery schedules with vendors and suppliers • Negotiates improvements in product quality following unfavorable test results on vendor goods
Project Management	• Leads team planning cutover from one product to another, e.g., coordinates transition from one type of packaging to another to minimize losses

Job Strategies: Within a manufacturing company, the purchasing function is generally in the manufacturing department, while in a services company it will be under the Controller or V.P. of Administration. Purchasing functions in hospitals and educational institutions are usually managed by an administrative executive.

Skills and experience in demand by the purchasing function include financial knowledge, sales experience, negotiating ability, cost control/improvement accomplishments, and data processing experience. Manufacturing and engineering experience can be pluses, depending on the type of organization. Someone with limited or nonexistent business experience should consider an educational institution for a first employer. Its purchasing requirements will not be as complex as those of a manufacturer, enabling one to adjust to the field without having to understand highly technical terminology. After gaining a few years of experience in this kind of environment, obtaining a purchasing job at a manufacturing company should be relatively easy.

Career Path

Purchasing Assistant—Entry-level position; assists purchasing agent in all areas except vendor negotiations

Purchasing Agent (Buyer)—Responsible for researching, evaluating, and negotiating with vendors; in a large company, a purchasing agent specializes in particular areas, e.g., all packaging, all plastics, all metal components

Director of Purchasing (Purchasing Manager)—Supervises one or more purchasing agents; establishes and administers departmental policies and budget; involved in negotiations for major contracts; liaison to Marketing in developing costs for new product programs; directs the implementation of computerized systems to enhance department productivity

Information Sources for Purchasing

Purchasing, 275 Washington Street, Newton, MA 02158, 617/964–3030.

Paul V. Farrell, ed., National Association of Purchasing Management, *Aljians Purchasing Handbook*, 4th ed. New York: McGraw-Hill, 1982. The bible of the field, this book describes the responsibilities of the function, policies, legal aspects of purchasing activities, etc.

Stuart Heinritz, Paul Farrell, and Clifton Smith, *Purchasing: Principles and Applications*, 7th ed. Englewood Cliffs, NJ: Prentice-Hall, 1986. This textbook provides an overview of the purchasing function, including procedures, how to manage purchasing activities in a world economy, and how to select and evaluate suppliers.

PurchasingWorld (monthly), 6521 Davis Industrial Parkway, Solon, OH 44139, 216/248–1125.

National Association of Purchasing Management, 2055 E. Centennial Circle, P.O. Box 22160, Tempe, AZ 85282, 602/752–6276. Publishes the *Journal of Purchasing and Materials Management*. Offers two free pamphlets on the field of purchasing: "Golden Opportunity" and "Purchasing as a Career."

SALES: In most companies the sales function is performed by both field and headquarters sales personnel. In addition, sales services (also called consulting sales services) are provided by manufacturers' representatives. These can be individuals or companies that arrange to sell manufacturers' products on a commission basis. A company would use representatives to augment its in-house sales staff, or to serve as its exclusive sales force if it has no sales personnel on its payroll. A more detailed discussion of the sales function is presented in Chapter 9, beginning on page 230.

FIELD SALES: All responsibilities listed here pertain equally to in-house sales representatives and manufacturers' representatives.

Tasks of the Sales Representative

Creative/Analytical	• Identifies customer needs and problems so that a product or service can be modified by marketing • Analyzes competitive products to determine strengths and weaknesses relative to own company's products or services • Overcomes customers' objections about prices being too high, competitive products performing better, too much trouble to switch suppliers, etc. • Designs sales presentations, e.g., copy, charts
Oral Communication	• Initiates contact with prospects over the telephone and through sales calls in person • Delivers sales presentations • Participates in trade shows, presenting products or services to buyers visiting the company's exhibit
Written Communication	• Writes letters to prospective customers introducing the company's products or services • Prepares written sales proposals (especially for technical products or services)
Negotiating	• Negotiates contract prices and terms for large orders • Negotiates schedules for product or service delivery and/or installation • Negotiates the resolution of customer complaints
Project Management	• Coordinates personnel contributing to proposal writing, development of sales quotations, product demonstrations, order processing, etc.

Job Strategies: Career changers with no sales experience can enhance their chances of establishing themselves in the field by aiming for industries where their experience in the fields they're leaving could be an asset. For instance, a teacher should consider approaching companies selling audiovisual materials or textbooks to educational institutions, since these kinds of companies would place a premium on someone's ability to understand the problems of its customer, the teacher. Similarly, a chemist would have an advantage in selling laboratory equipment to chemists. If your sights are set on a sales career in an industry totally unrelated to your present one, I recommend a two-step approach: first, obtain a sales job in an industry related to your present one; after gaining two to three years of experience in that industry, you should be able to make the transition to your desired industry.

To identify industries in which you would have a good chance of obtaining a sales job now, make a list of those vendors and suppliers with whom you or others in your organization interact. I'm confident that some of these businesses will appeal to you.

Career Path

Here is a typical career path for sales:

Sales (Account) Representative—Entry-level position; may entail informal on-the-job training or initial period of formal study; after designated training period, one would be given a territory and a sales quota

Senior Sales Representative—Responsible for larger territory, or more important customers

Branch Manager—First position is usually in a small office, since individual's managerial skills haven't been demonstrated, and company will want to minimize its risk; position is responsible for hiring, training, and supervising three to ten sales representatives, for establishing sales quotas, and for managing sales campaigns; will also participate in major sales calls and formal presentations

Regional (Zone) Manager—Responsible for two to seven branch offices spanning a geographically cohesive territory, e.g., the East Coast, the South; position sets quotas, manages budgeting function, and participates in major sales presentations and contract negotiations

(*Note*: Some companies have a three-tier system, typically with two to five regions; each region may have four to ten districts, each of which consists of several branch offices.)

Director of Sales (at headquarters)—Oversees all field and headquarters sales activities, the budgeting for entire department, and the establishment of territory sales quotas; acts as liaison to other departmental managers, e.g.,

Marketing, Manufacturing, in formulating company policies; reports to General Manager of a division, or to Chief Executive Officer of the company; position can lead to General Manager and CEO

HEADQUARTERS SALES: Headquarters sales personnel engage in activities to ensure the smooth operation of the field sales organization. Listed here are the primary tasks of these personnel, often called sales administrators. In a large company these tasks will be specialized into several job titles, e.g., Inventory Allocation Specialist, Sales Forecasting Specialist, Sales Meetings Specialist. For background information on the headquarters sales function, refer to Chapter 9, page 233.

Tasks of the Sales Administrator

Creative/Analytical	• Conceives of new ways to analyze sales data to help management make more judicious decisions; also, designs new sales report formats
	• Works with data-processing staff to design software for producing sales reports
	• Analyzes commercially available report-generating software packages to determine whether they meet the company's reporting needs and, if so, adapts them for company use
	• Analyzes national, regional, and branch sales data to identify strengths and weaknesses in products, sales office management, and competition, as well as seasonal factors affecting sales
	• Analyzes available inventory and makes decisions as to which customers will receive allocations of products in limited supply
	• Develops sales forecasts by product/model for three months, six months, one year
Oral Communication	• Delivers presentations at national sales meetings on new headquarters sales information systems
	• Delivers presentations to key customers and field sales personnel on new products or services
Written Communication	• Writes newsletter for distribution to sales force, which details company's and competitors' new product introductions and price changes

	• Prepares price sheets for company's products or services
	• Writes speeches to be delivered by headquarters sales personnel at national sales meetings
Negotiating	• Negotiates prices/terms with hotels, suppliers of audiovisual equipment, manufacturers of award plaques
	• Negotiates schedules with data-processing personnel for completion of computerized information systems to analyze sales data
	• Negotiates arrangements with trade show managements
Project Management	• Plans and organizes all aspects of regional and/or national sales meetings, e.g., hotel and travel accommodations, audiovisual support, agendas, purchase of plaques for presentation to top performers
	• Coordinates the preparation, production, and distribution of weekly/monthly sales reports to headquarters and field personnel

Job Strategies: The headquarters sales function draws upon a variety of skills commonly developed by individuals employed in other fields. Examples are analytical ability (any number-crunching job), events coordination, client/customer contact, experience working with desktop computers. Thus people with backgrounds in accounting/finance, computer programming, meetings planning, and market research should, depending on an employer's particular headquarters sales activities, be able to position themselves as strong candidates. You should target medium-size companies ($75–$200 million sales), since they would be likely to have formal headquarters sales functions but would not be contacted by as many job hunters as are larger companies. However, if a particular headquarters sales function—for example, sales forecasting, sales meetings, field communications—appeals to you more than the others, you'd be more likely to find a job dedicated to that activity in a large company.

Career Path

Sales Administrator—In a small- and medium-size company, position may require writing a newsletter for sales force on new products/services and on competitive developments, analyzing sales trends by product/service, and planning and organizing regional and national sales meetings; in a large company each of these activities is handled by a specialist dedicated to the particular function

Sales Administration Manager—Manages one or more sales administrators; in a large company this job is specialized to cover one of these areas: Sales Forecasting, Inventory Allocation, Sales Meetings, Field Communications, Contract Administration; develops and administers department budget

Director of Sales—Oversees all field and headquarters sales activities; establishes sales quotas and budgets for entire sales department; liaison to other department managers in providing direction to company (or division); position reports to General Manager of a division or Chief Executive Officer of the company, and can lead to those positions

(*Note*: Although I've shown two distinct career paths for field sales and headquarters sales, it's very common for people to zigzag between the field and headquarters functions by taking lateral moves or promotions along the way.)

Information Sources for Sales

David Mayer and Herbert M. Greenberg, "What Makes a Good Salesperson," *Harvard Business Review*, July-August 1964. Although not a recent article, the principles set forth in it have stood the test of time, as reflected in its being one of the publication's top ten best-selling reprints.

Sales and Marketing Management (published 16 times annually), 633 Third Avenue, New York, NY 10017, 212/986–4800.

Sales and Marketing Executives of Greater New York, 114 E. 32nd Street, Suite 1301, New York, NY 10016, 212/683–9755. Promotes the sales profession through workshops and meetings. Offers publications dealing with the field, and sells sales educational materials. Publishes special research reports.

Manufacturers' Agents National Association, P.O.B. 3467, 23016 Mill Creek Road, Laguna Hills, CA 92654, 714/859–4040. This is the association for manufacturers' representatives. It offers for sale a directory of its members and publishes a monthly magazine.

HUMAN RESOURCES: Best bets within the human resources function are personnel administration, recruiting/manpower planning (sometimes called "succession planning"), and training and development. More detailed descriptions of these functions are presented in Chapter 9, beginning on page 237.

PERSONNEL ADMINISTRATION AND RECRUITING/MANPOWER PLANNING: The tasks that follow are those of a personnel generalist, which is a position most likely to be found in a small-to-medium-size company. In a larger company, each personnel function will be specialized in a different job. An (R) at the end of any of the tasks that follow means that the responsibility is also applicable to a recruiter/manpower planner position.

Tasks of the Personnel Generalist and Recruiter/Manpower Planner

Creative/Analytical

- Conceives of innovative ways to recruit needed personnel (R)
- Screens many résumés sent in response to advertisements for presentation to functional managers (R)
- Analyzes qualifications of job candidates to ensure compatibility with position requirements (R)
- Performs cost-benefit analyses of proposed benefit programs, e.g., tuition refund, day care, dental plan
- Provides guidance to functional managers in dealing with employee-performance problems (R)
- Analyzes content of various jobs and develops compensation structures to reflect complexity of job requirements

Oral Communication

- Delivers presentations on pros/cons of various alternative benefit programs, e.g., dental plans offered by three insurance companies
- Conducts interviews of job candidates (R)
- Delivers presentations on strengths/weaknesses of candidates for a particular position (R)
- Conducts orientation programs for new employees
- Conducts telephone interviews of references provided by job candidates (R)
- Conducts career counseling and termination interviews of employees (R)
- Counsels supervisors and employees on union contract terms

Written Communication

- Writes company's employee-benefits booklet
- Writes company's new employee-orientation booklet
- Writes recruiting advertisements (R)
- Writes evaluations of job applicants (R)
- Writes job descriptions (R)

	• Writes announcements for employees explaining scope of benefits programs, modifications to benefits, and procedures for using the programs • Writes letters detailing terms of job offers to applicants (R)
Negotiating	• Negotiates fees and terms with suppliers of benefits • Negotiates fees and terms with employment agencies and executive recruiters (R) • Negotiates terms of job offers with finalist candidates (R)
Project Management	• Leads a team involved in identifying more productive organizational approaches for the company • Coordinates the design, production, and distribution of booklets on company policies, employee benefits, etc. • Provides direction to functional managers during company's annual manpower review, which evaluates employees in terms of their readiness for higher-level positions (R)

Job Strategies: Individuals interested in personnel generalist positions should approach companies with annual sales of $50–$200 million, hospitals, or universities. Skills and experience transferable to personnel administration are psychological training, social work background, and financial and accounting skills. The ability to use a desktop computer would be a strong advantage, since many companies develop data bases containing employee and applicant information.

Positions that entail recruiting/manpower planning exclusively are more likely to be found in companies with sales greater than $200 million, although this is not universally true. All skills important to the personnel administration function are similarly important in recruiting/manpower planning, with the possible exception of financial and accounting knowledge (unless, of course, one recruits personnel for these functions). However, assuming that one wanted to advance beyond a recruiting/manpower planning position, financial skills would be invaluable in handling the budgeting responsibility inherent in any managerial position.

In addition, a person who is very knowledgeable about a particular discipline and its requirements—for example, an electronics engineer—would be qualified to recruit personnel into that field.

Career Path

For personnel administration:

Personnel Generalist—Entry-level position most often found in a small or medium-size company; may entail any of the following duties: recruiting; research, evaluation, and implementation of benefits programs: preparation of job descriptions; salary planning; union relations

Senior Personnel Generalist—Performs all the duties of a personnel generalist, but with a higher level of authority

Director of Personnel (Human Resources)—Establishes budget for department; supervises personnel staff; interacts with functional managers to determine near- and long-term human resource needs; plays a major role in union negotiations and in developing benefits programs and compensation policies

For recruiting:

Recruiter/Manpower Planner—Recruits salaried and/or hourly employees, working with functional managers to establish screening criteria; responsibilities may include writing ads, hiring employment agencies, conducting interviews, checking references, making hiring recommendations, determining compensation to be offered to candidates, negotiating job offers; advises managers on performance, salary, and manpower reviews

Manager of Professional Recruiting—Supervises recruitment programs supporting all functional areas of a large company; works with functional managers to outline recruitment needs and methods; hires and acts as liaison to executive recruiters on middle-management and higher-level searches; screens top management candidates and makes hiring recommendations; develops and administers budget for department; position can lead to Director of Personnel

Other career opportunities and lateral paths:

Benefits and/or Compensation Specialist—Depending on the company's structure, will be responsible for either or both of these functions; duties could include researching and evaluating benefits programs offered by insurance companies, conducting analyses of other proposed benefits, e.g., day care, tuition-refund program, analyzing job functions and developing/revising descriptions, establishing salary structures for various jobs, preparing reports for government on employee benefits data

Benefits/Compensation Manager—Has full responsibility for designing benefits/compensation programs and/or for developing benefits/compensation policies and procedures, as well as for conducting negotiations with insurance providers; has budgetary responsibility for department; position can lead to Director of Personnel

TRAINING AND DEVELOPMENT: Training and development positions are found in both the end-user and consulting environments and typically entail responsibility for designing, conducting, and administering training programs. The tasks that follow are for a trainer in a company providing training consulting services to other companies. This is the easiest entry point for career changers and can be a stepping-stone to a training and development position within the end-user environment. Here are several ways in which positions in the two environments differ:

- A trainer employed by a consulting firm will generally present the same training program for one or more years to many client personnel, since this type of company has a limited number of program offerings.
- A trainer in a consulting firm will generally travel more frequently to deliver programs than his or her counterpart in the end-user environment, although an end-user company with geographically dispersed plants and offices may require extensive travel on the part of its staff.
- A training and development specialist within an end-user organization will often research, evaluate, and negotiate prices and terms with training consulting firms.

The training and development function is described in greater detail in Chapter 9, beginning on page 242.

Tasks of the Training and Development Specialist

Creative/Analytical	• Researches and analyzes materials in areas bearing on training needs, e.g., industrial psychology, time management, management theory and technique • Designs complete training programs, including case studies, audiovisual aids, role-playing exercises • Responds to questions posed by course participants • Analyzes participant evaluations of training programs for potential areas of improvement
Oral Communication	• Delivers training programs to managers and/or lower-level employees of client companies
Written Communication	• Writes materials for new training courses and writes modifications to existing training programs • Writes course leaders' instruction guides

Negotiating	• Hires and negotiates fees with hotels, audiovisual production houses, graphic designers, printers, etc. • Negotiates training schedules with client human resources personnel
Project Management	• Establishes schedule and resource (financial, human) requirements for the development of new training programs, as well as manages ongoing projects

Job Strategies: The best entry point for the training field is a position with a training consulting firm, since the competition for jobs in end-user companies is very keen, with many applicants having advanced degrees in human resources management or psychology. I recommend that you research training and development consulting firms in one or more of the industry directories available in many libraries.

Skills important to this function are public speaking ability, dynamic speaking voice, writing skill, leadership ability, and social adeptness. An interesting employment option is that of free-lance trainer. People who prefer flexible work schedules or who find difficulty in getting a salaried training position can sometimes find companies willing to train them in anticipation of having a greater demand for trainers than their full-time staff can satisfy. Independent training contractors typically receive a per diem rate (plus reimbursement of travel and living expenses) for their services.

Career Path

In a consulting company:

Training and Development Specialist—Responsible for conducting one or more training programs sold by his or her company; acts as liaison to client in coordinating registration data and communicating travel/lodging arrangements; travels 50–80 percent of the time to deliver programs at client locations or hotels throughout the country; sets up meeting rooms; acts as liaison to hotel management on facilities arrangements, bills, problems; in some companies, a trainer contributes to design of new training programs and/or redesign of existing ones

Program Manager—Responsible for the profitable marketing of one of the firm's training programs, i.e., researches and evaluates competitive offerings; studies business developments that may have implications for program design and makes modifications accordingly; coordinates development of training program and associated materials; has budgeting responsibility for program operation; trains and supervises one or more trainers

Vice President (or Partner)—Plays an important role in planning the company's business direction, budgeting, soliciting new business, and hiring and supervising professional staff; at this level one usually receives a percentage of the firm's profits, in addition to a salary

In an end-user organization:

Training and Development Specialist—Conducts assessments of training needs of various types of employees, e.g., management, new hires, manufacturing personnel; researches, evaluates, and recommends the use of outside training programs, as well as negotiates fees and schedules with companies offering such programs; contributes to design and presentation of in-house training programs, traveling to other company locations as needed; promotes training programs to managers throughout the company; arranges for physical facilities and for design and production of training materials

Program Manager—Manages all aspects of one type of training program designed to develop the skills of certain employees, e.g., new managers, middle-level managers, engineers; designs new programs within assigned area of responsibility, as well as develops modifications to reflect changing company needs; promotes these programs to managers throughout the company; reviews and approves outside training programs that meet the company's standards; may supervise one or more trainers, and sometimes also conducts training programs

Manager of Training—Supervises one or more program managers; interacts with functional managers throughout the company to identify training needs; oversees the creation or purchase of training programs to develop skills of all employee groups, from trainees through top management; may design and deliver training programs for higher-level personnel; develops and administers departmental budget; this position can lead to Director of Personnel

Information Sources for Human Resources

Neal Chalofsky and Carnie Ives Lincoln, *Up the HRD Ladder: A Guide to Professional Growth*. Reading, MA: Addison-Wesley, 1983. Describes how the human resource development system works. Offers theories and techniques for human resource development professionals to enhance their competence. Also provides guidance in writing a career plan.

Training; the magazine of human resources development (monthly), 50 South Ninth Street, Minneapolis, MN 55402, 612/333–0471.

Directory of Outplacement Firms, Kennedy & Kennedy, Inc., Templeton Road, Fitzwilliam, NH 03447. Presents an overview of the field. Provides details on firms serving corporations and individuals. Includes geographic and key executive indexes. (Because these firms often conduct group job-search training for fired employees, they should be targeted by job hunters.)

Training and Development Organizations Directory, Gale Research Company, Book Tower, Detroit, MI 48226. Describes almost 2,000 companies, institutes, and agencies offering training programs to the business, government, and not-for-profit sectors. Information is indexed by subject of training programs, location of companies, key executives, and organizations.

Training Business Directory, Hope Reports, Inc., 1600 Lyell Avenue, Rochester, NY 14606. Lists 4,700 companies and organizations marketing training programs to industry, with indexes by subject and geographical location.

American Society for Training and Development, Box 1443, 1630 Duke Street, Alexandria, VA 22313, 703/683–8100. Offers a free pamphlet entitled "Careers in Training and Development."

American Association for Counseling and Development, 5999 Stevenson Avenue, Alexandria, VA 22304, 703/823–9800. Offers a free pamphlet entitled "What is Counseling?"

American Society for Personnel Administration, 606 N. Washington Street, Alexandria, VA 22314, 703/548–3440. Offers a free pamphlet entitled "Careers in Resource Management."

PUBLIC RELATIONS: Public relations positions can be found in business corporations, educational institutions, hospitals, unions, and government agencies, as well as in public relations agencies (sometimes called "counselors"), which provide services to end users. Large companies specialize their public relations functions into "Investor Relations," "Community Relations," "Educational Relations," and other categories, as appropriate. Each of these functions is a potential target for those who aspire to public relations positions. A more detailed explanation of the public relations function is in Chapter 9, beginning on page 246.

PUBLIC RELATIONS SPECIALIST (OR PUBLIC RELATIONS WRITER): The responsibilities of a public relations writer in an end-user environment are detailed here. A major difference between this position and that of public relations writer in an agency is that the agency environment will provide exposure to a variety of clients representing a cross-section of business and, possibly, nonbusiness organizations. Also, agency work is usually project-oriented and is not likely to entail such activities as reviewing grant requests and writing employee newsletters.

Tasks of the Public Relations Specialist

Creative/Analytical	• Analyzes environmental impact of company's ongoing business activities and develops public relations programs to address them • Analyzes pending legislation for its effect on company's activities • Reviews requests for grants submitted to the company by charitable, civic, and cultural organizations • Analyzes costs associated with various public relations programs and contributes to development of departmental budget • Designs special events that enhance the organization's image with its various publics
Oral Communication	• Represents the company at professional and government association meetings, and at legislative hearings • Delivers presentations on proposed public relations projects, costs, and benefits • Represents the company on the boards of civic, cultural, and charitable organizations
Written Communication	• Writes newsletter for employees detailing company financial results, employee benefits, company special events, etc. • Writes company's annual report • Writes position papers for presentation to legislators in support of the company's lobbying efforts • Writes press releases detailing executive changes, new products/services, new manufacturing plants, the company's response to unfavorable publicity about its activities, etc. • Writes press kits to support major public relations programs • Writes speeches to be delivered by company executives
Negotiating	• Hires and negotiates fees with public relations consultants • Hires and negotiates fees with typesetters, photographers, graphic designers, free-lance writers

Project Management	• Establishes a schedule for the design, writing and production of public relations materials
	• Supervises the design, photography, and printing of annual reports
	• Coordinates the company's participation in charitable and community events
	• Organizes press conferences and special public relations events

Job Strategies: Since writing is such an important part of a public relations job, individuals interested in gaining entry into this field should be prepared to submit writing samples to a prospective employer. People who have had any of their writing published often succeed in making a very strong impact. It's easy to get articles published in regional publications, since editors are always willing to review proposals for stories consistent with their publications' editorial styles. Fees for these assignments will range from zero to a couple of hundred dollars, but the cachet of having an article published under one's name may be worth a lot when looking for a public relations job.

Other skills/experience known to be valued by the public relations function are research ability, financial knowledge (especially valuable for the investor relations function), experience working with community organizations, and project management skill.

When companies' public relations needs increase—due, for example, to strikes, legislation, product recalls—and place considerable demands on their public relations departments, they supplement their in-house capabilities by hiring public relations agencies. When these excessive demands fade, the companies will examine their public relations costs closely, and may discontinue or diminish the use of outside counsel. Also, some companies prefer to use public relations agencies for all their activities, because they feel that these firms have the experience and media contacts that justify the higher cost. If you are aiming for a public relations job, remember that, at certain times, political, economic, or other factors may make your targeted employer—and many other companies—give out more work to agencies. Conversely, if you find that there are few employment opportunities with agencies, that may mean that end-user companies are hiring more people to staff their in-house public relations operations.

You can find public relations agencies and corporate public relations operations listed in the directories presented in the Information Sources section, which follows. If you prefer an end-user environment, target organizations known to have a strong local presence—universities, hospitals, banks; they often have formal public relations functions. And, in general, bear in mind that companies usually have annual sales of at least $200 million before they establish public relations departments, although smaller companies sometimes have needs that prompt them to establish in-house public relations operations.

Career Path

In an end-user company:

Public Relations Assistant—Assists in writing/editing a company newsletter; conducts research to support special projects; writes press releases on executive appointments, and on company activities having public impact

Public Relations Writer (or Public Relations Specialist)—Writes/edits company newsletter; researches and writes position papers on major issues; writes employee communications; writes communications for the financial community, charities, and civic organizations; writes speeches for company executives

Manager/Director of Public Relations—Hires and works with public relations counsel and lobbyists; plays a major role in formulating the creative approach for the company's annual report; represents the company to professional and governmental organizations and to community leaders; analyzes and reports on public impact of proposed company programs and actions; develops and administers departmental budget

In an agency:

Public relations agencies are similar in organization to advertising agencies (see page 24). Account executive and higher-level personnel within a public relations agency are responsible for writing articles, press releases, press kits, etc. to support client projects. They also arrange for the placement of articles in targeted media. And, like their counterparts within advertising agencies, public relations account personnel coordinate internal agency resources to support accounts, as well as handle administrative duties.

Information Sources for Public Relations

Robert L. Dilenschneider and Dan J. Forrestal, *Public Relations Handbook*, 3rd ed. Chicago, IL: The Dartnell Corporation, 1987. Designed for both novice and seasoned practitioners, this book covers internal/external public relations, and hospital and medical school public relations. Case studies are included.

Robert T. Reilly, *Public Relations in Action*. 2nd ed. Englewood Cliffs, NJ: Prentice-Hall, Inc., 1987. This is a comprehensive overview of the field, including the various modes of public relations, e.g., publicity, communications, special events, financial public relations.

Public Relations News (weekly), 127 East 80th Street, New York, NY 10021, 212/879–7090.

National Directory of Corporate Public Affairs, Columbia Books, Inc., 1350 New York Avenue, Suite 207, Washington, D.C. 20005. This annual directory includes about 1,500 corporations involved in public affairs activities. It provides information on key personnel, corporate foundations and their primary interests, political action committees, and registered lobbyists.

O'Dwyer's Directory of Public Relations Firms, J. R. O'Dwyer Co., Inc., 271 Madison Avenue, New York, NY 10016. This annual directory lists over 1,400 public relations counselors and advertising agencies with public relations departments. An index directs the reader to firms having expertise in each of 15 specialized areas. The top 50 independent public relations companies in the country are ranked, as are the top 50 U.S.-based public relations operations.

O'Dwyer's Directory of Corporate Communications, J. R. O'Dwyer Co., Inc., 271 Madison Avenue, New York, NY 10016. Lists 1,600 industrial firms, with their *Fortune* and *Forbes* rankings, as well as the 50 largest companies in each of these categories: commercial banking, life insurance, diversified financial, retailing, transportation, utilities.

Public Relations Society of America, Inc., 33 Irving Place, New York, NY 10003, 212/995–2230. Publishes the *Public Relations Journal*. Conducts professional development programs. Offers pamphlet on careers in public relations, and a bibliography.

Other Good Bets for Career Changers
THE COMPUTER FIELD: No field has had more of a mystique than that of computers, probably because the computer is such a radically different tool. Because of this mystique, many people are afraid of learning about computers, thinking that it may be too difficult to master. But understanding the computer's capabilities is within your reach, I assure you. And even if you don't choose a career in computers, knowing how they work may enable you to enhance your performance in whatever field you enter, since they can benefit every discipline.

Although a computer science or similar degree is increasingly being required for professional jobs in the field, there are still opportunities for resourceful, intelligent people who have very limited or no formal training. While there are many types of professional jobs within the computer field, several present themselves as the best opportunities for career changers; I'll describe these shortly.

THE BENEFIT OF COMPUTERS: All organizations have routine tasks that must be performed. We've discussed some of them in earlier sections, including analyzing sales and market research data, and maintaining information on employees' skills to aid in promotion decisions. While these tasks can be performed manually, to do so would require so much time that by the time the manual information could be analyzed, it would be too late to take action. A computer is a tool that can perform arithmetic calculations, make logical decisions, and issue instructions to various output devices—printers, CRTs (video screens), disks, tape. It has been a boon to society (except, of course, when it generates an incorrect statement for your charge account) because it can do these tasks at extraordinary speed, saving substantial costs over human labor, as well as enabling much more timely business decisions.

CAREER OPPORTUNITIES IN THE COMPUTER FIELD: The following pages present descriptions of three computer-related jobs: systems analyst, computer programmer, and technical writer. Since some readers may have no prior experience in this field, I am using my own simple explanation of these jobs. You will find pointers to more detailed, precise descriptions under the "Information Sources" heading on page 52.

The Systems Analyst's Job: When an organization wishes to investigate a computerized method to address an information processing or analysis need, someone must analyze fully the scope of the need and determine:

- *what steps are involved in processing the information (e.g., accounting, payroll, sales, medical history) and in what order.*
For example, if a hospital wants to implement a system for billing its patients, it would need to collect data on laboratory test fees, room charges, telephone and television usage, etc., and channel these to a central location in the Accounting Department. But before a bill could be issued, the Admissions Department would have to provide Accounting with information about the patient's insurance coverage so the proper charges could be billed to the patient and his or her insurance company.

- *what analyses of data can be useful to other departments in the organization.*
For example, an order placed by a customer of a corrugated-box manufacturer would hold useful information for the Accounts Receivable Department (for invoicing purposes), for the Inventory Control Department (for reducing the amount of available stock), for the Marketing Department (which collects statistics on what products are selling best), etc. These departments would benefit by having the computer system generate reports containing the information relevant to their operations.

- *how information will be entered into and issued from the computer*
For example, it could be productive to have field sales personnel enter

order data into computer terminals located in their offices, and be able to access information on the status of their customers' orders. Someone must determine what kind of computer terminal would be most efficient and economical.

As you can imagine, getting the answers to these questions requires considerable interaction with personnel in the departments involved. Systems analysts make extensive use of charts that illustrate the information coming into the system, the processing steps and their sequence, and the output.

Let's look at a *Typical Workday of a Systems Analyst* in a large manufacturing company.

8:30–10:00	Meeting with Ed Ryan, Distribution Specialist, to learn his reporting needs (information, frequency) in conjunction with new order entry/warehouse distribution system
10:00–11:00	Integrate results of Ryan discussion into chart reflecting the order entry/warehouse distribution system's information processing steps
11:00–11:30	Prepare memorandum to Marcy Fine, Manager of Accounts Receivable, responding to her request that her department be allocated three computer terminals; advise her that two are planned initially and that an analysis of the productivity of those terminals in a few months may result in an additional unit being installed
11:30–12:30	Meeting with Alice Crippen, Programmer/Analyst assigned to new employee data base* application, to review systems approach and to discuss timetable for implementation
1:30–2:30	Review specifications of three computer terminals being considered for order-entry system; make phone calls to two vendors' technical support departments to get clarification of some points in user's manuals
2:30–3:30	Conduct training session for marketing staff in use of recently installed pricing system
3:30–4:30	Meeting with Andy White, Manager of Data Processing, to discuss need for additional computer capacity to be required by new order entry system
4:30–6:00	Prepare draft of request for proposal to be sent to three software vendors for design of credit and collections system which will generate periodic dunning notices to be sent to past due accounts

*A data base is a collection of information—for example, all employees, all inventory items, all students—relevant to a logically connected group of items.

The Programmer's Job: Once the system has been fully laid out in terms of the sequence of steps, reporting requirements, and data-access needs, one or more programmers will be assigned to write the software, i.e., the instructions to the computer that will meet the system specifications.

Using a specialized language, the programmer writes instructions (code). Unlike languages such as English, German, and French, computer languages include a very limited number of words or instructions, ranging from 50 to 100 or so, depending on their sophistication. Once you learn your first computer language and understand each of the commands, it's fairly easy to master additional languages.

The types of instructions the programmer can issue to the computer include performing arithmetic calculations, comparing alphanumeric data and making decisions as to whether to perform additional calculations, making decisions to bypass certain instructions and continue with others, and issuing output in the form of type, sound, and graphics. Whereas in the past programmers would handwrite their instructions on coding sheets for subsequent keypunching into cards by keypunch operators, nowadays programmers enter their commands directly into a computer using a keyboard and a CRT.

Programmers usually specialize in either business or scientific applications, and become adept at one or two computer languages commonly used in each of these environments. Thus someone may refer to himself as a COBOL programmer, COBOL being a language widely used in the business environment. But this person may also know how to use several other languages. Furthermore, programmers become associated with specific types of computers—so one can be a COBOL programmer in an IBM environment or a COBOL programmer in a Honeywell environment. Adapting to other manufacturers' computers is not difficult once you learn one, but employers usually prefer to hire programmers who have experience with their particular type of computer.

After working in an entry-level programming job, one can be promoted to a programmer/analyst position, which will entail—in addition to writing code—responsibility for designing the overall logic of the program. Most programmer and programmer/analyst jobs also require that maintenance programming tasks be performed, which means responsibility for handling any problems arising from programs they've previously written, or which were written by another programmer. Maintenance programming is important because errors (called "bugs") often arise due to logical mistakes introduced into the original design of the program. These may not surface until some unusual data are introduced into the computer. Since programmers often have responsibility for maintaining programs written by other people, preparing comprehensive documentation is an important part of any programming job. It can be in a form as simple as a sentence every once in a while in the program stating what the program is doing (e.g., "The state tax rates are being applied to each employee's gross pay") or as complex as a 100-page manual.

A *Typical Workday of a Business Programmer/Analyst* in a medium-size corporation could look like this:

8:30–12:00	Modifies code in payroll system—writes COBOL instructions to change two states' income tax formulas; adds instructions to print information showing year-to-date shares of company stock owned by each employee, purchased through automatic payroll-deduction program; tests both changes to make sure they are implemented accurately
1:00–1:45	Rewrites page 18 in payroll system manual to reflect changes in the payroll program described above
1:45–3:00	Meets with Phyllis Driscoll, Personnel Manager, to discuss her need for an employee-skills data base, i.e., type of information to be stored, types of analyses to be performed, formats of various reports (by skill type, by employee, by length of experience in job, etc.)
3:00–5:30	Call from Don Miller of Payroll Department regarding error in amount of deductions in the pay checks of two employees, both of whom live in Kentucky; researches cause of error in payroll program; determines that error is related to the way the program treats employees with less than six months' tenure; implements and tests correction; reports to Miller that program fix has been implemented

The Technical (Software Documentation) Writer's Job: Once the system has been designed and programmed, it's ready for use by those departments for which it was developed. In most non-data-processing organizations that develop systems for their own use, the programmer is responsible for writing operating instructions for the user departments in clear English.

On the other hand, companies that design and market software (programs) for the marketplace must go to considerably greater lengths in preparing their documentation, since ease of use is a strong factor in persuading people to buy their programs. For example, a secretary using a word-processing software package must be able to understand what each instruction in the word-processing command system can accomplish, and will be more productive in using the system to the extent that the instructions are written in clear language.

Responsibility for preparing written documentation to support software is assigned to a technical writer.* After meeting with the programmer to learn

---

*Only a fraction of technical writers are employed in computer-related jobs. The rest work in other fields requiring comprehensive documentation for technical products, e.g., aircraft, munitions, medical/surgical, photographic.

exactly what the program is designed to accomplish, he or she writes this information in a format that can be understood easily by the user of the software. While having a good understanding of programming can be an asset in gaining entry into the technical writing field, one who has an excellent command of the English language—coupled with the ability to ask the right questions of a programmer—can be very effective at this job.

A *Typical Workday of a Technical Writer* for a company producing software for the personal (desktop) computer market could look like this:

8:30–10:00	Meets with Jane Riley and Christopher Meeks, programmers who designed the company's new records management system for physicians and hospitals, to discuss design and scope of user's guide for the system
10:00–11:00	Writes changes for user's guide to the word-processing system to reflect an enhancement in the software; sends draft of changes to Bruce Chamberlain, programmer on the word-processing package, for his review
11:00–1:00	Reviews memorandum from Hal Fisher, Manager of Technical Support, detailing complaints from customers regarding confusing passages in word-processing system's user's guide; accesses word-processing software on the computer to confirm customer complaints; prepares memo responding to Hal Fisher confirming validity of these complaints and committing to date by which documentation will be revised
2:00–3:30	Prepares outline for user's guide for records management system for physicians and hospitals; forwards to Margaret Dorch, Technical Writing Manager, for her approval
3:30–5:30	Reviews current user's guides for mailing list and general ledger programs for confusing or incomplete instructions, following request from Margaret Dorch

Job Strategies for Programming and Systems Analysis: An article in *The Wall Street Journal** reported that many computer science jobs go unfilled today because fewer students are majoring in the field. But this declining interest means opportunities for career changers to enter the field. And this applies not only to people who were math and science majors, but to liberal arts graduates as well: the article cites a computer industry recruiting executive's belief that critical thinking ability is more important than a computer science degree.

Whether you are interested in a programming or systems analysis career, starting as a programmer is usually necessary. To determine whether you

*"Jobs Go Unfilled as Fewer Students Show Interest in Computer Science," *The Wall Street Journal*, November 27, 1987, p. 13.

have the aptitude to be a programmer, you can take some sample programmer aptitude tests, found in several books on the market. (One is listed under Information Sources, page 52.) See if your local library has one for you to study.

If you take the test and your test scores are favorable, you should take an introductory data-processing course that will provide you with a conceptual understanding of computers. If the subject interests you, take some courses in one or more computer languages, to be determined through discussions with data-processing faculty at a local college or university. If you perform very well in these studies, consider one or more of the following next steps:

- Undertake an extensive program of self-study. This is most feasible if you have your own personal (desktop) computer. When you've gained a high level of programming proficiency in one or more languages, identify companies that use these languages and market yourself to them as a junior programmer.
- Research which companies (usually large ones) in your area have in-house programmer training programs and present your qualifications as a candidate.
- Undertake a formal program of study in information systems or computer science. This can be accomplished in any of the following ways:

1. a certificate course in computers offered by an adult/continuing education division of a university;
2. a six-to-nine-month program offered by a private data processing school;
3. a two-year associate's degree program in data processing or computer science; or
4. a four-year bachelor's degree program, with a major in computer science or management information systems.

If you already have an associate's or bachelor's degree in any other field, you may be able to get a bachelor's degree in computer science by taking an additional number of courses, to be negotiated with the school you wish to attend. If you have a bachelor's degree in another field, you may be able to acquire a graduate degree in computer science or management information systems easily.

I should mention that individuals without programming skill but with experience in some business function are sometimes able to become systems analysts. This is most feasible when their employers are willing to give them on-the-job training.

Career Paths for Programming and Systems Analysis: The jobs described in the preceding pages can be found in three types of companies:

- those in the computer industry that produce hardware and/or software;
- service companies, which do contract programming and the like;
- end users: companies that buy or rent computers for their own purposes

For simplicity's sake, I will describe the career path only for typical end-user companies, but if the field interests you, keep in mind that similar employment opportunities exist in the two other segments.

Many end users combine systems analyst and programmer into single titles, with this likely career path:

Junior Programmer/Analyst
Programmer/Analyst
Senior Programmer/Analyst
Project Leader (Lead Programmer/Analyst)

If a company has separate programming and systems analysis jobs, a typical career path for systems analysis would be the following:

Junior Systems Analyst
Systems Anaiyst
Senior Systems Analyst
Lead Analyst

Project leaders and lead analysts will usually report to development managers or project managers, who are responsible for developing application software for selected functional areas of the company—or on a project basis for any department. Programming functions in businesses range from those employing a few people to several hundred. Depending on the company's size, several development managers or project managers will usually report to a systems manager, the information systems manager, or, finally, to the director of M.I.S. (Management Information Systems).

Job Strategies and Career Path for the Position of Technical Writer of Software Documentation: While a technical writer does not have to know how to program in order to be effective, grasping the conceptual basis of a computer is important. Therefore, you should complete one or more introductory courses, including one in programming fundamentals, so that you'll have the confidence to use software for which you'll be writing documentation.

A prospective employer would naturally require technical-writer applicants to show writing samples. The best examples would be reports, proposals, public relations pieces, or other materials that demonstrate

- an ability to organize written material in a logical fashion;
- an excellent vocabulary and skill in selecting the most appropriate word or phrase to communicate an idea;

- the ability to communicate complex thoughts in simple language; and
- an unpompous writing style (very important in data processing—companies strive for "user-friendly" documentation).

Software documentation writer positions can be found in companies marketing computer software to end users and in large companies that develop software for their own use. Within the former environment, companies marketing software to consumers, as opposed to those which market it to business, are the best types of organizations for technical-writer aspirants to target, since the consumer software packages will be easier to understand right away. Because there is always a lot to learn in one's first job in a new field, it's better to get one's "feet wet" with technical material that's easier to grasp. Individuals with a good understanding of specific business functions—for example, accounting, finance, or sales—may be able to leverage that knowledge to obtain technical writer positions within large end-user companies.

The typical progression for a technical writer is as follows:

Junior Technical Writer
Technical Writer
Manager of Technical Writing

Information Sources for the Computer Field

Mark Garetz, *Bits, Bytes, and Buzzwords*: *Understanding Small Business Computers*. Beaverton, OR: Weber Systems, 1983. Geared toward the beginner's learning needs, this book explains microcomputers, software, and peripherals.

Robin Bradbeer et al., *The Beginner's Guide to Computers*: *Everything You Need to Know About the New Technology*. Reading, MA: Addison-Wesley Publishing Company, 1982. This book was written for lay people. It provides readers with an understanding of the applications of the computer in everyday life and fundamental computer concepts. Readers are instructed in how to write simple BASIC programs.

David Fay Smith, *A Computer Dictionary for Kids and Other Beginners*. New York: Ballantine, 1984. Easy-to-understand language is used to explain computer terminology from A to Z.

Elayne Shulman, Richard Page, and Milton Luftig, *Computer Programmer Analyst Trainee*. New York: ARCO Publishing Co., 1987. Contains sample tests similar to those used by industry to measure programming aptitude.

Directory of Top Computer Executives, Applied Computer Research, Inc., 11242 N. 19th Avenue, Phoenix, AZ 85029. This semiannual directory is published in East and West editions. It names all *Fortune*-listed companies' data-processing executives, as well as executives managing mainframe installations with annual DP budgets of $250,000+. Each entry gives the executive's name, company, address, telephone number, area of responsibility, and types of computer systems.

Data Processing Management Association, 505 Busse Highway, Park Ridge, IL 60068, 312/825–8124. Offers a free pamphlet entitled "Your Computer Career."

American Society for Information Science, 1424 16th Street NW, Suite 404, Washington, DC 20036, 202/462–1000. Offers a free pamphlet entitled "Challenging Careers in Information."

National Science Foundation, Division of Science Resources Studies, Room L-611, 1800 G Street N.W., Washington, DC 20550, 202/357–9859. Offers a free taxonomy of computer jobs.

Association for Computing Machinery, 11 W. 42nd Street, 3rd Floor, New York, NY 10036, 212/869–7440.

American Federation of Information Processing Societies, 1899 Preston White Drive, Reston, VA 22091, 703/620–8900.

Society for Technical Communication, 815 15th Street, NW, Washington, DC 20005, 202/737–0035. Offers a free pamphlet, "Careers in Technical Communication."

Selected High-Growth Industries and Fields

In recent years I have watched the growth of several industries and fields that I consider particularly attractive to career changers because they draw upon many skills used in other types of work. These are:

SPORTS MARKETING: Sports marketing pertains to businesses providing financial support to sports events in order to enhance their corporate images and the sales of their products and services. Sports marketing firms— and sports marketing divisions of advertising agencies—sometimes seek corporate sponsorship of events planned by sports-oriented organizations, and businesses often initiate their involvement with sports events. Typical types of events sponsored include marathons, tennis matches, golf tournaments, skiing competitions, and polo matches. Key executives in sports marketing firms are actively involved in contract negotiations with sports organizations and corporate sponsors. They will also advise their clients on the type of sport and particular event that will maximize the company's exposure to its targeted segment. Sports marketing personnel manage all aspects of these events, including:

- establishing a schedule and budget for the event;
- writing copy for use in promotional brochures, advertising campaigns, and press releases;
- designing contests to promote the event to the public;
- negotiating terms with, hiring, and directing printers, graphic designers, and other suppliers producing materials (e.g., tickets, T-shirts) for the event;
- negotiating promotional support of local sponsors;
- negotiating television coverage;
- hiring personnel to staff the sports events; and
- coordinating on-site logistics.

Although this field may hold special appeal for sports enthusiasts, you don't have to be interested in sports to be successful in it. What you do need are writing ability, sales and negotiating skills, and the ability to manage time-critical projects successfully. This is not a field for people who love sitting behind a desk most of the time, since a lot of work must be done at the site of the events.

Job Strategies: To research firms specializing in sports marketing, study *Sports Market Place* (see Information Sources, page 55), a directory listing hundreds of organizations involved in various aspects of the industry. In addition, many advertising agencies have established divisions dedicated to sports marketing. Major sports marketing events, the agencies promoting them, and their corporate sponsors are reported in *Sports Marketing News*. (See Information Sources following.)

One way to test your interest in the field and make some good contacts that may lead to a job offer is to volunteer your services at a local sports event having commercial sponsors. Introduce yourself to the promotional company's on-site representative and offer to collect tickets, help out with security, or negotiate promotional support of local merchants.

Prepare writing samples that will demonstrate your ability to develop promotional materials. Any published samples you can provide will be an added plus. Present a local magazine or newspaper with some proposals for stories that fit in with its editorial style; if it's a sport-oriented story, so much the better. You may be paid a small fee or nothing for the story, but the fact that you will have a published article or two to your credit will be a strong asset in your job campaign.

Many advertising agencies have divisions dedicated to sports marketing— see page 24 for the typical advertising agency account management career path. The chief difference between the agency career path and that within sports marketing firms is that the latter are generally rather small organizations, so the account executive may report directly to the firm's owner.

Career Path

Many of these firms are organized along the lines of advertising and public relations agencies. As such, the career path is similar:

Junior Account Executive—Provides support on one or more accounts, serving as liaison on the design and implementation of sports promotional projects

Account Executive—Full responsibility for supporting one or more accounts; interface between client advertising/promotional personnel and company's in-house creative and production staff

Account Supervisor—Plays a major role in formulating the creative concepts for events; actively involved in negotiating corporate support for events; supervises one or more account executives

Information Sources for Sports Marketing

Sports Market Place, Sportsguide, Inc., P. O. Box 1417, Princeton, NJ 08542. This directory contains three sections:

> For over 50 sport categories, information is provided on U.S., Canadian, and international associations; professional leagues and teams; publications; and suppliers selling products related to the sport.

> The multi-sport section lists organizations/companies dealing with more than one sport according to ten categories, including publications, promotional/athlete/event management services, trade show and meeting calendar, etc.

> In addition, there are geographical, key executive, and alphabetical listings by sport or service.

Sports Marketing News, Technical Marketing Corporation, P. O. Box 453, Winchester, MA 01890, 617/729–0235.

See also, "Information Sources for Marketing" (page 25) for pointers to advertising agencies, many of which have sports marketing divisions.

PROPERTY MANAGEMENT: Owners of real estate—residential, commercial, industrial, retail—have as their prime objective enhancing the value of their properties. The job function devoted to accomplishing this objective is the property manager. Property manager positions are found both within corporations and institutions that own property, and in real estate service companies that manage properties on a contractual basis. Primary responsibilities include development of budgets for the operation and improvement of the property, preparation of specifications for services and products purchased for the property, vendor/supplier negotiations, tenant relations, and, if a real estate services company, sales presentations. Some property managers will also lease space and develop promotional programs, and will have considerable contact with real estate brokers. In major cities property managers will usually have to deal with unions.

This is not a nine-to-five job, since at any time some emergency at the facility could result in the property manager getting a call from a building manager with the need for a decision on how to deal with a power outage, bomb threat, snowstorm, etc. Individuals with experience in the heating, ventilation, and air-conditioning trades would have a strong advantage in obtaining a building manager position, which can lead to property management. Building managers always work right on the premises, since they have to be able to respond quickly to any emergencies or complaints about the facility. Property managers may or may not be stationed on the premises, depending on the size of the facility and the organization of the company.

The preference of employees to work close to home is leading to more construction of combination office, apartment, and retail complexes. This, in turn, is placing new demands on property managers in that they must address the needs of a diverse population of tenants with problems unique to their types of space.

Job Strategies: Career changers interested in the property management field should read national real estate publications such as the *Journal of Property Management* and the *Real Estate Forum* (see Information Sources, page 57) to develop a good understanding of the industry's issues and trends. Consider completing the Institute of Real Estate Management (IREM) course, Leasing and Management of Office Buildings. This one-week program will provide the foundation that may help convince a company of your qualification for an assistant property manager position.

Office complexes under construction or recently completed are likely to need property management personnel. You can research these through local real estate and business publications that announce awards of commercial office management contracts to real estate service companies.

Experience in managing projects, working under pressure, and negotiating arrangements with vendors and suppliers is valued by the property management function. Financial and data-processing skills may provide a significant edge in getting a first property management job, as could a civil engineering background.

Career Path

The following is a description of the career path for property management within a real estate services company. Positions in corporate real estate departments will entail similar responsibilities.

Assistant Property Manager—Entry-level position; provides support to the property manager in all his/her responsibilities

Property Manager—Develops and administers budgets for the operation and improvement of the property; designs and delivers presentations to owners (if employed by a management company) to win contracts to manage their buildings; prepares specifications for services provided by contractors; reviews proposals, negotiates modifications to fees and terms, directs contractors in the performance of their work; monitors regional real estate market conditions so as to establish competitive rents; handles relations with the property owner (if a real estate services company) and rent collection; may also supervise a building manager located at the property site

Senior Property Manager—Oversees two to four property managers; in a real estate management company will also play a key role in proposal development, sales presentations, and in contract negotiations with property owners

Certified Property Manager—Held by someone who has completed a series of three courses offered by the Institute of Real Estate Management (IREM), has been employed in the field for at least five years, and has demonstrated the highest level of technical, financial, and sales/marketing knowledge; usually manages a very large facility (500,000 square feet and up)

Information Sources for Property Management

Real Estate Forum (monthly), 12 West 37th Street, New York, NY 10018, 212/563–6460.

National Roster of Realtors Directory, Stamats Communications, Inc., 427 Sixth Avenue SE, Cedar Rapids, IA 52406, 319/364–6032. Lists all realtor (R) members of the National Association of Realtors. Describes the functions, publications, courses, chapters, and key personnel of eight professional associations.

Institute of Real Estate Management, 430 North Michigan Avenue, Chicago, IL 60611, 312/661–1930. Publishes the bimonthly *Journal of Property Management* and an annual membership directory. Also awards the Certified Property Manager professional designation.

Building Owners and Managers Association International, 1250 Eye Street NW, Suite 200, Washington, DC 20005, 202/289–7000.

International Association of Corporate Real Estate Executives, 471 Spencer Drive South, Suite 8, W. Palm Beach, FL 33409, 305/683–8111. Publishes a directory of corporate real estate executives.

EMPLOYEE-ASSISTANCE PROGRAMS: The National Institute on Alcohol Abuse and Alcoholism has estimated that the annual costs of lost employment and reduced productivity attributed to alcoholism amount to over $70 billion.* It's no wonder, therefore, that companies have taken action to address alcoholism in the workplace, as well as other personal problems that translate into productivity losses. Their response has taken the form of programs—called employee-assistance programs, or EAPs—that provide employees with referrals to professionals in a wide range of disciplines, including substance-abuse counseling and other mental health services, budget and debt counseling, career counseling, and legal services.

While some companies manage their own employee-assistance programs, hiring their own professional staffs, the majority of the more than 9,000 EAPs in the United States are contractual arrangements between end-user organizations and EAP consulting firms and social service agencies, which also offer EAPs.

At an EAP consulting firm, a program administrator is assigned responsibility for supporting client companies in a particular region. His or her job will include training the client's management in procedures for referring employees to the service. In some EAP consulting firms the program administrator will get involved in marketing the service to corporations as well. Some firms may also have a counselor reporting to the program administrator who will handle only assessment, referral, and counseling, with no administrative responsibility. While some EAPs hire professionals in various disciplines on a contractual basis, most will refer employees to external professionals. Other EAPs provide 3–6 sessions of employee counseling before referring the individual to external professionals.

The assessment and referral services are completely free to the employee, but the employee pays the fee charged by the professionals to whom he or she is referred. In instances where employees' problems have become obvious through poor performance and other signs, they are strongly encouraged to seek help through the program, since they may lose their jobs if the poor performance caused by the problem continues. All employees are told about EAPs, and an employee's *voluntary* contact with the EAP is kept confidential.

Because of the newness of the EAP industry, the backgrounds of its counseling and administrative professionals vary widely (as do salaries), ranging from recovering alcoholics with business experience to social workers with backgrounds in counseling alcoholics. However, as the industry is growing, more formal requirements are evolving, and one of the two primary professional associations (see Information Sources, page 60) for the field has initiated a certification program. In a discussion I had with George "Bud" Wassell, CEAP, the EAP Director of Meriden-Wallingford Hospital in Con-

---

Sixth Special Report to the U.S. Congress on Alcohol and Health (National Institute on Alcohol Abuse and Alcoholism, January 1987), p. 23.

necticut, he pointed to the increasing demand for a master's degree in counseling or social work for individuals holding program administrator positions, as well as experience working with alcoholics. Another credential widely accepted in the EAP field, Certified Alcoholism Counselor, can be obtained through a combination of alcoholism counseling experience and formal study. (For information on the credentialing process in your state, contact the state agency responsible for alcohol and drug education and information.) In addition, there is a greater emphasis today on psychiatric training, so as to be able to deal with crisis situations. Lastly, any experience within the business world can be very helpful in rounding out one's qualifications.

Job Strategies: One way to obtain information on EAP companies is through the two associations serving the profession: Employee Assistance Society of North America and the Association of Labor-Management Administrators and Consultants on Alcoholism, Inc. (See Information Sources following.) Contact them to determine whether there are chapters in your area and, if so, explore the possibility of participating in workshops and other activities. Each association also publishes a membership directory. Since mental health agencies, alcoholism counseling agencies, and treatment centers get referrals from these programs, they may be another source of information about area EAPs. Many states have commissions on alcohol and drug abuse, which may be helpful, too.

End-user companies and EAP consulting firms value counseling and social work backgrounds in considering applicants for program administrator positions. More and more graduate programs in counseling and social work are offering concentrations in the EAP area. Experience working with alcoholism is very important, which is one reason why recovering alcoholics may also be considered for counseling and administrator positions.

Career Path

EAP Counselor—Can exist either within an EAP consulting firm or the employer environment; EAP counselor is responsible for assessing the scope of the problem, providing counseling where appropriate, and directing the employee to outside professionals who can provide additional help

EAP Program Administrator—Can exist either within an EAP consulting firm or in the employer environment; Program Administrator is responsible for designing, implementing, and managing EAP programs, as well as for assessment and referral services

Clinical Director (Manager)—More commonly found in an EAP consulting firm (but not in all) than in an end-user company; Clinical Director is responsible for designing the company's program, and for training and supervising the staff of program administrators

Corporate Manager of EAP—Exists in a large end-user organization; responsible for designing and administering an in-house EAP, developing and administering budgets, and staffing (including hiring of outside contractors)

Information Sources for Employee-Assistance Programs

National Council on Alcoholism, 12 West 21st Street, New York, NY 10010, 212/206–6770. Publishes a directory of their affiliates with EAPs.

Association of Labor-Management Administrators and Consultants on Alcoholism, Inc. (ALMACA), 1800 North Kent Street, #907, Arlington, VA 22209, 703/522–6272. Awards the Certified Employee Assistance Professional (CEAP) credential.

Employee Assistance Society of North America (EASNA), P. O. Box 3909, Oak Park, IL 60303, 312/383–6668.

EAP Digest (bimonthly), Performance Resource Press, 2145 Crooks Road, Suite 103, Troy, MI 48084, 313/643–9580.

MEETINGS AND CONVENTIONS: The design, marketing, and management of meetings and conventions has developed over the past ten years into a large, sophisticated industry, providing excellent opportunities for people seeking new careers. One major type of meeting, the trade show, is an event where companies marketing products and services to a particular industry present them to buyers by renting space in a large exhibit hall. An indication of the growth of the meetings and conventions industry is the increase in annual trade shows since 1976 from approximately 900 to about 3,000. But the industry isn't limited to trade shows; hundreds of professional associations—for example, the American Bar Association and American Psychological Association—hold major national meetings, and corporations conduct large meetings for sales personnel, distributors, and dealers.

Trade shows and major professional association conventions are large-scale events, requiring careful planning of physical facility requirements, advertising, and promotion. Says David Cheifetz, President of Conference Management Corporation, "Trade shows are essentially living magazines, since they present information on topics of interest to a particular industry, and advertisements of products and services for the industry." As you can imagine, therefore, many of the skills required for successful magazine production are similarly important for a successful trade show or convention, including graphic design and copywriting, for example, as well as the design of seminars to attract attendance.

One can be employed in this industry by a corporation or association sponsoring the meetings, by a hotel that promotes its facilities for meetings and conventions, or by a company engaged solely in planning and running trade shows and conventions. If employed within the sponsoring corporation or association, one is usually called a meetings planner, with responsibility for planning and directing all aspects of the event. This could entail developing the creative theme and seminars for the meeting; hiring and directing graphic designers, copywriters, and typographers; and coordinating travel and lodging arrangements. Trade shows are marketed through direct mail and via the telephone, so skills in these areas are important, too.

Positions within companies that plan and manage trade shows and conventions are likely to be more specialized, with one person responsible for designing the seminar (a seminar programmer), one responsible for selling exhibit space to companies interested in promoting their products and services to meeting attendees, and another responsible for coordinating the facilities arrangements.

Job Strategies: The greatest opportunities in this field can be found in companies marketing trade shows and conventions. The most important qualification sought by these companies in candidates for seminar programmer positions is the ability to write well. Applicants must be prepared to show writing samples that demonstrate their ability to write both informational and promotional materials. A journalism, magazine editing, or direct marketing background would be a plus.

The operations end of the business requires the ability to plan every aspect of a major time-critical project to ensure its successful completion. Skill in negotiating fees and terms with carpenters, electricians, and other contractors is important. A background in corporate facilities management would be a definite advantage in being considered for an operations position. A sales background in any field would be an asset in gaining an exhibit sales position in a meetings planning company.

Someone interested in obtaining a meetings planner position in a trade or professional association can research key executives in these organizations through the American Society of Association Executives. (See Information Sources following.) A corporate meetings planning position would fall under the headquarters sales function. (See page 233 for detailed information on this functional area.) However, a headquarters sales job that entails only the planning of meetings is most likely to be found in a large company.

Career Path

Following are descriptions of commonly found positions in the meetings and conventions industry:

In a company that plans and manages trade shows and conventions:

Seminar Programmer—Responsible for developing creative concepts and preparing promotional material for seminars on topics of interest to meeting attendees; conducts research to identify potential seminar leaders and negotiates arrangements with them

Project Manager—Has overall responsibility for the profitability of a commercial trade show and supervises a team consisting of a sales representative, seminar programmer, and operations manager; establishes a budget for the event and formulates marketing strategies to ensure maximum attendance at the event and associated seminars

Other career opportunities and lateral paths in a meetings planning company:

Sales Representative—Sells exhibit space to companies marketing products and services to the professionals or companies attending the trade show or convention; can lead to project manager

Operations Manager—Is responsible for all logistical aspects of the meeting or convention, e.g., researching, selecting, and conducting negotiations for the facility; coordinating the shipment of equipment to the site with truckers and airlines; hiring and directing carpenters and electricians; resolving on-site problems of exhibitors; position can lead to a project manager job

In a trade or professional association, or in a corporation that organizes its own sales meetings:

Meetings Planner—Responsibilities include marketing the event to members (corporate sales meetings do not have to be marketed, since employees are required to attend them) and developing promotional and/or informative materials; selection and preparation of the meeting site, negotiations with hotels, airlines, exhibitors; coordination of on-site activities during meeting, etc.

Information Sources for Meetings and Conventions

Robert W. Lord, *Running Conventions, Conferences and Meetings*. New York: AMACOM (div. of American Management Association). This out-of-print book is now available from Books on Demand (division of University Microfilm International), Ann Arbor, MI. Readers are given step-by-step guidance in planning and organizing successful meetings, i.e., program subjects, speakers, use of convention bureaus, hotel arrangements, etc.

Trade Show/Convention Guide, Budd Publications, Inc., P. O. Box 7, New York, NY 10029. This publication lists trade show management companies, associations involved in the industry, trade shows and convention facilities by state, a calendar of events, and shows categorized by industry.

Tradeshow Week, 12233 W. Olympic Boulevard, Suite 236, Los Angeles, CA 90064–1039, 213/826–5696.

Meeting News (monthly), 1515 Broadway, New York, NY 10036, 212/869–1300.

Meetings and Conventions (monthly), 1 Park Avenue, New York, NY 10016, 212/503–5700.

American Society of Association Executives, 1575 Eye Street NW, Washington, DC 20005, 202/626–2723. Offers five-day course on convention management, which covers budgeting, site selection, strategies for promoting the event, etc.

Meeting Planners International, 1950 Stemmons Freeway, Dallas, TX 75207, 214/746–5222.

Society of Company Meeting Planners, 2600 Garden Road, #208, Monterey, CA 93940, 408/649–6544.

The Value of Talking to Practitioners

Through your reading of the previous sections, as well as your library research, you may find one or more career options that seem appealing. But the reading part of your research should be supplemented by interviews with people doing the kinds of work in which you are interested. If you can get referred to these people through personal contacts, all the better, but if you can't, don't let that deter you. Conduct research to identify managers and executives in organizations (Chapter 3 explains how to do this); contact them by phone and tell them you are in the process of evaluating alternative career options, that you've identified the field of human resources, or advertising or data processing, for example, as one where your skills can be applied effectively. Add that you've done a lot of library research, but that at this point you really need to talk to people in the field, since you have a number of questions that your research could not answer. Try to arrange an interview, at which you can pose your questions—ask to see job descriptions for positions within their functional areas. In addition to helping you determine whether you would enjoy the work, these documents will be invaluable in preparing you for a job hunt, should you decide to target the field.

Never try to transform this kind of meeting into a job interview, since the basis on which you were granted the interview was for information—not a job. If you do try to, the interviewer will probably feel manipulated and will therefore be resentful rather than cooperative. Of course, if the interviewer intitiates a discussion of a job opening, by all means follow through.

Literature to Help You Identify Career Options

The following reference and other books are available in many public libraries:

The Occupational Outlook Handbook. U.S. Department of Labor, Employment and Training Administration, 200 Constitution Avenue, NW, Washington, DC 20210. Spend at least a few hours leafing through this wonderful book, which contains detailed descriptions of over 500 commonly performed occupations. You'll learn about the skills and education necessary for success in many fields, what a typical workday consists of, the amount of money you can earn, the long-term job outlook for each field, and professional associations to contact for further information.

Dictionary of Occupational Titles. U.S. Department of Labor, Employment and Training Administration, 200 Constitution Avenue, NW, Washington, DC 20210. This book contains brief descriptions of hundreds of jobs. Each job is assigned a number that can be used to look up the same job in the *Occupational Outlook Handbook*, which contains a much lengthier description.

Guide for Occupational Exploration. U.S. Department of Labor, Employment and Training Administration, 200 Constitution Avenue, NW, Washington, DC 20210. Contains a summary list of interest areas, work groups, and subgroups the reader can look up to find career options. For example, you could refer to the sections on "Business" or "Oral Communications" to find careers compatible with these areas.

William E. Hopke, ed. *The Encyclopedia of Careers and Vocational Guidance*. Chicago: J. G. Ferguson Publishing Company, 1984. This three-volume set includes a review of careers and advice on selecting one.

Paul Downes, ed., *Chronicle Career Index*. Moravia, NY: Chronicle Guidance Publications, Inc. Published annually; list sources of career and vocational guidance literature on specific careers. Many items are free.

Business Periodicals Index. H. W. Wilson Company, 950 University Avenue, Bronx, NY 10452. Under specific topics—for example, "Personnel Management" or "Market Research"—you will find lists of articles on these subjects in business periodicals.

Patricia G. Schuman, *Materials for Occupational Education*: *An Annotated Source Guide*, 2nd ed., New York: Neal-Schuman Publishers, 1983.

U.S. Employment Opportunities, Washington Research Associates, Inc., 2103 N. Lincoln Street, Arlington, VA 22207. This is an annual publication providing overviews of the prospects for selected industries, along with implications for job hunters. It lists employers with openings in the covered industries. Quarterly updates of economic prospects are also published.

Health Careers Guidebook. Washington, DC: U.S. Department of Labor, Employment and Training Administration, 1979. Describes the responsibilities and associated compensation for 450 executive, administrative, and managerial positions in the health-care field. Also includes names and addresses of employers who hire for these positions.

Health Careers: Where the Jobs Are and How to Get Them. New York: Fawcett Books, 1982.

Marti Prashker and S. Peter Valiunas, *Money Jobs! Training Programs Run by Banking, Accounting, Insurance, and Brokerage Firms and How to Get into Them*. New York: Crown Publishers, Inc., 1984. This book describes career opportunities in a variety of financial environments and provides details on many corporate training programs.

Joan Anzalone, ed., *Good Works, A Guide to Careers in Social Change*, 3rd ed. New York: Dembner Books, 1985. Contains a directory of socially oriented organizations, including descriptions of their objectives, types of projects, budget size, and staffing.

Eric Kocher, *International Jobs*. Reading, MA: Addison-Wesley Publishing Company, 1983. Describes job opportunities in the federal government, not-for-profit organizations, U.S. corporations, and international communications organizations.

Harvard Business Review, Harvard Business School, Soldiers Field, Boston, MA 02163. This journal presents innovative practical approaches for dealing with problems encountered in the management of companies and organizations in the private, public, and not-for-profit sectors. Its articles are highly readable—even by someone with no business background.

There are many books on the subjects of individual careers. Check your local bookstore or library for those relevant to the vocations appealing to you. Also, virtually all professions and industries have publications tailored to their needs. To find those of interest to you, consult your library's periodical directory.

Researching Educational/Training Programs

If your targeted field requires a formal course of study, you'll want to be sure the program you choose can satisfactorily prepare you for entry into the profession. In researching the quality of graduate or undergraduate programs, consult with faculty members in the field you are considering and, in addition, ask them for the names of several people who graduated from the program one to three years previously. Ask the graduates how well the program prepared them for their field, how the quality of their education was viewed by experienced practitioners in the field, and how easily they were able to obtain their first job.

You can also consult the following books in researching the quality of many graduate and undergraduate programs:

Dr. Jack Gourman, *The Gourman Report—A Rating of Graduate and Professional Programs in American and International Universities*, 4th rev. ed. Los Angeles: National Education Standards, 1987.

Dr. Jack Gourman, *The Gourman Report—A Rating of Undergraduate Programs in American and International Universities*, 6th rev. ed. Los Angeles: National Education Standards, 1987.

In each of these Dr. Gourman uses a point valuation system that considers eleven criteria important in providing academic education.

The National Directory of Internships contains information on 26,000 internships available in 65 fields spanning the private, public, and not-for-profit sectors. Many of the internship descriptions specifically mention that midlife applicants are welcome. The directory can be purchased from the publisher:

National Society for Internships and Experiential Education, 3509 Haworth Drive, Raleigh, NC 27609, 919/787–3263.

FINDING FINANCIAL AID OPPORTUNITIES: The following books offer valuable information on sources of scholarships, fellowships, loans, and grants:

S. Norman Feingold and Marie Feingold, *Scholarships, Fellowships, & Loans*, Vol. 8. Arlington, MA: Bellman Publishing Co., 1982.
Foundation Grants to Individuals and *The Foundation Grants Index*. New York: The Foundation Center, 1986.

It may seem that we talked about the steps involved in changing your career (page 11) a long time ago. We've dealt in great detail with the first step, namely, understanding your capabilities and finding work environments that draw upon them. I am sure that you now have the confidence to complete the first step successfully. Here are the rest:

Step 2—Develop your Career Criteria

To get you started, I have developed a list of items I suggest you consider in formulating your criteria; presumably you will have additional considerations unique to your needs. As you read this list, jot down some notes on your response to each item.

Compensation
What annual compensation do I need as a minimum after I enter a new field? What will I want to earn five years from now? Ten years?

Near- and long-term outlook for job security in the field
How important is job security to me?

Educational requirements, now and later
How willing am I to undertake a program of study now to gain entry into a new field? Suppose I can enter the field without further study, but will have to pursue higher education to advance. How willing am I do to that? Will I have the financial resources to undertake the educational program?

Compatibility with your aptitudes and interests
What aptitudes and interests do I have that I want to use in the new career— for example, creativity, writing ability, public speaking ability, mathematical or logical ability, project management skill, mediating/negotiating skill, leadership skill, foreign language proficiency, interest in social or environmental matters?

Type and degree of commitment required by the field
Some fields typically require a greater level of dedication than do others. This can take several forms, e.g., long work days, working without breaks, intellectual and physical demands. For example, attorneys practicing in many law firms and beginning investment bankers are required to work as many as 100 hours weekly. On the other hand, jobs in retail sales will have more limited, predictable work schedules that coincide with the operating hours of the store.

Ask yourself this question: What degree of effort and commitment to a career am I prepared to make?

Satisfaction of personal/psychic needs
How important is it that my work allow me to make a contribution to society, or support my political beliefs? What are my self-image and status needs? How much control do I need over the work I do? Over my work schedule? What is my work style, e.g., loner, enjoy working with one person, or in small/large groups?

Practical considerations
How important is it that I travel (overnight)? That I don't travel? How important is it for me to have a job that gets me out of the office during the workday?

In developing your list, be careful not to include in it criteria for evaluating a specific job—for example, some of my clients have included on lists they've brought me such items as "a lot of light when I'm working," and "a nicely appointed office with modern furniture." These are factors that can range widely within one field and which should be considered later when evaluating a job *offer*, not a career option.

In developing your list try to include at least 15–20 criteria. While they all may not be equally important to you, we will discuss shortly how to evaluate the relative importance of each factor in making your decision. As you conduct your research into possible career options, evaluate the degree to which each satisfies each criterion.

Step 3—Making the Decision

After completing your career research and developing your criteria you will be ready to make a decision as to whether you want to make a change to a new career, and, if yes, which one it will be. Both decisions can be made in the same step, since determining whether you should leave your present work is akin to considering your current career as an option.

Making this decision properly requires a process that will enable you to measure each option fairly. Begin by assigning a weighting factor, from one to ten, to each of the criteria you developed in Step 2 to reflect their relative importance to you. For example, if work content is of the highest importance to you, and salary is slightly less important, assign work content a value of ten, and salary an eight or nine. If it's minimally important that you work in an environment that is not too high pressure, you could assign this criterion a point value of one, two, or three. If you have a preference not to travel, which is as important to you as the work content, then assign a ten to this criterion also. If long-term job security is fairly important to you, but slightly less important than salary, this category would be assigned a seven or eight.

Now construct a table, listing all your criteria in the rows on the left side, and have each career option head a column. Based on the information you've gathered about these career options, assign one score per criterion (from one to ten, with ten being the most favorable) to every career option shown on the table. Each score should reflect the extent to which you believe the particular criterion is met by each career option.

Once you've completed this step, multiply each point value in the career criterion box by the weighting factor you earlier ascribed to each criterion. When you finish adding up the column entries, you will have a total weighted score of attractiveness for each career option.

Figure 1 illustrates the use of this technique as applied to a teacher considering market research and sales as possible career options.

Testing Your Interest in a Field
Some degree of uncertainty is associated with a career change, but you can take steps to reduce dramatically the risk of your not liking the targeted work. Here are a few ideas:

- *Volunteer your services as a part-time intern.*
  If your schedule allows, whether through vacations or during your work week, try to negotiate an arrangement with a local firm engaged in work that interests you.

Figure 1. An example of a comparative analysis of three career options

Criterion	Weighting Factor	Option 1: Teaching		Option 2: Market Research		Option 3: Sales	
		Score	Weighted Score	Score	Weighted Score	Score	Weighted Score
Compensation now	6	2	12	5	30	6	36
Compensation in 5 years	9	3	27	7	63	9	81
Not a high pressure atmosphere	6	7	42	3	18	1	6
No need to relocate	10	10	100	10	100	6	60
No need to travel	5	10	50	7	35	3	15
Uses my communication and analytical skills	8	7	56	9	72	6	48
Interesting, non-repetitive work	10	1	10	7	70	5	50
Gets me out of the office	7	1	7	7	49	10	70
Long-term job security	6	10	60	8	48	5	30
No further formal education required for advancement	4	4	16	6	24	10	40
Offers future opportunity for self-employment	5	2	10	8	40	4	20
Total Weighted Score			390		549*		456

*Most Attractive Option

- *Get a part-time or temporary job for after hours or during vacations.*
  I know of a number of people who worked on a temporary basis—some as secretaries or clerks—and so impressed the company management that they were offered permanent, full-time professional positions.

- *Take a leave of absence, if possible.*
  Some organizations will allow this kind of arrangement, although you do run the risk that your position in the company will be negatively affected if you return.

Even if you cannot use any of the above approaches, you really don't have much to lose, since you can probably find work in your old career if the new one doesn't work out. To move ahead in life you must take risks.

Step 4—Develop Your Plan of Implementation

Many important decisions—especially those resulting in a major expenditure of time—are best implemented with a formal plan. A plan for making your career change should include these elements:

- a determination of which industries you seek entry into, and which organizations within those industries seem to offer work environments where you can gain the best exposure to the field, and be most productive and happy;
- an evaluation of alternative strategies for contacting executives in these organizations and selection of the method best for you;
- a set of job-hunting documentation, including a résumé, a cover letter and thank-you letter that can be tailored to individual situations, list of references, and salary history;
- extensive preparation for the job interview;
- salary negotiation skill;
- a method for evaluating one or more job offers objectively; and
- a schedule of implementation. In developing your schedule, divide your campaign into a number of manageable steps and make a commitment to set aside some number of hours weekly toward completing each. This method is more likely to motivate you to continue than if you were to set only a final date by which the entire project will be finished. How long it will take you to achieve your goal will depend on a number of factors, e.g., the current demand for personnel in the field you target, whether you have transferable skills from your present work, how much time you can spend each week on your campaign. Thus I cannot give you advice for your particular situation. However, it might be helpful if I told you about a client of mine, a teacher seeking a new career. He

spent approximately fifty hours conducting research into several fields through library visits, attending meetings of professional groups, and sending for and studying literature provided by professional organizations. An additional thirty hours were spent in arranging and participating in interviews with seven executives in his targeted fields before he narrowed his objective to the field of market research. My client's eighty-hour project, which was conducted over a period of three months, entailed a total cost of about $235, for these items: toll calls, photocopies, mailings to professional associations, three books, transportation, parking, and luncheon meetings.

I would like to assure you that the entire process is not as difficult as it may seem, but people do tend to feel overwhelmed when they face an unknown situation. *Information* is what closes the gap between the known and the unknown, while reducing anxiety about taking a new major step. And information—presented in step-by-step fashion—is what you will find in the following pages.

3

The Job Hunt

EVALUATING VARIOUS APPROACHES

In my opinion, every job hunter is capable of obtaining employment through his or her own efforts, but in order to conduct a proper job-hunting campaign, one usually has to spend a lot of time in researching and contacting employers, and in writing a résumé and letters. Using professional services can sometimes reduce significantly the time spent on these activities—and that may be very important to you. Let's compare the pros and cons of using these services versus managing your own job search; I hope you'll conclude after reading the following pages that you should conduct your job campaign yourself.

Professional Services

Services that assist job hunters fall into two categories:

- *Career services* help job hunters identify alternative career options, devise job strategies, target employers, write or guide the client in writing résumés and letters—but they do not find a job for the client. Companies included in this group are typically called outplacement services and career consultants or counselors.
- *Placement services*, such as employment agencies and executive recruiters, act as go-betweens for job hunters and employers. Employment agencies are most often paid a fee by the employer, but in some cases collect their fees from the applicant. Executive recruiters, who work on behalf of employers, specialize in finding middle- and higher-level management personnel and executives; recruiters always collect their fees from the employer.

Let's look more closely at how each of these two types of services works.

Career Services

Many outplacement companies are hired only by companies that are about to terminate the jobs of employees, as a fringe benefit to the employees; however, you may be able to find one that will work directly for you. Their fees may be as high as 15 percent of the job hunter's total annual compensation, and some companies require a minimum fee of $3,500 or more. Services include:

- assistance in dealing with the psychological aspects of being laid off or fired, and with the anxiety associated with seeking a new job;
- office space and secretarial support;
- assistance with developing résumés and cover letters;
- access to directories and other sources of data on companies and executives;
- mailing of résumés and letters to targeted employers; and
- coaching in interview skills and salary-negotiation techniques.

Although outplacement firms usually assist clients in managing job-search campaigns only, some also offer advice in changing careers. On the other hand, career consultants, which are usually smaller operations than outplacement companies, offer extensive career-planning services and, in some cases, job search guidance similar to the type offered by outplacement firms. Some career consultants charge a flat fee for a package of services; others offer a menu of services, each of which can be purchased for a flat fee—or on an hourly basis.

Some people feel more motivated to work at job hunting when they have the kind of support provided by these companies, but several of the services they provide are available from other sources—either free or at a much lower price. Secretarial and mailing services can provide you with all the clerical help you need at a reasonable cost; free access to directories is available through any good public or university library; publicly held companies will gladly send anyone copies of their annual reports. As you will learn further on, mass mailings are usually a waste of time. In addition, the use of this kind of service may become a crutch, weakening your own efforts to accomplish your objective. Naturally, if your company is paying for such a service, you should use it to whatever extent you find helpful.

CHECKLIST OF CONSIDERATIONS WHEN SELECTING A CAREER SERVICE: Before you engage a career consultant or outplacement service, get the answers to these questions:

1. How extensive is the experience of the consultant or company in your area of interest?

Specifically, if you are looking for guidance in selecting a business career or a new job in the business world, you will be best served by someone with a business background. Such a person is likely to be familiar with the titles and responsibilities of jobs for which you may be qualified, and have a good understanding of the hiring procedures and selection criteria for these jobs.

2. Does the company offer services that encompass all your needs?

For example, if you know what your skills are you shouldn't need aptitude testing. But you do need someone who can match your aptitudes to the right fields.

3. How much will the services cost?

Fees for career and outplacement services vary widely. To ascribe a value to a service by calculating how much time would be provided and determining an hourly fee doesn't really help, since a company that has a much higher hourly fee than others may also satisfy your needs better, making an arrangement with it a better value. Also, if a company offers several services as a package and you don't need all of them, try to negotiate the purchase of just those you do need.

4. Is there a contract to sign?

If so, I suggest you read it very carefully. Do not allow yourself to be pressured into signing a contract. Question every item in it that appears ambiguous or incomplete, and stipulate that you want it modified to reflect any oral clarifications given to you. In many states, consumers have three days after the signing of a contract to change their minds and get a full refund of any deposit paid. Check with your local consumer protection agency for the applicable law and be sure you understand how, if at all, you can extricate yourself from the contract, and what it will cost you.

5. Will the service be provided by someone other than the person with whom the initial interview and financial arrangements are discussed?

In some outplacement companies intake counselors negotiate the sale of the service, while others actually provide the service. Because career guidance is a highly personalized service where the right chemistry is important, prior to engaging the service you should insist on meeting the counselor with whom you would be working. Additionally, you may want to get written confirmation that your agreeing to do business with the company is contingent upon your ability to work with that person throughout the program. Try to negotiate the option to extricate yourself from the contract and pay a prorated amount of money for the services rendered to date if that person is no longer available.

6. If access to the hidden job market is claimed, proceed with caution and explore further.

I've always been suspicious of companies promoting access to the hidden job market, because it implies that they procure employment for individuals—while in most states, only employment agencies are allowed to charge for matching applicants and employers. A company that markets access to the hidden job market, if it is not an employment agency, may merely be providing the client with a list of, or access to, directories of companies or mailing lists of executives. If so, there is nothing hidden about this information—you can probably find all the directories you need in a good public library and purchase the names you need directly from a mailing list company.

Placement Services: Employment Agencies and Executive Recruiters

An employer will hire an agency or recruiter to locate a candidate who fits a particular skills profile if it decides that the service would be able to conduct the search in a more cost-effective manner and with better results than the company itself would. Employment agencies conduct their searches on a contingency basis; this means that a fee is paid to an agency only if its candidate is hired by the employer. The types of positions with which agencies usually deal range from general office help to middle management. Many agencies specialize in certain types of jobs, e.g., data processing, engineering, marketing, sales. Fees that range from 10 to 30 percent of the selected candidate's first year's compensation are typical in the agency business, with the higher percentages being paid for higher-level personnel. I should add that some agencies collect their fee from the applicant—not the employer.

Executive recruiters (informally called "headhunters") generally deal with jobs from the middle-management level to top executives, with some taking on slightly lower-level searches as well. They are also used by companies to find individuals in rare specialties. Unlike an agency, a recruiter is usually paid on a retainer basis. A typical contract specifies that the recruiter will receive a fee of anywhere from 25 to 40 percent of the position's anticipated first year's cash compensation. Typically, one-third is paid at contract signing, one-third paid one month later, and the balance paid when the recruiter has produced (depending on the contract terms) two or more candidates. Notice that I said "produced" candidates. Even if the company does not hire the satisfactory candidates presented by the recruiter, a fee is still paid.

There are many variations on these fee arrangements for both agencies and recruiters, since sometimes recruiters and agencies will try to make their fees more attractive than their competitors', and sometimes companies will negotiate arrangements more favorable to themselves.

Large recruiting firms assign individuals to handle various business specialties. If you are seeking a job in your field at a middle-management level or higher—or if you are employed in a rare specialty—and want to be placed by an executive recruiter, call the firm to determine the name of the person who handles your functional area. That individual will probably suggest that you send your résumé, but this isn't cause for optimism. If your qualifications do not satisfy any of the company's search assignments, it's likely that your résumé will be filed away under the area of your specialty. It will be retrieved if and when a future search assignment is consistent with your qualifications.

One reason that executive recruiters aren't enthusiastic about dealing with job hunters who initiate contact with them is that if the individuals are hired, they may tell the client that *they* initiated the contact with the recruiter—yet the recruiter will have charged a "search" fee. While it's not very common for this kind of contact to prove fruitful, it is possible. If you do plan on contacting a recruiter—or an agency, for that matter—it's important to sell them on your attractiveness as a candidate.

The most significant implication of the agency/recruiter business is that if you are changing careers, you cannot expect to be helped by these companies. Why? The applicant is not the agency's or recruiter's client; the client is the company paying the fee to the agency or recruiter. If you are a career changer, it's extremely unlikely that an agency or recruiter will feel able to collect a fee by promoting you, since suggesting that the company hire an applicant with no background in the field could jeopardize the recruiter/company relationship. The client's management knows that it can place an ad—at a much lower cost than a professional's fee—seeking former teachers, accountants, actresses, etc. to fill any open positions.

But suppose you are not changing fields; should you contact an agency or recruiter? Even in this case, as a general rule, I suggest not. Imagine that you are the executive who must fill the position you want. You are presented with two candidates; candidate number one comes to you through an employment agency; candidate number two contacts you directly. Remember, if you hire the first candidate, you must pay a fee that could run into many thousands of dollars. Assuming that the candidates have comparable qualifications, do you have any more assurance that the agency-sponsored applicant will perform better than the one who got in touch with you directly? Of course not, so why pay a large premium? Furthermore, implicit in the savings realized by the employer in not having to pay an agency fee is an opportunity for the applicant to negotiate a more favorable salary.

In fairness to agencies and recruiters, I should tell you that they do offer some advantages. Since they are constantly contacting companies, they know of positions opening up; also, employers do find it advantageous to use them in a number of instances—for example, if they don't want key employees to know that management is planning to replace them and believe that an advertisement might betray that fact. An agency or recruiter can praise you to an employer in a way that you might feel uncomfortable doing yourself, but which might be necessary in order to convince the employer to meet you. If you are in a work situation that leaves you little time for job hunting, once a go-between has met you and reviewed your qualifications he or she can market you without your losing valuable work time.

Probably the most compelling argument against relying on agencies and recruiters is that you are the one person who has your interest most at heart. A go-between's primary interest is the fee he or she will gain upon placing you. Agency and recruiting people are often privy to information about a company's high turnover rate or financial problems, but being completely candid with an applicant about this information may cost them thousands of dollars. By relying on a middle person, you may gain the advantage of having someone else do your leg work—but may sacrifice the opportunity to discover for yourself whether you would want to spend the next several years of your career with a particular employer. Of course, working through an agency or recruiter doesn't preclude your conducting research on a prospective employer, and obviously the industry wouldn't have grown to its current large level if there weren't a need for its services, but it is my belief that most people can generate better results on their own.

Managing Your Own Job Search

Many people obtain their own jobs by

- responding to advertisements, or
- initiating contact with employers.

I advise my clients to answer advertisements that appeal to them, but to focus their job-hunting efforts on identifying and contacting employers on their own. Let's consider each of these methods, so that you can decide for yourself how you should spend your job-hunting time in order to generate the best job as quickly as possible.

Responding to Employers' Advertisements

Are ads really worthwhile as a means of obtaining employment? Very definitely yes, as many of my clients (and I) can attest, but the highly competitive nature of this avenue means that getting a job through ads is a long shot—even if your credentials are good and your résumé well-written. Many ads in *The New York Times* and *The Wall Street Journal* generate hundreds of replies, while those in the *National Business Employment Weekly* may get several thousand. Even ads in local newspapers in my region, Fairfield County, Connecticut, generate a couple of hundred responses. However, since responding to ads entails relatively little time and expense, it is a method you should use—as long as you do not rely on it as your main route to a job.

For career changers, though, responding to ads is almost always a waste of time. Imagine that you are the individual recruiting for the position. Your responsibility is to identify those applicants who most closely match the requirements of the job. If you are doing your job properly, you'll eliminate those résumés that do not show experience in the line of work pertaining to the job. Since you can only interview a limited number of candidates, why waste time with those without formal qualifications? If you are a career changer, competing against résumés is a highly unfavorable situation, since your credentials will always pale by comparison. But don't let this bother you; there is another very effective way for you to get your foot in the door, which I will be talking about later.

If you do answer to ads—especially when responding to a publication that generates many responses—wait 10 to 14 days after the ad appears before you respond if you know or believe the advertiser to be a medium- or large-size company. Most of the responses will be received during the week after the ad appears. Any résumé reviewed along with 50–100 or more the same day isn't as likely to command as much attention as that which is reviewed along with only a dozen or so. Realize, too, that a professional position will usually not be offered to an applicant within a week after the ad is placed. The selection process is very thorough and can last from several weeks to several months—well beyond the time your résumé is received.

There is another very good reason for not responding immediately. Some executives have come to place less value on résumés that are received immediately in response to an ad. The ability to respond that quickly implies either a state of readiness that makes the applicant seem too anxious—possibly unemployed—or that the applicant is a habitual job hunter, someone who floods the market with his or her résumé. This type of applicant appears less attractive than someone who is not actively looking; in the latter instance the individual would presumably prepare a résumé only after seeing an appealing ad, and the response could not be sent immediately.

In addition to the disadvantages I've described, there are also the pitfalls of blind ads and bogus ads.

BLIND ADVERTISEMENTS: A blind ad is one that uses a post office box number, without revealing the identity of the advertiser. Companies place such ads for a variety of reasons. They may be replacing an employee and do not want to reveal that fact; or they do not want the burden of sending rejection letters to many applicants, and would feel obliged to do so if their name were associated with the ad. From the job hunter's perspective, though, a blind ad presents a problem: suppose his or her own employer placed the ad?

To address this concern, some companies that place blind ads include the statement "Our employees know of this opening" to provide potential respondents with the confidence to answer the ad. One trade publication tells respondents to its ads to indicate on the outside of their envelopes those companies which should not receive their submittals. Would that more publications adopted this very considerate practice.

BOGUS ADVERTISEMENTS: Bogus ads are advertisements for jobs that do not exist. Why would anyone pay money to place such an ad?

- One reason could be to gather competitive intelligence. It is not unheard of for companies to learn their competitors' secrets by interviewing their employees for dummy jobs. A *Fortune* article quoted a recognized authority on trade secrets as saying: "The candidate is not deliberately revealing secrets and is not being hired to do so. But secret information—

or portions of it—leaks out. If a company interviews enough people, it can often obtain an accurate picture of a competitor."* And, reports the article, such an unethical practice is legal as long as the employee is not specifically asked for trade secrets.

- In some cases the advertiser is not really a prospective employer but is an executive recruiter or employment agency that has placed the ad for research or marketing purposes. An executive recruiting firm is successful to the extent to which it has timely and accurate data on many potential candidates. Some recruiters will, therefore, advertise a position for which they do not have a contract. Some employment agencies also advertise in order to gather research—or to attract employers who might be seeking applicants with qualifications similar to those described.

Initiating Contact with Employers

I firmly believe that going after your targeted job yourself is the method that promises the best results. I have already talked about the temptation to skip research when relying on an agency or recruiter. Another important benefit of pursuing a job yourself is the favorable impression you'll make on the employer by having researched the company on your own and initiating contact without using an intermediary. If there is one attribute that is vital in the business world it is aggressiveness. Business executives like aggressive employees, since they are most effective at getting things done in organizations where many groups vie for limited resources. What better way to communicate clearly that you have this attribute than by going directly to the employer?

Furthermore, of all the functional areas in a business organization, the two most aggressive are sales and marketing, making it even more important for candidates for jobs in these areas to initiate contact on their own. If you don't take my word for it, listen to Nick DiBari, a former top-producing salesman at Storage Technology and a marketing vice president for Comdisco, where he played a major role in increasing the company's sales from $50 million to more than $600 million:

> How you get to see the decision-making interviewer is by far the most important part of the marketing interview. The "Five Great Steps of the Selling Process" would certainly start with the attention step, which sets the stage for whether or not the listener will really listen to what you have to say. Putting it bluntly, get rid of your headhunter immediately. There is absolutely no place in the sales and marketing world for placement services. Deep down inside, the decision-making interviewer (obviously avoid nondecision-making

*Steven Flax, "How to Snoop on Your Competitors," *Fortune*, May 14, 1984, p. 130.

interviewers) really wants to see just how you engineered this meeting with him. He's not just looking to place or replace a "body." He's looking for a "total package." A person with controlled aggressiveness, ingenuity, competitiveness, stamina, confidence, respect, intelligence, street-smarts, and a high self-esteem. To net it out—if you can't figure out a way to get to see the "right" guy, then you don't deserve the job opportunity he may have to offer.*

It's possible that you have never used this method to obtain employment, so I can appreciate that you might be a little reticent about trying it. But I will shortly show you, step by step, how to do it successfully.

Although I am confident that you can conduct a job hunt on your own, the other methods can be used to supplement your efforts. Respond to any ads that seem worthwhile, since that will not be a very time-consuming activity in itself—although you should still research any employer who responds to your submittal in order to avoid going on unproductive interviews. If you are under a tight schedule to get a new job, an outplacement firm or career consultant can often quickly provide you with knowledge and resources you'd have to spend a lot of time gaining on your own. And a well-selected agency or recruiter can screen prospective employers for you. But be very careful not to rely on it exclusively. Several months later you may come to realize that the placement service has failed, and meanwhile you have made no progress on your own.

THE ADVANTAGES OF RELYING ON YOUR OWN EFFORTS: While many of life's endeavors have desirable ends or objectives, the means to attaining these objectives often appear singularly undesirable. Most people regard the job-hunting process in this way, which is probably why they are tempted to dump responsibility for the project into the laps of professionals. But the process of job hunting should be viewed as a constructive, enriching experience. For one thing, it's very common to come out of the job-hunting process with a number of contacts that may prove very worthwhile in the future.

Second, upon completion of a successful job hunt on your own, there is a tremendous feeling of satisfaction in having generated an opportunity mainly through your own efforts. You may also gain an awareness of new capabilities acquired through negotiating interview appointments and job-offer terms— in addition to learning research techniques which you may be able to apply on your new job to enhance your performance. Lastly, approaching a job hunt with enthusiasm and a positive attitude will be reflected in the favorable

*"Closing the Job Interview," *Sales and Marketing Management*, November 12, 1984, p. 63. Reprinted by permission of *Sales & Marketing Management Magazine.* Copyright: November 12, 1984.

impression you make on those whom you contact for jobs. If you feel anxious or pessimistic, you will involuntarily reveal it to those with whom you speak over the phone and during interviews. With a positive attitude as a foundation, you will have a significant edge over those of your competitors who view the job-hunting process with horror. And you can enhance this advantage by incorporating these elements into your research activities:

- Keep meticulous, thorough records of all companies researched. Note the dates, names, titles, organizations, and content of discussions with everyone with whom you have contact.
- Be sure to thank anyone who assists you with information, introductions, or advice—whether in person or over the telephone—with a typewritten note.
- Keep the momentum going. Get into the habit of doing something on your job search every day, and you will be surprised at how much progress you make.

CONDUCTING AN EFFECTIVE RESEARCH PROGRAM

The Hierarchical Method

One approach to finding a new job is to use a hierarchical strategy, the components of which are:

- identification of high-potential industries, unless your career is clearly associated with a particular industry;
- identification of sound companies in those industries that are within your preferred geographical area; and
- research to determine which executives in those organizations have the authority to hire for the functional area you are targeting.

Targeting Industries That Meet Your Needs
An annual directory, *Standard & Poor's Industry Surveys,** contains a detailed analysis of every major domestic industry, including commentary about the status of the industry, its problems, and outlook. Also included are charts comparing the financial performance of leading participants in the industry. The *United States Industrial Outlook*, published annually by the U.S. Department of Commerce, describes the current situation, outlook for the year, and long-term prospects for over 350 manufacturing and service industries.

*Detailed information on all directories referred to in this chapter can be found in the Appendix (page 277).

A number of industries have been identified as strong growth areas by *The Wall Street Journal* because they provide services and products greatly in demand by the baby-boomer generation. They are:

Food companies (specifically, those that market baby food and convenience-food products)

Restaurants and fast-food chains

Resorts and travel companies marketing services within the U.S.

Home entertainment

Toys and games

Clothing

Real estate

Furniture and equipment

Home appliances

School books and supplies

Auto*

Locating Employers Within Your Targeted Industries

Established by the government to aid in assessing the strengths of industrial groups, the Standard Industrial Classification (SIC) code is one of the job hunter's most valuable tools. Every industry in our economy has been assigned a SIC code, which can be two to seven digits in length, reflecting subdivisions within larger industry categories. For example, SIC code 384 designates the Surgical, Medical, and Dental Instruments and Supplies industry; SIC code 3841 is one subdivision of 384, Surgical and Medical Instruments and Apparatus. The *Standard Industrial Classification Manual*, published by the Office of Management and Budget of the federal government, lists all major SIC codes and the industries within them. Turning to page 250 of the latest *Standard Industrial Classification Manual*, we find the types of businesses within SIC code 3841 (See Figure 2).

Now suppose you wanted to find all companies in the United States that fall under SIC code 3841. You could refer to Dun's Marketing Services' 1988 edition of the *Million Dollar Directory—Series Cross Reference by Industry*, specifically, the section "Businesses by Industry Classification." An excerpt

---

*"As Birth Rates Rise, So Should Certain Stocks," *The Wall Street Journal*, June 12, 1986, p. 31. Reprinted by permission of *The Wall Street Journal*, © 1986, Dow Jones & Company, Inc. All Rights Reserved.

384 SURGICAL, MEDICAL, AND DENTAL INSTRUMENTS AND SUPPLIES

3841 Surgical and Medical Instruments and Apparatus

Establishments primarily engaged in manufacturing medical, surgical, ophthalmic, and veterinary instruments and apparatus. Establishments primarily engaged in manufacturing surgical and orthopedic appliances are classified in Industry 3842; those manufacturing electrotherapeutic and electromedical apparatus are classified in Industry 3845; and those manufacturing X-ray apparatus are classified in Industry 3844.

Anesthesia apparatus
Biopsy instruments and equipment
Blood Pressure apparatus
Blood transfusion equipment
Bone drills
Bone plates and screws
Bone rongeurs
Bronchoscopes, except electromedical
Cannulae
Catheters
Clamps, surgical
Corneal microscopes
Cystoscopes, except electromedical
Diagnostic apparatus, physicians'
Eye examining instruments and apparatus
Fixation appliances, internal
Forceps, surgical
Gastroscopes, except electromedical
Hemodialysis apparatus
Holders, surgical needle
Hypodermic needles and syringes
IV transfusion apparatus
Inhalation therapy equipment
Inhalators, surgical and medical
Instruments and apparatus, except electromedical: medical, surgical, ophthalmic, and veterinary
Instruments, microsurgical: except electromedical
Knives, surgical
Metabolism apparatus

Muscle exercise apparatus, ophthalmic
Needle holders, surgical
Needles, suture
Operating tables
Ophthalmic instruments and apparatus
Ophthalmometers and ophthalmoscopes
Optometers
Otoscopes, except electromedical
Oxygen tents
Pelvimeters
Physiotherapy equipment, electrical
Probes, surgical
Retinoscopes, except electromedical
Retractors
Rifles for propelling hypodermics into animals
Saws, surgical
Skin grafting equipment
Slit lamps (ophthalmic goods)
Speculums
Sphygmomanometers
Stethoscopes and stethographs
Suction therapy apparatus
Surgical instruments and apparatus, except electromedical
Surgical knife blades and handles
Surgical stapling devices
Tonometers, medical
Trocars
Ultrasonic medical cleaning equipment
Veterinarians' instruments and apparatus

Figure 2. Excerpt from the *Standard Industrial Classification Manual*, published by Statistical Policy Division, Office of Management and the Budget, U.S. Government.

from page 8820 of that directory, displaying the names and addresses of some companies in this SIC code, is shown in Figure 3.

Note that any one company can operate within several industries; the SIC code next to each company name in Figure 3 designates the major industry category of the company.

If you have a preferred geographical area, take note of the locations of

```
▲BAXTER INTERNATIONAL INC              P 470
   One Baxter Pky                      SIC 2834
   Deerfield, IL 60015
   Tel (312) 948-2000
 INTERTECH RESOURCES INC               P 2609
   2275 Half Day Rd                    SIC 3841
   Deerfield, IL 60015
   Tel (312) 940-7789
 SMITH & NEPHEW INC                    P 4621
   1845 Tonne Rd                       SIC 3841
   Elk Grove Vig, IL 60007
   Tel (312) 806-0080
 GOOD-LITE CO*                         P 2124
   1540 Hannah Ave                     SIC 3841
   Forest Park, IL 60130
   Tel (312) 366-3860
 SQUIRE COGSWELL CO INC                P 4738
   3411 Commercial Ave                 SIC 5084
   Northbrook, IL 60062
   Tel (312) 272-8900
▲ABBOTT LABORATORIES*                  P 25
   Abbott Pk Rt 137 Wkgn Rd            SIC 2834
   North Chicago, IL 60064
   Tel (312) 937-6100
 MARSHALL ELECTRONICS INC              P 3200
   600 Barclay Blvd                    SIC 3841
   Prairie View, IL 60069
   Tel (312) 634-6300
 INTERNATIONAL DGNSTC IMAGING*         P 2596
   1100 Remington Rd                   SIC 8911
   Roselle, IL 60173
   Tel (312) 885-1100
```

Figure 3. Excerpt showing some companies listed under Standard Industrial Classification 3841, from the *Million Dollar Directory, Series Cross-Reference by Industry*, Dun's Marketing Services, p. 8820. Copyright © 1988, Dun & Bradstreet, Inc. Reprinted by permission.

these organizations to see which are in that region as you scan the list of companies in any SIC code that interests you. Thus, for example, if you were interested in the Chicago area, Abbott Laboratories in Figure 3 would present itself as a prospective employer. A next step in this detective process would be to get more information on the company. Continuing with our example of Abbott Laboratories, we find considerable detail about the company on page 25 of the 1988 edition of Dun's Marketing Services' *Million Dollar Directory—America's Leading Public and Private Companies*, Series A-F, shown in Figure 4.

There are many directories catering to particular fields and industries. See the Appendix (page 277) for a list of those useful to job hunters in many fields. To locate directories relevant to your needs that do not appear on that list, refer to the *Directory of Directories*, available in many libraries.

STUDY NEWS DEVELOPMENTS PERTAINING TO TARGETED COMPANIES: To learn about newsworthy developments pertaining to any of the companies in your targeted geographical area, you could then refer to the *Predicasts® F&S Index® United States Annual*, which provides pointers to articles in the business press. Turn to the page containing the SIC code that interests you, and review the list of articles to see if any pertaining to your targeted employers have been written; if so, refer to the publication

D-U-N-S 00-130-7602   IMP EXP

▲ • ABBOTT LABORATORIES* (IL)

Abbott Pk Rt 137 Wkgn Rd, North Chicago, IL

Zip 60064	*Tel* (312) 937-6100
Sales 3360MM	*Emp* 34700
Tkr Sym ABT	*Exch* BSE CIN MSE NYS PBS

CHEMICAL & AGRICULTURAL PRODUCTS DIV Mnfr Bulk Products for Use In Care of Animals & Poultry Agricultural Pesticides Plant Growth Regulators & Biological Insecticides & Industrial Chemicals Bulk Pharmaceuticals Bulk Chemicals & Related Products
DIAGNOSTIC DIV Mnfr Radioactive Pharmaceuticals Serum Hepatitis Detection Systems Diagnostics & Chemical Reagents Blood Analyzers Microbiology Systems
HOSPITAL PRODUCTS DIV Mnfr Hospital & Laboratory Products Including Intravenous & Irrigating Fluids & Related Administration Equipment Venipuncture Products Anesthetics Critical Care & Suction Equipment & Other Specialty Products for Hospitals
PHARMACEUTICAL DIV Mnfr Antibiotics Hypnotics Cardiovascular Agents Vitamin & Nutritional Products Anorectics Anti-Anxiety Agents & Numerous Other Pharmaceutical Preparations
ROSS DIV Mnfr Adult & Pediatric Nutritional Products Prepared Infant Formulas & Personal Care Products
SIC 2834 2831 2833 2023 3841 5122 Discover Develop Mnfr & Sell a Broad & Diversified Line of Human Health Care Products & Services
Bk CitiBank NA, New York, NY
Accts Arthur Andersen & Co, Chicago

*Robert A Schoellhorn	*Ch Bd CEO*
*Duane L Burnham	*V Ch B CFO*
*Jack W Schuler	*Pr COO*
*Charles J Aschauer Jr	*Ex VP*
*Thomas R Hodgson	*Ex VP*
Laurence R Lee	*Sr VP Adm Sec*
Richard H Morehead	*VP*
Robert C Barnes	*VP Corp Engg*
Paul N Clark	*VP Pharmaceutical Opers*
John E Condon	*VP Corp Qlty Assurance*
O Ralph Edwards Jr	*VP Prs*
James L Farlander	*VP Corp Mtls Mgt Pur*
Kenneth W Farmer	*VP Mgt Info Svcs Dt Pr*
Richard Gast	*VP Ross Pdts*
Richard B Hamilton	*VP Public Affairs*
Robert S Janicki	*VP Pharm Pdts Rsch & Dev*
Joseph S Jenckes	*VP Washington DC*
John C Kane	*Vp Chem & Agr Pdts*
Richard W Kasperson	*VP Corp Regulatory Affrs*
John G Kringel	*Vp Hosp Pdts*
John F Lussen	*VP Taxes*
David W Milligan	*VP Dgnstc Pdts Rsch Dev*
David A Thompson	*VP Diagnostic Opers*
James A Hanley	*VP Tr*
Lester E Hammar	*VP Cont*
Lael F Johnson	*VP Genl Counsel*

K Frank Austen MD, James F Bere, Joseph V Charyk PhD, Philip de Zulueta, David A Jones, Boone Powell Jr, Arthur E Rasmussen, W Ann Reynolds PhD, William D Smithburg, William L Weiss

Figure 4. Excerpt from *Million Dollar Directory—America's Leading Public and Private Companies, Series A-F,* Dun's Marketing Services, p. 25. Copyright © 1988, Dun & Bradstreet, Inc. Reprinted by permission.

containing the article. You can also use the company name as a reference. For example, continuing our research of Abbott Laboratories, you could refer to the *Predicasts®* 1988 Quarterly/April-June publication and find the titles, publications, and dates of articles written about Abbott Laboratories for that period; see Figure 5.

While your public library may not have the publications containing these articles, it can usually refer you to other libraries in the area that do. Furthermore, you may be able to get information from the company itself. All publicly held companies publish annual reports; all you need do to obtain one is to write or call the company. This document will provide you with information about the company's new product development activities, plant expansion programs, executives, and financial performance. Public libraries also maintain files of annual reports and newspaper articles on regional and national companies.

Abbott Laboratories

Industrial Biocide business has been acquired by Angus Chemical	Jrl Comm 04/08/88 p13B
Sells industrial biocide business to Angus Chemical	Am Paint 04/11/88 p22
Sells industrial biocides business to Angus Chemical	Chem Mkt R 04/11/88 p23
Sells industrial biocides business to Angus Chemical	S&C spec 05/00/88 p71
Sells idle latex glove plant in Spartanburg, SC, to Baxter Healthcare	R&P News 05/16/88 p3
Has sold its industrial biocides operations to Angus Chemical	Adhesives 06/00/88 p46
And British Bio-Tech to jtly develop tests for infectious diseases	New Sci 03/17/88 p25
To jtly research diagnostic tests with British Bio-Technology	Eur Chem N 03/21/88 p23
To jtly develop human diagnostics	Biotechnol 05/00/88 p457
Genentech seeks to invalidate patents on plasminogen activators	WSJ (NJ) 03/18/88 p15
Says Genentech's TPA blood-clot dissolver infringes Abbott's patents	Mod Health 03/25/88 p7
Is sued by Genentech over tissue plasminogen activator patents	Chem Week 03/30/88 p12
Genentech is suing to invalidate patents over clot-dissolving drugs	D&C Ind 05/00/88 p78
Signs diagnostics R&D agreement with British Bio-Technology	Chem Ind 03/21/88 p167
Has nearly finished $37 mil fermentation expansion, Illinois & PR	Chem Mkt R 03/21/88 p53
Chief executive compensation data, 1987	Forbes 05/30/88 p154
CEO performance profile	Fin World 04/05/88 p96
Sales of in vitro lab diagnostic tests & equip to doctors (table)	NY Times N 05/15/88 pF6
Sales/earnings compiled with major drug store vendors for 1987 (table)	ChainDrugR 03/28/88 p6
EPS estimate, 1988	Fin World 04/05/88 p6S
Profits per employee data	Forbes 04/25/88 p192
Earnings projtn, 1988	Forbes 04/25/88 p256
Ranked in top 10 Fortune 500 pharmaceuticals cos by 1987 sales (table)	Fortune 04/25/88 pD50
Net sales, profits & assets in 1987 (table)	Chem Week 04/27/88 p42
Financial analysis	Value Line 03/25/88 p208
Investment rating data, 1988	Fin World 04/19/88 p70
Financial ranking data, 1987	Fortune 04/25/88 pD50

Figure 5. Excerpt from *Predicasts® F&S Index® United States*, 1988 Quarterly/April-June. Copyright © 1988, Predicasts®. F&S Index® trademark of Predicasts®. Reprinted by permission.

The hypothetical research effort we just tracked was geared toward finding a company in your targeted industry that was in your preferred geographical area. If location is secondary to your finding a sound, high-growth employer in an industry you've already decided to target, you could bypass the *Million Dollar Directory* and go straight to the *Predicasts®* index to use any SIC code to identify companies generating newsworthy developments in new product development, marketing, finance, and other categories.

USING THE SIZE OF AN ORGANIZATION AS A CRITERION: The largest companies hold a strong attraction for a lot of people, since they offer excellent benefits, as well as the cachet of working for a name everyone knows. However, one negative inherent in targeting a leading company is that many other job hunters have the same idea, resulting in a volume of résumés that far exceeds the company's hiring capacity. Compounding this problem is the fact that large companies have fairly sophisticated systems for developing home-grown talent, making the job prospects for outsiders even gloomier.

A good strategy for job hunters, therefore, is to contact companies in the $75–$200 million range, since they are usually large enough to have formal functional areas in place (I say "usually" because there are some industries where this generalization may not apply), yet may not have human resource development programs in place to address attrition, which they experience just as much as do larger companies. These companies frequently offer compensation packages competitive with larger companies', since they often have to make a special effort to induce applicants to forgo joining larger firms. Thus, as you research companies in your targeted industries, pay special attention to companies in this range that seem to be well-managed.

Researching Information on Executives

Having read articles about newsworthy developments generated by prospective employers, you will develop a list of a number of attractive companies, and be ready to obtain information on executives in them. As a general rule, if you are targeting a medium- ($75–$200 million annual revenues) or large-size ($200 million+ annual revenues) company (or division of a company), initiate contact with the highest-ranking executive managing the function you want to penetrate. If you seek employment in a smaller company, contact either the highest-ranking executive of the targeted function, or the president. One exception to this rule: if you are aiming for a field sales job, contact the top-ranking field sales executive in your preferred geographical area. While you could initiate contact with the vice president or director of sales in the headquarters of the company, approaching the field sales manager would probably generate results faster. Lastly, if you are seeking the job of the highest-ranking executive of a particular function, contact the chief executive officer (CEO) or division general manager.

If you don't know the name of the department that includes the position you seek, the chart on page 208 may help you, but remember that department names—and functions within them—vary from company to company, so you must always confirm this information with the company itself. Switchboard operators and receptionists are often good sources for this information.

To research executives, your next directory stop could be Dun's Marketing Services' *Reference Book of Corporate Managements*. For example, Figure 6 shows an excerpt from the page containing more detailed information about management at Abbott Laboratories.

By having access to the backgrounds, both educational and business, of executives whom you are targeting, you might find that you have an employer or alma mater in common with one of them. You could then develop your résumé, letter, and initial approach in a way that would capitalize on that common denominator.

The "Change" Strategy

Studying Executive Changes as Harbingers of Job Opportunities

Whenever there is a change in organizational management at a high level, you can be sure that changes at lower levels will be forthcoming, for these reasons:

- Employees at lower levels are fired because the new executive is dissatisfied with their performance.
- Employees at lower levels are dissatisfied with the new management and quit.
- A restructuring of the organization results in jobs being gained/lost.

A study supporting this cause-effect phenomenon was presented in a *Harvard Business Review* article. The author analyzed organizational changes implemented by 14 high-level executives—including district, marketing/sales, divisional, and group general managers—of companies whose sales ranged from $21 million to $3 billion. The functional areas determined to be affected by the most significant changes of the first three years of these executives' tenure included

- reorganization of chief engineer's department affecting engineering, construction, and installation;
- introduction of product management;
- sales service training;
- revision of mission scope and revamping of marketing strategy affecting marketing and sales;

D-U-N-S 00-130-7602
ABBOTT LABORATORIES
Abbott Pk Rt 137 Wkgn Rd
North Chicago, Il 60064
SIC 2834 2831 2833 2023 3841 5122   *TEL.* (312) 937-6100
Discover Develop Mnfr & Sell a Broad & Diversified Line of Human
Health Care Products & Services
CH BD CEO*- SCHOELLHORN, ROBERT A, b 1928; m; Philadelphia
Coll of Textile & Science; 1947–1973 American Cyanamid Co, Pr
Lederle Laboratories; 1973-present Abbott Laboratories*, Ex VP Hosp
Gp, 1976 Pr COO, 1979 Pr CEO, 1981 Ch Bd CEO; Dir; also Dir
Pillsbury Co; Ch Bd Health Industry Manufacturers Assn, ITT Corp &
PMA.
V CH B CFO*- BURNHAM, DUANE L, b 1942; 1963-University of
MN, BS; 1972-University of MN, MBA; 1969–1975 Maremont Corp;
1975–1982 Bunker-Ramo Corp, Pr CEO; 1982-present Abbott Lab-
oratories*, CFO Ex VP, now V Ch B CFO; Dir.
PR COO*- SCHULER, JACK W, b 1940; m; 1962-Tufts Univ, BS;
1964-Stanford Univ, MBA; 1964–1969 Texas Instruments France;
1964–1970 Texas Instruments Germany, Mgr Discreet Devices;
1970–1972 Texas Instruments Asia, Genl Mgr; 1972 Texas Instruments Corp, Mgr Strategic Plng Semi-Conductors; 1972-present Abbott Laboratories*, 1972 Dir Sls & Mktg Diagnostic Div, 1974 Div VP
Sls & Mktg, 1976 VP Diagnostic Opers, 1983 Gp VP, then Ex VP, now
Pr COO; Dir.
EX VP*- ASCHAUER, CHARLES J JR, b 1928; m; 1950-Northwestern
Univ, BBA; 1951-Centre d'Etudes Indestrielles, MBA; 1951–1955 USN
Lt; 1955–1962 Mc Kinsey & Co Inc, Principal; 1962–1967 Mead John-
son & Co, VP Mktg Mead Johnson Laboratories Div; 1967–1970 Mare-
mont Corp, Pr Auto Gp; 1970–1971 Whittaker Corp, VP Gp Ex; 1971-
present Abbott Laboratories*, VP Corp Plng, then Corp VP & Pr Hosp
Pdts Div, 1976 Gp VP, 1979 Ex VP; Dir; also Dir Benefit Tr Life In-
surance Co & Stearn Chemical Corp.
EX VP*- HODGSON, THOMAS R, b 1941; m; 1963-Purdue Univ,
BSChE; 1964-University of MI, MSChE; 1969-Harvard Univ, MBA;
1972-present Abbott Laboratories*, Asst to Pr, 1973 Dir Sup Pdts &
New Business Dev Hosp Pdts Div, 1976 Genl Mgr Faultless Rubber
Co, 1978 VP Genl Mgr Hosp Pdts Div, 1980 VP Hosp Pdts, 1983 Gp
VP, now Ex VP; Dir.
SR VP ADMN SEC- LEE, LAURENCE R, b 1928; m; 1946-University
of Chicago, PhB; 1951-University of Chicago, JD; 1947– 1948 Army;
prior 1955 Miller Gorham Wescott & Adams, Associate; 1955-present
Abbott Laboratories*, 1963 Sec Genl Counsel, 1970 VP Sec Genl
Counsel, 1981 Sr VP Admn Sec; also Dir First Nat Bk of Lake Bluff.
VP- BARNES, ROBERT C, b 1927; m; 1949-Northwestern Univ,
BSChE; 1966-University of Chicago, MBA; prior 1951 S C Johnson &
Son; 1951-present Abbott Laboratories*, 1963 Mgr Process Engg,
1965 Dir Office Svcs, 1966 Dir Corp Engg, 1969 VP Corp Engg; also
Dir First Fed Svgs & Ln Assn of Waukegan IL.
VP- CONDON, JOHN E, b 1928; 1951-University of Dayton, BS; 1956-
Ohio State Univ, MS; 1967-George Washington Univ, ScD; 1969 Fed-
eral Executive Inst; 1962–1972 National Aerospace Administration,
Dir Office Reliability & Qlty Assurance; 1972-present Abbott Labora-
tories*, VP Corp Qlty Assurance.

**Figure 6. Excerpt showing some of the executives listed in Dun's Marketing
Services'** *Reference Book of Corporate Managements,* **pp. 7–8. Copyright
© 1988, Dun & Bradstreet, Inc. Reprinted by permission.**

- manufacturing rationalization*;
- sales systems and procedures;
- rationalization and restructuring of production operations;
- restructuring of sales operations;
- manufacturing operations, production engineering, quality control, and product planning.†

A significant number of personnel changes implemented by the surveyed managers took place within the first six-month period, the "taking hold" stage, and during what the author calls the "reshaping" stage, which began anywhere from thirteen to eighteen months after assuming the position. Figure 7 shows the total number of personnel and structural changes implemented by these managers within their first three years in the new positions and clearly demonstrates the positive correlation between the two types of changes.

In my opinion, an appropriate heading for this list is "Employment Opportunities." Although some of the personnel changes reflected in Figure 7 were probably promotions or lateral moves of existing personnel, I am sure that there were many new hirings. I consider the search for high-level management changes the most valuable strategy you can use to unearth job opportunities, and, fortunately, finding these situations is fairly easy. Newspapers have columns in their business sections that detail executive changes; this applies not only to major publications such as *The New York Times* and *The Wall Street Journal*, but also to local newspapers. Trade publications— newspapers and magazines serving particular industries—also have columns detailing executive changes. Researching executive change information in back issues of publications would be a good idea, since, as the *Harvard Business Review* study indicates, there can be a considerable time lag between the executive's assumption of his or her duties and the implementation of organizational and personnel changes. To find trade publications serving your targeted industry, refer to a periodical directory in your local library. If you read in the business news columns that John Jones left Company A and was appointed executive vice president of Company B, consider both these companies as prospective employers, since Company A will be replacing Mr. Jones with another executive.

Capitalizing on General Business News to Find Opportunities

Many changes—both in organizational structure and general business activity—are reported in a broad array of business publications, notably *The*

---

*Rationalization programs are streamlining and cost-cutting activities.

†John J. Gabarro, "When a New Manager Takes Charge," *Harvard Business Review*, May-June 1985, p. 118. Copyright © 1985 by the President and Fellows of Harvard College; all rights reserved. Reprinted by permission.

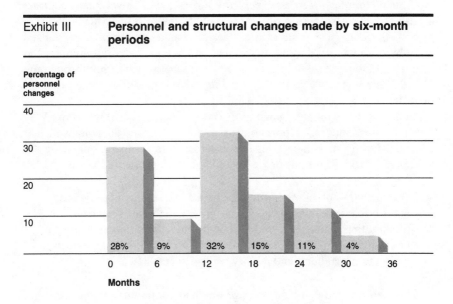

Exhibit III   **Personnel and structural changes made by six-month periods**

Percentage of
personnel
changes

40

30

20

10

	28%	9%	32%	15%	11%	4%	
	0	6	12	18	24	30	36

Months

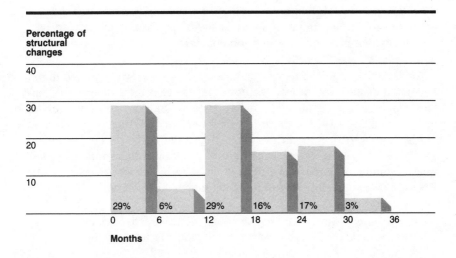

Percentage of
structural
changes

40

30

20

10

	29%	6%	29%	16%	17%	3%	
	0	6	12	18	24	30	36

Months

Figure 7. Reprinted by permission of *Harvard Business Review*. An exhibit from "When a New Manager Takes Charge," by John J. Gabarro, May-June 1985. Copyright © 1985 by the President and Fellows of Harvard College; all rights reserved.

Wall Street Journal, Business Week, Forbes, and *Inc*. Government contract awards, business expansion programs, establishment of new manufacturing plants—these are just some of the types of changes that can be capitalized upon by resourceful job hunters. To demonstrate just what job hunters can gain from reading these publications, I would like to "walk" you through the May 9, 1988 issue of *The Wall Street Journal* and point out some potential opportunities.

An article on page one, headlined "The California Tan May Go the Way of California Condors," reports on the decline in interest in suntans in that state and further says that "sales of sun screens are booming, outpacing the old tanning lotions and oils in a $400 million market oriented at the sun."*

> *Opportunity*: Job hunters with experience marketing or selling products to retailers can capitalize on the growth in the sun screen market by targeting manufacturers, as should other practitioners likely to be in demand by these companies, such as toxicologists, chemists, production planners, and quality control specialists.

Here's an article beginning on page one and continuing on page ten that contains a special bonus: an analysis of the quarterly performance of 34 industries, which includes financial results of leading companies in them, as well as explanations for the earnings results.

> *Opportunity*: Job hunters targeting these industries can search the analyses for information about business expansions or industry trends that may translate into job openings.

An article on page two reports that the executive who was expected to run Federated Department Stores, Inc. for Campeau Corporation departed, "intensifying management disarray,"† so opportunity knocks for other executives of large retailing businesses to throw their hats into the ring.

Also on page two is an article about Boeing finding corrosion damage on old 737 jets. It further states "The Federal Aviation Adminstration . . . last week expanded an order for airlines to step up inspections of early-model Boeing 737s for possible corrosion, metal fatigue and cracks."‡

> *Opportunity*: Structural engineers and nondestructive testing specialists could conduct research to identify those airlines owning early-

---

**The Wall Street Journal*, May 9, 1988, p. 1. Reprinted by permission of *The Wall Street Journal*, © 1988, Dow Jones & Company, Inc. All Rights Reserved.

†*The Wall Street Journal*, May 9, 1988, p. 2. Reprinted by permission of *The Wall Street Journal*, © 1988, Dow Jones & Company, Inc. All Rights Reserved.

‡*Ibid.*

model Boeing 737s (but if you read *The Wall Street Journal* a week later, you would have found an article reporting the number of 737s owned by specific airlines) and negotiate consulting contracts with them—or they could refer to the *Consultants and Consulting Organizations Directory* to identify consulting firms providing aircraft inspection services that might hire them as subcontractors.

An article on page four reports that a high-rise sprinkler law for Los Angeles will be proposed by two city legislators in the aftermath of a recent fire that killed one person and caused millions of dollars in damages.

> *Opportunity*: Firms marketing sprinkler systems are probably gearing up for the windfall business expected from the law. Typically rather small companies unsophisticated in marketing, they might welcome being approached by job hunters experienced in business-to-business marketing and sales techniques.

"Periodicals Address Asians—in English"* proclaims the headline of an article on page 25. We learn that *AsiAm*, a Los Angeles-based publication targeting young and middle-age affluent Asian-Americans, reports that its ad pages are running at about ten per issue—double the number two seasons previously. In addition, the magazine has gotten the business of some major companies.

> *Opportunity*: Individuals seeking advertising sales positions who live in areas where many leading consumer products companies are headquartered could present their qualifications to *AsiAm* management.

Moving our eyes to the right of this article we find an item heralding the development of erasable optical disks that will allow personal computers to store hundreds of times as much data as is possible on the current floppy disks. Maxtor Corporation of San Jose, California is singled out as the one company that has overcome obstacles that have made these disks much slower than magnetic disks. An industry source claims that this development "puts Maxtor firmly 12 months ahead of the competition."†

> *Opportunity*: We can assume that Maxtor will apply considerable effort to ensure that its lead over the competition is as large as possible, so that it can garner the lion's share of the erasable optical

---

The Wall Street Journal, May 9, 1988, p. 25. Reprinted by permission of *The Wall Street Journal*, © 1988, Dow Jones & Company, Inc. All Rights Reserved.

†*The Wall Street Journal*, May 9, 1988, p. 25. Reprinted by permission of *The Wall Street Journal*, © 1988, Dow Jones & Company, Inc. All Rights Reserved.

disk market. Maxtor management will no doubt want to fill any open positions quickly to avoid delaying the commercial launch of such a critical product. Therefore, job hunters with related engineering, manufacturing, sales, and marketing experience could present their qualifications as possible backup candidates.

According to an article on page 28 about RJR Nabisco, Inc., its firing of the Saatchi & Saatchi DFS, Inc. advertising agency will result in a major share of $117 million of its advertising business going to FCB/Leber Katz Partners and to two units of the New York-based Interpublic Group of Companies.

> *Opportunity*: Advertising industry account service, creative, and production personnel could approach these two agencies for jobs immediately, since acquisition of such a large volume of business will probably require them to expand their staffs.

Turning to page 29 and the "Who's News" column, we find a number of announcements of executive appointments that could prove fertile ground for job hunters, since major changes at lower levels in the organization are likely to occur. (See the findings of the *Harvard Business Review* study on page 88.) Also included is the following item:

> ABBOTT LABORATORIES (North Chicago, Ill.)—Don G. Wright, formerly vice president, scientific affairs and quality assurance, of the company's hospital-products division, was named vice president, corporate quality assurance, of this maker of health-care products, succeeding John E. Condon, who retired.*

This announcement underscores the importance of always confirming information gained through library research—a job hunter targeting Mr. Condon at Abbott Laboratories who did not verify the *Million Dollar Directory* information presented in Figure 4 (page 85) would have obsolete information as of this date, if he or she did not read this issue of *The Wall Street Journal*.

An article on page 43 reports that Laventhol & Horwath, a major accounting firm, will pay $15 million to settle an anti-racketeering class-action lawsuit. As the auditor for a failed tax shelter that cost 2,850 investors more than $20 million, Laventhol & Horwath is the first major accounting firm to lose a jury trial under the federal Racketeer Influenced and Corrupt Organizations Act of 1970.

---

*The Wall Street Journal, May 9, 1988, p. 29. Reprinted by permission of *The Wall Street Journal*, © 1988, Dow Jones & Company, Inc. All Rights Reserved.

Opportunity: As a consequence of the Laventhol & Horwath case, all accounting firms will be evaluating whether the risk management functions they have in place are adequate to protect them from similar suits. No doubt some will find themselves lacking, and consequently, job opportunites for risk management professionals with relevant experience will be created. In addition, accountants without risk management experience who seek a change from their work should seize this opportunity to market themselves as qualified to identify and reduce auditing risks.

Beneath this article is a small item that lists eight companies that won military contracts ranging from $12.8 million to $54.2 million for computer, communications, flight training simulation, and munitions equipment.

Opportunity: While a company usually expands its work force in anticipation of a contract being signed, the tight time constraints of a government contract—and penalties for delays—coupled with the employee turnover that every company experiences, could result in job opportunities for engineering and manufacturing professionals, and computer programmers, to name a few.

Not a bad harvest for one day's read! And you can be sure that a regular, careful reading of *The Wall Street Journal* and other national and regional publications will yield a treasure trove of leads you can use in your job hunt. By following through on these you'll have a tremendous advantage in being considered as a candidate without competing against hundreds of others.

Using School, Business, and Social Contacts

Being graduated from the same school tends to create instant rapport. You could contact fellow alumni who you believe might be able to help you. Even if you're targeting a job in finance and there's an alumna/alumnus in your area who's a marketing executive, don't discount this person as a lead, since he or she may provide you with an introduction to someone in your targeted area.

Many alumni associations publish directories providing detailed information on the whereabouts, professionally and geographically, of graduates. Even in cases where directories aren't published, alumni associations will sometimes provide this information. If it's made available only at the school location, you could hire a student to research those people of interest to you.

Use your membership in business or professional organizations to build your network of contacts. If you are unaware of which organizations cater to people in your field, refer to the *Encyclopedia of Associations* for the national headquarters of these groups. They will direct you to local contacts.

Prepare a list of all the people you know through your social and community activities—from your church or synagogue, club, PTA, volunteer activities, as well as retail merchants and professionals. Each person knows a hundred other people who could prove valuable in your job-hunting campaign.

Ask your contacts for advice that could assist you in your job hunt, as well as for introductions to people they know who might be able to provide you with leads. Approaching them this way—as opposed to asking them for a job—exerts less pressure on them and is more likely to result in a sincere effort on their part.

INFORMATION SOURCES

Many mailing list companies sell lists of companies and executives based on specified criteria of industry type, functional area, company size, ZIP code, etc. While it may cost a few hundred dollars to obtain this information, it may save you a lot of time going through directories yourself.

Job hunters with desktop computers and modems can similarly save time in researching companies by accessing some of the many business data bases providing information on thousands of companies. For example, users of some data bases can query the system for companies whose sales lie in a particular range—this would be useful to identify medium-size companies, which I suggested (see page 87) were good targets. Some of the on-line services offering access to data bases charge only for usage, i.e., no start-up or minimum charges.

See the Appendix, page 277, for pointers to mailing list and on-line services companies, as well as for a comprehensive list of reference books.

4

How to Present Yourself on Paper

THE SUPERMARKET ANALOGY

What does a lineup of cereal boxes on a supermarket shelf have to do with job hunting? Plenty! When you go into a supermarket to buy cereal, what causes you to make your purchase decision? You'll decide which product to buy based on a number of factors, including the attractiveness of the packaging, the price, the claims made on the box, e.g., contains no sugar, is high in fiber, is endorsed by an athlete you or your child may like, and, most important, how these attributes compare to those of other cereals on the same shelf. Similarly, you, as a job hunter, are marketing a product: *you*. You have packaging (your dress, speech, demeanor), a price (your required salary), product claims (the statements in your résumé and letter attesting to your experience and qualifications), and testimonials (your references).

Appreciating this analogy between the marketing of a product and the marketing of a job candidate is necessary to understand the importance of distinguishing yourself from all the other products vying for the consumer's purchase decision—in this case, the employer's job offer. Thus in thinking about how you will prepare for your presentation to the marketplace, always ask yourself this question: am I presenting myself to the prospective employer in a way that will make an impression that is superior to the other "products" on the "shelf"? Some candidates behave as though they were answering a loud "No!" to this question by

- using plain copier paper for their résumés, as opposed to spending a bit more money and getting a fine-quality paper;
- responding to an advertisement by sending a résumé without a cover letter;

97

- sending a weak cover letter with a very well written, strong résumé; or
- submitting a handwritten list of references instead of a typed list.

Actions that constitute a "yes" answer to the question posed include

- always obtaining, when possible, the recipient's name and title before sending a cover letter, as opposed to addressing it "Dear Sir";
- sending two copies of your résumé in response to an ad, on the assumption that the recipient will generally have to make another copy for someone else in the organization (this will ensure the aesthetic quality of both copies circulated); and
- bringing extra copies of your résumé with you to an interview.

As you read the following pages on how to prepare your résumé and cover letter, you may find the material a little dry, since it's very much a "how-to" section. But please bear in mind that your reward for reading the whole section carefully will be the ability to make a superior impression on any prospective employer.

THE ADVANTAGE OF A RÉSUMÉ

Let's first consider whether, in fact, a résumé is necessary. A survey of the ads in any newspaper will show that the vast majority of employers ask applicants to submit résumés. The very few organizations offering the applicant the option of calling initially will probably require a résumé in the event they grant an interview.

Furthermore, while the primary purpose of a résumé is to generate interviews, even in those cases where interviews are arranged through contacts a résumé is usually required. Regardless, however, of whether a résumé is required, it is highly desirable for you to use one. Most companies have developed their own job application forms that, I'm sure you'll agree, look pretty much alike. They ask you to describe your responsibilities in an amount of space that usually requires you to omit some information. Also, since an application form forces all candidates to use the same format, it makes it extremely difficult for one candidate to distinguish himself or herself sufficiently from the competition.

On the other hand, the résumé, which can really take whatever form you believe will present your background in the best light, affords you a wonderful opportunity to set yourself apart from everyone else. Unfortunately, most people do not capitalize on this opportunity. Instead, they write résumés that resemble a collection of answers to the standard questions on a job application form.

A résumé must be viewed as a promotional piece. As part of your packaging, it provides a succinct listing of your claims, so that the buyer can determine how well you will meet his or her needs, and whether you are worth the money being asked or offered. Of course, the aesthetics of the résumé are very important as well, just as the attractiveness of a cereal box can be a critical factor in the decision to buy. We'll go into detail on the aesthetics of the résumé later, but let's first review a few aspects of a résumé-writing project.

WHEN TO PREPARE YOUR RÉSUMÉ

While you might assume that the best time to write your résumé is when you need it, the truth is that it is exactly the opposite—the best time is when you don't need it. If you have been fired, the associated anxiety and time pressure is not at all conducive to the relaxed, objective state of mind that will produce a résumé showing you in the best light. Even if you have not been fired, you should write your résumé when you do not need it for two reasons:

- Describing your responsibilities and accomplishments is much easier if the information is fresh in your mind. Each new accomplishment or increase in responsibility should signal the need for an update of your current position description. This ensures that all pertinent information—especially quantifiable results—will be included, whereas if you wait until you need the résumé immediately, the information may be, at best, hazy and, at worst, unavailable.
- Many companies test new products and services in limited markets before they spend a lot of money promoting them nationally. Test-marketing provides a company with valuable feedback on consumers' reactions, which can be used to improve advertising approaches and the product itself. You can derive comparable benefits from test-marketing your résumé, and for this reason you should prepare it well in advance of needing it to allow you enough time for a test. Your test market should be people whose judgment and knowledge of your field you value.

THE LANGUAGE OF THE RÉSUMÉ

Because the résumé is a promotional piece, use language that makes the most of your background. Many people use rather weak wording to describe their responsibilities and accomplishments, deflating their value in the eyes of the employer. An example of wording that does not describe one's performance in a promotional manner would be:

Purchased all office equipment.

The following statement says essentially the same thing, but communicates a more active role in the purchase of the equipment:

Researched and evaluated office equipment vendors for best prices and quality; negotiated all prices and terms.

Another example of a rather passive way of explaining a responsibility would be:

Responsible for the company's records-retention function.

This is a stronger way of expressing the same thing:

Devised and implemented a company-wide records-retention program that ensured compliance with legal, financial, and regulatory requirements.

And compare:

Liaison between Accounting and M.I.S. departments.

with this:

As liaison between the Accounting and M.I.S. departments, formulated accounting and credit/collection data-processing requirements; established schedules for the production of reports.

A résumé should be written in the first person—not the third. For example, the statement:

"Manages accounting staff of eight."

implies that "He" or "She" is the subject of the verb "manages," which would mean that someone else was making this statement about you. Since you are writing about yourself, use the first person. Thus, in the example above, the correct word to use is "manage" or "managed," if a past activity.

As a rule, avoid the use of "I" or "my" in a résumé, unless you feel it's necessary to express a particular point.

THE LENGTH OF THE RÉSUMÉ

Generally speaking, a résumé should be limited to two pages, unless you are targeting the academic, medical, or scientific fields, where longer résumés are acceptable—but even then, don't exceed three pages, exclusive of your publications. For individuals with extensive business backgrounds, a good way to keep the résumé to two pages is to summarize the earliest three or four positions in one paragraph, with the dates associated with this paragraph being the start date of the first position covered and the end date of the last position covered. Another solution to the problem of having information that exceeds two pages is to have the résumé typeset. (Refer to page 147 for details on this approach, as well as a caveat pertaining to its use.)

It might be worthwhile at this point to address a commonly held belief that a résumé must be limited to one page. I routinely prepare résumés one and one-half to two pages in length for clients—with excellent results. I believe that the one-page myth came about because most résumés are poorly written. People have become so bored with reading them that, subconsciously anyway, they know it's easier for someone to shorten a bad two-page résumé to one page than it is to transform a bad two-page résumé into a good two-page résumé. As long as your résumé is well-written and contains information meaningful to the reader, it can be two pages.

NECESSARY PREPARATION FOR WRITING THE RÉSUMÉ

We now come to the most critical part of writing a résumé. In writing anything—whether a play, proposal, letter, or résumé—you must keep the audience's perspective in mind. In this case we want to write the résumé— the "package" copy, harking back to my supermarket analogy—with the "consumer"—the employer—in mind. So you should do the following:

1. Write or get hold of a job description for the position you want.
2. Put yourself in the employer's shoes and think long and hard about each component of the job description.
3. Write down, one by one, all conceivable qualifications that would contribute to the employer's conviction that an applicant would be well qualified for the job. Distinguish between those items that are musts, versus those that, while not musts, are characteristics that would make the candidate highly desirable. Bear in mind that this is not a list of the qualities you feel you have for the position, but rather of those items important to the employer.

I call the entire list—of musts and additional valuable characteristics together—the "employer's scoring points" or the ESP. As an example, let's suppose you are applying for a position as an advertising and sales promotion manager for a consumer products company—specifically, a health and beauty aids manufacturer. Putting yourself in the position of the hiring manager you might develop a list that looks like this:

Employer's Scoring Points (ESP)

Musts

1. Experience overseeing the development of advertising and sales promotion programs within a health and beauty aids company (at least four years)
2. Managerial experience (at least two years, but preferably more)
3. Demonstrated ability to keep project costs within budget
4. Experience in finding, evaluating, and contracting for outside services such as photography, typesetting, graphic design, advertising, and sales promotion support (at least one year)

Other Valuable Characteristics (in order of approximate importance)

5. Experience developing and administering advertising budgets larger than $3 million
6. M.B.A. degree in Marketing
7. Experience coordinating the production of video promotional programs to be used in conjunction with sales activities
8. Experience organizing participation in trade shows
9. Ability to work well in a large company, supporting many functional managers in their product programs
10. Experience working in an advertising agency
11. Excellent command of English
12. Excellent platform skills, so as to be able to deliver presentations to top management in my absence
13. Conceptual understanding of microcomputers, so as to direct the use of spreadsheet and graphics software packages
14. Good working relationships with the suppliers my company uses

After you finish your list, evaluate how well your qualifications stack up against the ESP. In areas where you are weak or totally lacking, try to offset the liability. For example, one of my clients was targeting a middle-management position in manufacturing, while his background had been as a staff specialist in manufacturing, with no formal managerial experience. When we developed his ESP, it was obvious that managerial experience was essential. Our solution: my client had been responsible for leading task forces for several projects, so we stressed this point, making it clear that the sum total of his experiences as a task-force leader was comparable to formal managerial experience.

By the way, often an ESP item cannot be expressed easily in writing. For example, an employer seeking an individual to sell financial planning services to wealthy people would naturally want someone with whom these people would feel comfortable, someone with a high degree of social skills and presence, and a manner of speaking that would imply that he or she was well-educated. These traits are best communicated in an interview, rather than by a résumé. Therefore, when developing your ESP, think carefully about which qualifications sought are best reserved for the interview.

If you are targeting more than one type of job or field, develop an ESP list for each. Compare the items on each list, and if you find that there is a lot of overlap in the key areas, you can probably get away with using one résumé—as long as you don't use an objective (see page 109 for further details). However, if the important hiring criteria differ, you will have to develop a résumé for each area you target.

THE FORMAT OF THE RÉSUMÉ

The traditional format for presenting your employment background is the reverse chronological approach, starting with the dates, title, organization, city, and state of the most recent position, followed by a description of responsibilities and accomplishments, and so on. People seeking new careers, however, are handicapped by this format. Say you've been a teacher and are now looking for a public relations job. The first item the reader will see— and on which the greatest importance will be placed since it is the most recent experience—will be the teaching background, which will be irrelevant to the employer's needs. But perhaps as a volunteer for a community organization you've written press releases and stories about the organization's activities that have been published in local newspapers. You would benefit from a format that would allow you to describe your writing experience before your professional employment. And that is exactly what the functional résumé format enables you to do. It highlights several skill areas before presenting details about your title, the length of the position, and your employer. For example, if you want to describe your sales abilities, you would have a section called "Sales" in which you would include a compilation of the most important sales duties and accomplishments extracted from *all* your employment experiences.

Skeletal examples of the chronological and functional résumé formats, respectively, appear on the following pages. I've placed a number adjacent to each component of the résumé and will use these numbers in the discussion following.

Deciding which format to use is a fairly simple matter. If you are targeting a type of employment consistent with what you are doing now or have done most recently, use a chronological format; if you are changing careers, or if

THE CHRONOLOGICAL FORMAT

(1) Name

(2) Street Address
City, State ZIP

(3) Telephone Number(s)

(4) Objective

(5) Professional
Profile _____
_____

(6) Strengths: _____
_____

_____

(7A) Professional
Experience

(7A.1) Start Date-   Header Line #1: Your Title, Organization, City, and
End Date   State (current or most recent employer)

(7A.2) Describe your responsibilities here. _____
_____

Key Accomplishments
•* _____

• _____
_____

• _____
_____

Start Date-End Date   Header Line 2 (your previous employer)
_____
_____

Key Accomplishments
• _____

• _____
_____

(Follow with all the jobs you wish to add.)

*I use a bullet to highlight accomplishments; a bullet can be made on a typewriter by typing
the letter "o" in lower case and blackening it in with a ballpoint pen. With larger typefaces,
however, a lower-case "o" may be too large. Other symbols that can be used to highlight
important points in résumés and letters are the period, asterisk, and lozenge. If listing three
or more items, you could number them 1, 2, 3, etc.

8 Other Experience

Start Date-End Date _____

_____

_____

9 Education _____

_____

10 Professional _____
Education _____

11 Patents _____

_____

12 Publications _____

_____

13 Memberships _____

_____

14 Military _____
Service _____

15 Community _____
Activities _____

16 Personal _____

_____

17 Honors _____

_____

18 References _____

_____

THE FUNCTIONAL FORMAT

(1) Name   (2) Street Address, City, State ZIP   (3) Telephone Number(s)

(4) Objective

(5) Professional Profile _____

_____

_____

_____

(6) Strengths: _____

_____

_____

(7B) Key Responsibilities and Accomplishments

(7B.1) SKILL CATEGORY #1 . . . Describe responsibilities and accomplishments relevant to this skill category. _____

_____

_____

_____

SKILL CATEGORY #2 . . . _____

_____

_____

_____

_____

SKILL CATEGORY #3 . . . _____

_____

_____

_____

_____

(7B.2) Professional Employment

Start Date-End Date   Header Line #1: Title, organization name, city, state (current or most recent employer)

Start Date-End Date   Header Line #2 (above information for previous employer)

Start Date-End Date   Header Line #3 (next earliest employer, etc.)

(Follow with all the jobs you wish to add.)

(8) Other Experience

Start Date-End Date _____
_____
_____

(9) Education _____
_____

(10) Professional _____
Education _____

(11) Patents _____
_____

(12) Publications _____
_____

(13) Memberships _____
_____

(14) Military _____
Service _____

(15) Community _____
Activities _____

(16) Personal _____
_____

(17) Honors _____
_____

(18) References _____
_____

you would like to emphasize certain skills in a way that the chronological format will not allow, use a functional format. I should tell you that some people don't like to read functional résumés. They immediately suspect that the applicant using a functional format is trying to hide something. However, since only a small minority of people harbor negative feelings toward the functional résumé, the advantage offered by this format should more than offset any disadvantages.

WRITING YOUR RÉSUMÉ

The numbered sections following correspond to the same numbered sections on each of the preceding résumés. The first three—name, address, and phone number—are presented in a different way on each of the preceding skeletal outlines so that you can choose the one that appeals more to you. But bear in mind that the method used in the functional format will not allow you to include your home and business telephone numbers, unless your name is very short.

1. Name

If you customarily use a nickname and have included your legal name on the résumé, the interviewer would probably address you by a name you never use, and you would probably tell him or her what your real name is. But this creates an awkward initial moment in the interview, one you can very easily eliminate. For example, if your real name is Norman, but everybody has called you Ted since you were a child, list your name as follows:

Norman (Ted) Aldrich

2. Address

Use a street address. Avoid post office box numbers, since that could imply that you're transient, unstable, or hiding something.

3. Telephone Numbers

It's important to have proper phone coverage during a job hunt, so any number appearing on your résumé should not be busy for longer than ten minutes, and it should always be answered. Consider engaging an answering service or buying an answering machine to provide coverage on your home phone. Among your circle of friends you may know someone who has graduated to an answering service and left his or her machine in a closet. As an alternative to a machine you could arrange with a self-employed friend to use his or her number on the résumé. If so, label this number "Messages."

It is not uncommon for people to include their business phone numbers, if they have sufficient office privacy and know that their employers don't disapprove of personal calls. If you are busy when someone calls, say that you are not free to speak and ask if you can return the call at a more convenient time.

4. Objective

Try to consider the objective from the employer's perspective. He or she is looking for a candidate who will stay in the job long enough to justify the time and money spent recruiting and, if necessary, training the employee. Therefore, the employer will be most interested in knowing whether the applicant has an objective consistent with the position available. If not, the employer will not feel confident that the applicant will be around for the long term.

Next, examine the objective from the standpoint of *your* needs. If you do not have a specific focus, choosing an objective that is general enough to encompass all the jobs you are willing to consider will result in a wishy-washy approach that certainly won't impress an employer with your single-minded commitment. Conversely, should you specify "sales promotion," for example, and an opportunity for an interview in advertising comes up, your objective would only be a liability. The interviewer would know that advertising is not your first choice, and would believe that if you accepted an offer, the likelihood is strong that as soon as the job market for sales promotion opened up, you would be gone.

The solution to the problem of a too-specific or too-general objective is simple: move the objective from the résumé onto the cover letter if your résumé is transmitted by mail, or explain the objective in your initial discussion with the employer. This way, the employers get what they want, i.e., objectives tailored to their needs, and you get what you want: a résumé that can be used in all instances (unless there is insufficient overlap on your ESP lists).

If, after analyzing the trade-offs, you believe that an objective is appropriate for your situation, then use one, but do not talk about seeking a "challenging, growth opportunity." This phrase—or some variation—is not only a cliché; it also reflects a strategic error. Naturally, you are looking for a challenging, growth opportunity. But, again, let's look at it from the employer's perspective. An employer is looking for someone who can *contribute to his or her needs* on a long-term basis. Here is an example of an objective that communicates the "contribution" factor:

Objective   A financial analyst position in a multinational company where career opportunities exist to permit my long-term contribution.

Try to convey this kind of impression in your own objective, while limiting its length to about twenty-five words.

5. Professional Profile

Just as the résumé is a synopsis of employment history, the professional profile—which will be the first section of your résumé (if you forgo using an objective) is a synopsis of the résumé. The profile allows you to editorialize about your background and promote yourself in a way that will be consistent with what the employer is seeking. Strive to include in your profile all the Musts on your ESP list and, if appropriate, the top one or two important items under the Other Valuable Characteristics heading. (See the discussion of the ESP on page 102.) This rule is illustrated in the following example of a profile for our mythical advertising and sales promotion manager:

> Professional Profile
>
> Advertising and sales promotion manager for leading manufacturer of health and beauty aids (annual revenue: $250 million); manage in-house creative/production staff of six, as well as make extensive use of outside services. Consistent record of excellence in developing cost-effective creative programs that contribute to significant market-share increases. M.B.A. in Marketing.

In the above example, one of the items on our ESP list, "experience developing and administering budgets larger than $3 million," is implied by the sales volume of $250 million, since companies typically spend 3–10 percent of their sales volume on advertising and promotion. But the rest of the items on the list are directly supported.

To familiarize you further with the format of the profile, here is an example of one for a purchasing manager:

> Professional Profile
>
> Purchasing manager for manufacturer of industrial and food chemicals; annual revenue: $500 million. Background as senior buyer for military contractor and for paper manufacturer. Consistent record of excellence in negotiating favorable contracts that contribute to profitable product programs.

Career changers are presented with a particular challenge in formulating their profiles, for they must deemphasize the specific responsibilities in the field they wish to exit in favor of more general qualities applicable to their targeted field. Here, for example, is a possible profile for a teacher with experience representing his organization to professional associations, and who is seeking a public relations position:

Professional Profile	Teacher with extensive background representing school to state and national professional organizations on policy and legislative matters. Editor of monthly newsletter for local teachers' association. Proven ability to learn quickly, work productively, and produce high-quality results on challenging assignments.

Here is a profile for a salesperson who seeks a position as a training specialist for a consulting firm selling a management-training program to companies in many industries:

Professional Profile	Individual with sales background within the data-processing industry. Extensive experience in writing proposals and in designing/delivering major sales presentations to all management levels. Knowledgeable about the operations and needs of many manufacturing and services industries.

6. Strengths

This is the section that really allows you to blow your own horn. Use it to promote your proficiencies, addressing those important items on your ESP list that have not been included in your profile. Turning to our advertising and sales promotion manager example (see ESP list on page 102), here is an appropriate strengths section:

Strengths: Thoroughly familiar with advanced video equipment, with experience establishing an in-house facility. Excel at designing and organizing exhibits for national trade shows. Proven ability to work effectively with both marketing and nonmarketing management in developing creative solutions for promotional use.

An example of a good strength to include for a marketing manager in the consumer electronics industry is:

Demonstrated ability to develop business plans that include comprehensive analyses of the economic, competitive, and consumer factors driving the audio and video markets.

For a sales manager:

Proven ability to dramatically turn around poorly performing territories through a combination of upgraded sales training and innovative promotional programs.

For a personnel recruiter:

> Skilled at evaluating the qualifications of engineering and data-processing personnel.

For a controller of a manufacturing company:

> Skilled at redesigning materials management systems for improved cost-effectiveness.

7A (Chronological) & 7B (Functional) Formats: Presenting Your Employment Experience

All positions that can be classified as "professional"—as opposed, for example, to jobs held during college—should be included in this section. Sometimes people have upgraded themselves from secretarial or blue-collar employment to professional careers. In such instances the content of the experience prior to the beginning of your professional career isn't important for a prospective employer to see, but the fact that you were employed during that period is important, since employers tend to be suspicious of gaps in employment. One good way to include this information is to put it under the heading "Other Experience" (Number eight on skeletal outline of résumé) just after the "Professional Experience" section. Indicate the dates of this nonprofessional experience and write a one- or two-sentence description of the jobs you held during that period.

Formulating Your Responsibilities and Accomplishments

If you believe your job search will be best served by using a chronological résumé, develop a description of each of your jobs that includes both responsibilities and accomplishments. If you have decided that a functional format will serve your purposes better, select three or four skill areas which you know the employer is seeking, and describe separately under each heading those responsibilities and accomplishments that support your claim of having these skills. Regardless of which résumé format you choose, you will develop your responsibilities and accomplishments the same way.

A responsibility is what you are supposed to do; an accomplishment is an action that supports your having discharged a responsibility in a superior fashion. Thus an example of a responsibility is:

> Manage internal sales force of 35, as well as 15 independent representative organizations; develop marketing plans targeting mass merchandisers, discounters, department stores, and catalog showrooms.

An accomplishment reflecting the excellent way you handled that responsibility would be:

> Devised several promotional programs and revamped pricing. Result: achieved a 32 percent increase in distribution in all channels.

Note that if you are describing a responsibility pertaining to your current employment, it should be done in the present tense. However, all accomplishments associated with present responsibilities should be expressed in the past tense.

Here is a responsibility for a sales administration specialist:

> Provide administrative and technical support to field sales representatives, distributors, and industrial customers.

with this relevant accomplishment:

> Initiated a monthly newsletter for the field sales organization which provides timely information on competitive product introductions, pricing changes, and other developments.

Another example of a responsibility would be:

> As controller of the Sports Equipment Division, contributed to the development of budgets and strategic plans.

An accomplishment that describes how the individual carried out the above responsibility is:

> Devised and implemented a system for comparing the performance of capital investment projects with forecasted results.

Here is another example of a responsibility:

> As office manager for branch of a truck sales and leasing company employing 25, administer sales commission program and serve as liaison between branch and headquarters staff in interpreting commission policies and resolving problems.

and a possible accomplishment:

> Instituted a system for auditing commission payments, which identified $8,000 in overpayments.

THE IMPORTANCE OF QUANTIFYING ACCOMPLISHMENTS: This brings me to a very important point. All business employers are seeking people who can save and/or make money for them. Within the not-for-profit and public sectors profits don't have to be made, but costs must still be controlled or these organizations will not be able to continue to provide their services. Therefore, always try to quantify your accomplishments in ways that express your being able to make or save money for an organization. This is extremely important in any position in which performance is obviously measurable—for example, sales, marketing, controllership, construction-management positions—and is also important in other positions where performance may not be thought of as quantifiable. For example, a personnel manager may be measured on the extent to which he or she contributes to a reduction in turnover; an engineer may be measured on his or her ability to develop ideas for cost improvements in manufactured products. And, of course, any manager who has a budget to administer will surely be measured on the extent to which he or she keeps costs within budget.

EXAMPLES OF QUANTIFIED ACCOMPLISHMENTS APPLICABLE TO VARIOUS FIELDS: To get your creative juices going, scan this list—organized by functional category—of types of accomplishments that can be quantified to see if any pertain to your situation.

Sales
- Achieved 155 percent of sales quota in 1988.
- Increased the number of accounts by 35 percent.
- Received an award for generating the most revenue—of 45 sales personnel—during the first half of 1988.

Sales Administration/Support
- Designed a computerized sales analysis system that provided sales trend data in 50 percent of the time associated with the former manual system.
- Saved a key account worth $650K annually by upgrading the level of service provided to them.
- Conducted a training program for secretaries that enabled them to handle 65 percent of customer inquiries and problems, allowing the professional staff to concentrate on more complex matters.

Marketing
- Designed a cost-effective promotional allowance program for a luggage line that was directly responsible for a 90 percent increase over 1987 sales.
- Implemented pricing strategies that were instrumental in the company achieving a $1.5 million increase in profitability during 1988.

- Introduced two new hair dryer models that captured 4 percent of the market in 1988.
- Designed an innovative trade show exhibit that generated 45 percent more business than the previous year's exhibit.

Finance/Accounting
- Implemented a computerized inventory system that contributed to an increase in annual inventory turns from 4.2 to 6.
- Implemented inventory controls that were directly responsible for a 45 percent reduction in inventory write-offs.
- Installed a computerized synthesized-voice collection system that enabled the company to maintain its collection rate . . . at an annual savings of $50K in labor costs.
- Planned and managed a major corporate reorganization and consolidation that resulted in a savings of over $1.5 million annually.

Human Resources
- Designed a bonus system for middle managers that was directly responsible for a 75 percent reduction in annual turnover at that level.
- Researched and negotiated terms with a health insurance carrier for coverage identical to the current policy—at 8 percent lower cost.

Engineering
- Designed a procedure that reduced the costs of packing an electronic component from $1.89 to $1.17, saving approximately $72,000 annually.
- Designed a modification for an industrial stapling machine that reduced rejected parts significantly, increasing the production rate by 11 percent.
- Was awarded a patent for my design of a mechanism for releasing measured amounts of cleaning fluid from a plastic container. This device was recognized as the key contributor to a five-point increase in market share in the past two years.

Manufacturing
- Served as leader of a task force that identified opportunities to increase raw material yields by 12 percent.
- Redesigned several machine controls, achieving a 15 percent increase in production output.
- Researched, identified, and eliminated the cause of a high percentage of rejects in the manufacture of porcelain dishware, saving the company $75,000 annually.

Purchasing
- Renegotiated two major packaging contracts, saving 14 percent over previous costs.

- Initiated and coordinated implementation of standardized on/off on four coffeemaker models, allowing economies of scale in purchasing which resulted in an annual savings of $65K.

Public Relations/Communications
- Designed and managed a campaign that resulted in a 60 percent increase in new members.
- Developed a press kit that resulted in a 50 percent increase in newspaper coverage for a major product program over a similar program's press coverage the previous year.

Strategic Planning
- Researched, evaluated, and negotiated the acquisition of a producer of polyethylene packaging. Result: providing in-house manufacturing capability enabled the company to save $355,000 over vendor-supplied packaging.
- Conducted a study that provided direction for a major change in the company's distribution strategy, which was credited with increasing sales by 18 percent.

And here are some quantifiable accomplishments within the not-for-profit sector.

Social Services
- Wrote three major grant requests which were successful in obtaining $650K in funds.
- Designed and managed a fund-raising program that generated $150K within three months.

Education
- Planned and implemented the computerization of the college's registration system, saving 35 percent in annual labor costs.
- Negotiated state funding that enabled the Computer Science Department to purchase 16 new computers, contributing to a 28 percent increase in department enrollment.

THE IMPORTANCE OF COMPARING YOUR PERFORMANCE TO A STANDARD: In addition to quantifying your performance, try to compare it to some standard in a way that makes your performance look better. For example, if you were to tell me that, as a sales manager for a computer manufacturer, you increased sales by 125 percent in one year, this isn't enough to impress me with the fact that you are a superstar. For all I know, your predecessor managing the same territory achieved an annual increase the previous year of 185 percent. Thus, in quantifying your accomplishments, always try to compare your results to:

- the results that were expected of you, e.g., you finished a project in seven months, although it was forecast to take twelve months; you achieved 145 percent of the sales quota assigned to you;
- the performance of the function in periods prior to your appointment, e.g., over the 1986–88 period you increased your territory's sales volume by 150 percent, as compared to a 38 percent increase in the two years before you assumed responsibility for the territory; and/or
- your peers' performance, e.g., during the fourth quarter of 1988 you received an award for generating the highest sales of 285 representatives in the country; of 8 product planners in the company you implemented the highest amount of cost savings in your product line; during the 1986–88 period you were awarded the most patents of 16 engineers in the company.

7A.1 (Chronological) and 7B.2 (Functional): The Header Line (Dates, Title, Organization, City, State)

Although there is no set format, here are several approaches for presenting the header line—consisting of the starting and ending dates, your position title, the organization, city, and state—for each of your employment experiences:

1/86-present   *Systems Analyst*, Andrews Brothers, Inc.,
                      Des Moines, Iowa

                      or

1/86-present   ANDREWS BROTHERS, INC.,
                      DES MOINES, IOWA
                      Systems Analyst.

                      or

                      ANDREWS BROTHERS, INC.,
                      DES MOINES, IOWA   1/86-present
                      Systems Analyst.

The main difference among the above formats is that the third example doesn't highlight the dates. It may be advisable to use if the dates would reveal that you have not been employed continuously throughout your career, or if most of your employment experiences are of short duration. Sometimes people omit months from the dates of their employment in an attempt to conceal gaps, but personnel recruiters are usually suspicious of dates without months, so if you do not have any gaps be sure to include them.

An additional consideration is that the third approach requires less space for the margin, enabling you to present more information on one page than the other two styles allow.

Another point to consider: if you have held more than one position at the same company, and if you were to present the dates, title, organization, city, and state for each, the reader of the résumé would not know this until he or she read the header lines for the earlier positions. A better method is one that informs the reader immediately of the length of your entire tenure with the organization, as the following example does:

ANDREWS BROTHERS, INC.,
DES MOINES, IOWA

7/82-present

1/86-present	*Systems Analyst*
2/84-1/86	*Junior Systems Analyst*
7/82-1/84	*Accounting Clerk*

In the above example of multiple positions held in one company, indenting the position descriptions will help the reader link each job to the company named in the header line. Also, whenever the type of business in which the company is engaged would not be immediately evident to the reader, it's a good idea to include a parenthetical descriptive sentence or two just beneath the company name line. For example:

ANDREWS BROTHERS, INC., DES MOINES, IOWA
(A leading institutional food distributor serving the Midwest.)
7/82-present

or

BRISTOL-MYERS COMPANY, NEW YORK, NY
(Multinational company marketing pharmaceutical, nutritional, health/beauty, and household products; annual revenue: $4.8 billion.)

Notice that in the second example I included the annual sales, whereas in the first I did not. The guideline I use when working with my clients is that if the company is publicly held—which means that its financial data are in the public domain—we may include the revenue information on the résumé. If it is privately held, the information is probably considered proprietary. Another way to convey information about the size or the sales of a privately held company, while not disclosing confidential data, is to talk about the company being, for example, "the leading producer of professional hair-care products in the United States."

Sometimes, job hunters are very concerned about the confidentiality of their submittals to prospective employers. If you believe that news of your job-hunting activities may get back to your employer, instead of giving the name of the organization, describe it in a general way, e.g.,

6/83 to present   A major multinational manufacturer of computer peripherals.

or

1/85 to present   A 500-bed, not-for-profit voluntary hospital located in the New York metropolitan area.

It is rare that information about an employee's job hunting is communicated to one's current employer, but it does happen. This method will protect you until you are ready to divulge your employer's name after finding out more about a job opportunity.

Dealing with Promotions

Earlier I showed you how to itemize various positions held in the same company, using an indented format. If each of your positions was a promotion over the previous one, this must be communicated to the reader, since it will show a pattern of advancement that will imply your ability to handle higher levels of responsibility. But while it's very important to communicate the fact that you were promoted, it isn't always necessary to allot an entire paragraph to each of several earlier positions. If you have held more than one position in a company, and if the earlier positions are fairly minor in terms of the responsibilities they entailed, incorporate their description within that of the more recent one in the following manner:

4/85-present   *Manager*, Classic Clothes, Inc., San Diego, CA
Began as Saleswoman for this junior apparel store. Promoted to Assistant Manager in 6/86 and Manager in 9/87.

Notice that the dates in the margin reflect the *entire* employment period. A variation on this approach that does not specify the dates of the promotions is:

9/70-present   *Controller*, Ogden Luggage Company,
Chicago, IL
Began as Junior Accountant; received three promotions to positions providing experience in Credit and Collections, Accounts Receivable and Accounts Payable, before receiving promotion to Controller in 9/82.

Without giving the dates associated with the intermediate promotions, the above example provides the reader with information as to the experience this individual had in the company.

7A.2 *The Chronological Presentation of Your Experience*

I usually precede this section of the résumé with the title "Professional Experience," but you may prefer "Professional Employment." Many people use the term "Work Experience," but I feel that "Work" conveys a lower-level impression. I do recommend, however, that a recent college graduate, who usually doesn't have experience that could honestly be labeled "professional," use "Work Experience" or "Employment."

Each job description should contain the header information and, just beneath it, a description of your responsibilities and accomplishments. Since the employer will place the greatest weight on your most recent position, try to include the greatest number of accomplishments under that job heading—about two to six—with at least two under the previous position. Since space is a consideration (you should limit the résumé to two pages) and since the earlier positions are of decreasing importance to the prospective employer, highlighting accomplishments in those positions is not as important.

Begin the section dealing with each position by describing your responsibilties *only*, limiting the description of each position's responsibilities to ten lines. If you must use more, divide the description into two sections of relatively equal length, grouping related responsibilities in the same paragraph. List the accomplishments beneath the description of your responsibilities, using one of these approaches:

1. Skip a space after you finish describing your responsibilities, and use this method:

Key Accomplishments

- Managed growth of East Coast territory to achieve a 145 percent increase in sales (18 percent above quota).
- Developed a sales training program for my region, whose success was reflected in its implementation throughout the division's nine regions.

2. Instead of skipping a space after the last line of the paragraph describing your responsibilities, continue on the same line with the opener for the accomplishments, followed by a bulleted list as before. For example:

Conducted training for new distributors. *Key accomplishments*:

The second approach is good to use if space is tight, since it will save two lines over the first method.

3. The next approach is useful if you have only one accomplishment worth highlighting for a particular job. Skip a line after the description of your responsibilities and use this method:

Key Accomplishment: Received an award for identifying $50K in labor and material cost improvements for the company's largest-volume hair dryer.

7B.1 The Functional Presentation of Your Experience

After developing your responsibilities and accomplishments with a view toward matching every item on the employer's scoring points (ESP) list, select three or four functional skill areas and distribute your responsibilities and accomplishments among the appropriate categories. Each category can include statements about different positions you have held, as long as the reader is told the position with which they are associated. Precede the presentation of your functional skill areas with the title:

Key Responsibilities and Accomplishments

Here is a sample Human Resources skill paragraph:

Human Resources . . . In current position as manager of private medical laboratory, hire professional and administrative staff. Research and select training and development consultants to conduct courses in supervisory skills, record-keeping, and time management. In previous position as personnel specialist in a large hospital, was responsible for recruiting professional and secretarial staff to support accounting and plant engineering functions; specifically, formulated job descriptions, screened applicants, negotiated salaries, and conducted orientation programs.

Here is a Marketing skill paragraph using a bulleted approach:

Marketing
• Currently, as Marketing Manager for Advanced Sporting Goods Company, direct a professional staff of 18 in managing home exercise equipment, tennis and golf product lines—have achieved market share increases of 5 and 12 points in the golf and tennis categories, respectively.
• As Product Manager for Advanced Sporting Goods, managed the company's entry into the home exercise equipment market. Within two years established the company's presence in this industry by becoming the third largest producer, with 18 percent market share.
• In prior position as Product Planner for Stateline Products, played a key role in launching a line of self-cleaning outdoor grills that generated $12 million in sales—exceeding forecast by 21 percent.

7B.2 LISTING YOUR EMPLOYERS IN THE FUNCTIONAL RÉSUMÉ: In the functional format, all the information that would appear beneath the header line in a chronological résumé is mapped into the functional skill categories. Thus, the section containing information about one's employment would usually consist of header lines only. For example:

Professional
Employment

8/87-present	*Manager*, Healthcheck Laboratories, Ossining, NY
6/85-7/87	*Personnel Specialist*, Taylor Hospital, Tarrytown, NY

To describe several positions within the same company, use this format:

Healthcheck Laboratories, Ossining, NY
5/81-present

8/86-present	Manager
10/83-7/86	Senior Medical Technologist
5/81-10/83	Medical Technologist

You can use the same approach for describing several promotions as I earlier presented for the chronological approach (see page 120), e.g.,

6/72-present   *Controller,* Ogden Luggage Company, Chicago, IL

Began as Junior Accountant; received three promotions to positions providing experience of increasingly greater responsibility in Credit and Collections, Accounts Receivable, Accounts Payable, before receiving promotion to Controller in 9/86.

8. Other Experience

One decision many job hunters face is whether to include mention of part-time jobs (including self-employment) held concurrently with a full-time professional position but which do not bear on one's profession. On the one hand, the fact that you held a second job will surely show that you're a highly motivated person—a strong asset in applying for any job. On the other hand, employers having professional job openings tend to believe that applicants with part-time employment obligations will often have their minds on the *other* job while they're supposed to be working for them. And, too, the employer may be suspicious that the applicant is trying to develop the part-time job to a level where it can provide a full-time income, concluding that the person will be a short-timer. For this reason I recommend that you omit any mention of part-time employment in which you are currently engaged, although I see no negative consequence in describing employment experiences that have ended. If you are currently engaged in part-time work that is your only experience in a field in which you are seeking full-time employment, it would be important to communicate this to a prospective employer. However, it should be explained in a cover letter clearly stating that you undertook the employment in order to test your interest in the new field and to gain experience that would prepare you for the full-time position you now seek.

9. Education and 10. Professional Education

As with your employment descriptions, list your education in reverse chronological order. If you received a degree from a school you attended for four years, you needn't indicate the number of years you spent there; all that's necessary is to state the degree, year received, and, if relevant to your work, your major. However, if you interrupted your employment to attend school on a full-time basis, you may want to include the start and end dates of the schooling to account for your time during that period. Once you obtain an interview appointment, you may be asked to fill out an application form. If so, you will probably be asked to list all schools attended and the associated dates, in which case you should provide complete information. If you attended a college prior to the one from which you received your degree, you do not have to include this school on the résumé; however, if the school you previously attended was one that would make a favorable impression on the reader, you could state beneath the section detailing the later school something like this:

Prior study at Wesleyan University in Middletown, CT

Professional courses you attended that were conducted by outside organizations should be listed. You can include them either in the education section or, as I prefer, in a new section entitled "Professional·Education" or "Continuing Education."

My rule of thumb as to whether to include grade-point averages and school activities is that if you finished school five or more years ago, don't include them. On the other hand, if you were a member of a professional or honorary society or were the recipient of a scholarship or fellowship, it is appropriate to include this information throughout your career.

Here are sample Education and Professional Education sections for a financial manager:

Education	M.B.A. Finance, 1981, University of Connecticut, Stamford, CT B.S. Business Administration, 1973, City College of City University of New York, NYC Recipient, Gladstone Award for Excellence in Finance Member, Beta Gamma Sigma

Professional Education	American Management Association Courses:
1988	Data Processing for Non-Data-Processing Managers
1987	Managerial Skills Workshop
1987	Time Management, New York University Continuing Education Center

Other suggestions:

- If you are at a fairly junior level—within three years out of school—and have superior educational credentials, you may want to have your Education section follow the Strengths (number 6) section.
- If you are at a middle or senior level and went to a prestigious school, have your Education section follow your Professional Experience section, but mention the education at the end of your Profile, e.g., "M.I.T. B.S.E.E., Stanford M.B.A."
- If you majored in a field that differs from the kind of work you have performed in your career, omit mention of the major, unless you are changing careers and your major pertains to your objective.
- If you completed an associate's degree program prior to completing a bachelor's program, omit mention of the associate's degree since some people do not appreciate two-year college degrees. On the other hand, if you garnered many honors in an associate's degree program, include the degree, since the honors are important.
- If you financed 50 percent or more of your education, include mention of this if you completed your education less than five years ago.

11. Patents and 12. Publications

Itemize these accomplishments, including the dates and titles/descriptions. Be sure to include any co-authors/inventors.

13. Memberships

In general, limit these items to professional memberships, preferably those that are current. If none are current and you believe that mention of former memberships/affiliations will be helpful, then list them, but indicate the dates of your memberships. Also state whether you held any office or committee chairmanship.

14. Military Service

If your military service was unrelated to your present field, I suggest listing it after any professional memberships. Show the dates of your service, the branch of the armed forces, and your rank at time of discharge; add any honors you received. On the other hand, if you completed military service that prepared you for your present profession, it should be treated as professional experience.

15. Community Activities

Include mention of significant community activities only. For example, going door-to-door in your neighborhood for the American Heart Association would not qualify as a résumé item. On the other hand, if you organized a fund-raising drive to benefit local charities or were instrumental in setting up a community shelter for the homeless, include these. Describe only those activities that would not be considered controversial.

Political and Religious Activities
Do not include these unless you know that a prospective employer is looking for these experiences, e.g., if it's a political or religious organization that has the job opening.

16. Personal

Years ago it was very common for people to include personal information on their résumés—their age, marital status, number of children, etc. And employers typically asked personal questions of applicants. Title VII of the Civil Rights Law enacted in 1964 prohibits employment discrimination on the basis of sex, age, ethnic origin, and religion. What this means is that companies can ask only job-related questions in interviews. For example, if a job requires the use of Spanish, the interviewer may ask the applicant if he or she knows how to speak Spanish. However, the interviewer should not ask the candidate where he or she learned how to speak the language, because that information might reveal his or her ethnic origin.

Questions that elicit information about the applicant's sex, age, ethnic origin, or religion are considered discriminatory. If you are asked such questions and are not offered the job, you could have grounds for a discrimination complaint. On the other hand, if you include your age on the résumé and then do not get the offer, you would not have such grounds, since the employer did not ask a question that elicited this information. (It is lawful for an employer to ask you your age for insurance purposes after you are hired.)

Make no mistake about it: employers are often curious about your personal data. If you are a woman of child-bearing age, they may want to know whether you are planning to have children, since that might mean that all the money they invested in training you would be for naught. Also, the employer may be prejudiced in favor of married people. My approach to dealing with personal information is almost never to include it. The exceptions are situations where I feel that providing a certain piece of personal information would be advantageous to my client. For example:

- If an employer is considering hiring a woman for a professional position and believes that the woman is married, he or she will assume that her husband is similarly in a professional position and may be transferred to another location. If the wife follows him, the employer will have to fill the position again, and will resent the money and time invested in that woman. Therefore, I will often recommend to my divorced and single female clients that they include a line of personal information— most of the items being included to justify a full line of information— to communicate this fact. The personal data might look like this:

Personal   U.S. citizen; excellent health; divorced; travel acceptable.

- If a recent college graduate with no professional experience is targeting a position in a fairly competitive environment—e.g., sales, marketing— and if the candidate has been involved in competitive sports, I will include these in a line of personal information, e.g.,

Personal   Interests: tennis, racquetball, football, fencing

17. Honors

It's a good idea to end the résumé on a strong note. If you have received any honors or awards from civic or professional organizations, or were a National Merit Finalist or Fulbright Scholar, include them here, and make this entry the last on your résumé. In the next section you'll learn that it isn't necessary to end the résumé with a "references" line.

18. References

The statement "References available upon request" or some facsimile is found in many résumés. My feeling is that it is assumed that if the employer asks for references, you will usually provide them. (See page 146 for advice on presenting [and withholding] references.) There are times, though, when including such a line is advisable. If you've held many positions for relatively short periods of time, it would be a good idea to include mention of references being available, since that might help dispel any notion that you left for poor performance. If the last item on your résumé is a rather weak one—for example, a description of your first job as a junior draftsperson—as opposed to an honor such as a scholarship or patent, etc.—including such a line will provide a nice ending to the résumé. Lastly, a references line is good for filling one more line if your résumé is very short.

RÉSUMÉ SAMPLES

A little later you'll learn how to prepare and present your references. But first, let's look at a few examples of résumés that put into practice the principles I have presented. The first résumé was prepared for a client—let's call her Corinne Walsh—who came to me for assistance twice, about a year and a half apart. I chose her résumé to show you because it exemplifies why a functional format is sometimes better than a chronological one.

The first time she consulted me, she explained that she wanted to position herself as a strong candidate for both advertising and public relations jobs— using one résumé. That would not be feasible with the chronological approach, since the reader wouldn't see the description of her public relations experience until the second page, making its impact weaker. On the other hand, the functional format allowed me to highlight her public relations background on the first page.

I developed a list of sixteen employer's scoring points (ESP) for "Corinne." One ESP Must (see page 102) was skill as a communications generalist, since she was receptive to an advertising or public relations job. Another ESP Must was the ability to capture attention through creative devices. I therefore included the fact that she had found her husband through an advertisement, both to grab the reader's attention *and* to put in a plug for her copywriting ability. The résumé generated many interviews, with people curious to meet her, and she obtained a position in advertising within a short time.

The next time she came to me she had decided to focus her career on advertising, and wanted to advance to a higher level in the field. The chronological format was the clear choice, since it would highlight her current advertising position on the first page. Although I placed greater emphasis on her advertising background, I mentioned her public relations experience in the profile, since many advertising agencies also provide those services; it could only enhance her value to them. Although it wasn't very likely that her next job would entail copywriting, my client opted to retain that strength, since it had generated many interviews. Here is the functional résumé my client used initially, followed by the chronological one:

Corinne E. Walsh   85 Hastings Road, Atlanta, GA 55721   404/555-3782

Professional Profile	Versatile communications professional, currently employed as creative director of small advertising agency, with additional account executive responsibility. Background as copywriter for consumer products firm and as public relations/ marketing director for company providing health-care services. Consistent record of excellence in designing communication programs that yield significant, results.
	Strengths: Accomplished in many facets of advertising, i.e., consumer, business-to-business, direct mail, video, radio/ TV, trade shows. Proven ability to negotiate favorable prices/ terms with suppliers. Skilled in writing captivating, effective copy on any subject—as partially reflected in my finding my husband through an advertisement.

Key Responsibilities and Accomplishments

ADVERTISING . . . As creative director of small advertising agency, supervise staff of six involved in supporting accounts within the data processing, security, and banking industries. Designed highly successful multimedia campaign for Adams International Security, using direct mail, print, and radio. Also serve as account executive for some clients. As copywriter for Kitchen-Ease, Inc., a leading manufacturer of professional cookware, designed and wrote trade and consumer ads, business-to-business brochures, direct-mail pieces, press kits; developed scripts for educational and promotional video productions.

PUBLIC RELATIONS/MARKETING . . . As public relations director of private, walk-in medical center, designed consumer information pamphlets on a variety of health-care topics. Managed all marketing aspects of the center, i.e., delivered presentations to major companies; negotiated contracts for employee health-care programs. My efforts played a major role in the center generating $350K revenue in its first year of operation.

MANAGERIAL . . . Throughout all supervisory assignments, have demonstrated the ability to develop and administer budgets in a cost-effective manner. Excellent at providing direction to typographers, graphic designers, and printers, to ensure on-time completion of projects. Founded and managed own advertising agency and art gallery in Atlanta, handling all creative and business management aspects of both companies.

Corinne E. Walsh—Page 2

Professional
Employment

5/85-present	*Creative Director*, Smith Vetter Maxwell, Inc., Boston, MA (An advertising and sales promotion agency serving consumer/industrial companies and educational institutions)
2/81-5/85	*Copywriter*, Kitchen-Ease, Inc., Atlanta, GA (Manufacturer of premium cookware for professionals)
9/78-2/81	*Director—Marketing/Public Relations*, Walk-In Medical Center, Atlanta, GA
6/75-9/78	*Owner/Manager*, Castaway Art Gallery, Atlanta, GA
6/71-5/75	*Copywriter*, Bryant, Wilson and Higgins Advertising, Atlanta, GA
Education	B.A. 1971, Georgia State University, Atlanta, GA Major: English

Professional
Education

1985	Advertising Seminar, Georgia State University
1985	Graduate Writing Internship, Georgia State University
1984	Introduction to Computers, Georgia Institute of Technology
Honors	National Merit Scholarship Finalist

Corinne E. Walsh
2265 Mountainside Avenue,
Elk Grove Village, IL 60201
312/555-1234

Professional
Profile

V.P./Creative Supervisor for leading direct-mail firm; responsible for developing multimedia campaigns for health-care, high-technology, and consumer-products accounts. Background as creative director of advertising agency and as public relations/marketing manager of company providing health-care services. Consistent record of designing communications programs that yield significant results.

Other strengths: Accomplished in many facets of advertising, i.e., consumer, business-to-business, direct mail, video, radio/TV, trade shows. Proven ability to negotiate favorable prices and terms with vendors and suppliers. Ability to write captivating, effective copy on any subject—as partially reflected in my finding my husband through an advertisement.

Professional
Experience

10/86-present

V.P./Creative Supervisor, Market Direct Worldwide, Chicago, IL
Began as Senior Copywriter; promoted in 8/87 to V.P./Creative Supervisor. Responsible for supervising two art directors and one copywriter in designing and implementing print, direct mail, TV, and radio advertising campaigns from concept through finished product. Design and deliver new business presentations; evaluate clients' advertising needs and develop creative approaches; establish and administer budgets for TV/radio productions; continue to provide copywriting support on projects. *Key Accomplishments:*

* Designed a direct-mail package for Good Health International, a health maintenance organization, that achieved the lowest cost-per-lead of any direct-mail package ever used by the company.
* Designed a print campaign for Advanced Electronics that produced results 400 percent better than their previous agency's performance.
* Created a two-minute TV spot for a lawn-care company; its success led the client to authorize another sixty-second spot, as well as radio and direct-mail support.

Corinne E. Walsh—Page 2

5/85-10/86	*Creative Director*, Smith Vetter Maxwell, Inc., Boston, MA Supervised staff of six involved in supporting accounts within the health-care, security, and banking industries. Hired and negotiated terms with graphic designers, printers, and communication consultants. Designed highly successful multimedia campaign for Adams International Security, using direct mail, print, and radio.
2/81-5/85	*Copywriter*, Kitchen-Ease, Inc., Atlanta, GA Designed and wrote trade and consumer ads, direct-mail pieces, and press kits for this leading manufacturer of professional cookware. Also developed scripts for sales training and promotional video productions.
9/78-2/81	*Director—Marketing/Public Relations*, Walk-In Medical Center, Atlanta, GA Designed consumer information pamplets on a variety of health-care topics for this private, walk-in medical center. Managed all marketing aspects, i.e., delivered presentations to major companies; negotiated contracts for employee health-care programs. My efforts played a major role in the center generating $350,000 revenue in its first year of operation.
6/71-9/78	Was employed during the last three years of this period as Owner/Manager of an Atlanta advertising agency; initially was employed as copywriter for another Atlanta agency.
Education	B.A. 1971, Georgia State University, Atlanta, GA Major: English
Professional Education	
1985	Advertising Seminar, Georgia State University
1985	Graduate Writing Internship, Georgia State University
1984	Introduction to Computers, Georgia Institute of Technology
Honors	National Merit Scholarship Finalist

I wrote the next résumé for a client whom I will call Jay Lamb here, a man who has a sales and marketing background in the health and beauty aids industry. I prepared his ESP list with a view toward having his background appeal to any consumer products company—not just health and beauty aids manufacturers. One ESP Must was "strength in all distribution channels used by consumer products companies," so I emphasized in the strengths section his experience selling through distribution channels commonly used by other consumer industries as well. Since many companies use both in-house and manufacturers' representative sales forces—each requiring somewhat different management approaches—I included this as a strength.

Because marketing and sales executives are measured primarily on quantifiable results, I sought to express in those terms as many of his accomplishments as possible. Note that every accomplishment but one includes a numerical measurement of his performance—market share increase, sales ranking in a geographical market, inventory reduction, etc. And the one accomplishment that is not expressed specifically in numerical terms is implied by mentioning his reversal of a negative profit trend.

Jay Lamb	**9 Seaview, Islip, NY 10514**	**516/555-6583**

Professional Profile	Accomplished sales/marketing executive with extensive background in the health and beauty aids industry. Currently marketing manager for company with $250 million annual revenue. Consistent record of promotions for excellence in meeting volume, profit, and market-development objectives.
	Strengths: Thoroughly familiar with national accounts within the supermarket, drug, discount, and variety segments. Proven ability to launch innovative product introductions that establish a leadership position for a company. Highly experienced in managing manufacturers' representatives, food broker organizations, and internal sales groups.

Professional Experience	The Robertson Corporation, New York, NY (Manufacturer of health and beauty aids, selling to supermarket, discount, drug, and variety trade. Annual sales exceed $250 million.) 2/82-present
3/86-present	*Marketing Manager.* Manage product planning, sales planning, market research, pricing, and advertising and sales promotion functions pertaining to a line of 65 products. Oversee development of information systems to support these functions. Manage staff of 15.

Some accomplishments:

- Managed the introduction of the Personal Best line of shampoos, conditioners, and coloring products to the Philadelphia and New York markets. Attained 100 percent distribution on full line of SKUs in both markets and have established the product line as a top seller in both markets—with one product achieving the number-1 position in its category.
- Instituted national sales incentive contests—one reduced inventories by 1.1 million cases of products in 90 days, more than covering the budget.
- Formulated new pricing strategies for the New You line of hair coloring products to capitalize on competitive weaknesses. Result: achieved an 8 percent increase in profitability for the line—vs. no profit improvement in the 2 years prior to my tenure.

Jay Lamb—Page 2

The Robertson Corporation, cont.

1/84-3/86   *Field Sales Manager—Northeast.* Designed and implemented marketing and sales programs supporting a $90 million territory encompassing eight states. Directed three regional sales offices employing 22. Revamped this territory from a conservatively managed, stagnant one to one characterized by aggressive, innovative sales planning and execution. Key accomplishments:

- Restructured the northeastern distribution system, reversing an East Coast plant's negative profit trend.
- Generated volume increases of 26.8 percent (1984) and 32.1 percent (1985), exceeding corporate objectives by 35 percent and 22 percent, respectively.
- Introduced a new combination shampoo/conditioner package, which attained the number-1 share position in the Boston and New York markets.

2/82-12/83   *Chicago Regional Sales Manager.* Had full P&L responsibility for sales in metropolitan Chicago—total volume: $28 million. Reversed a negative sales trend, achieving increases of 42 percent and 39 percent for 1982 and 1983, respectively.

6/77-1/82   *District Sales Manager*, Wallace Corporation, Atlanta, GA
Began as salesman in the Cleveland area for this manufacturer of stationery supplies. Promoted in 1980 to District
Sales Manager in Chicago. Directed sales staff of four in
promoting the company's product line to stationery stores,
department stores, and mass merchandisers. While in this
position, exceeded sales quotas by 8-34 percent, consistently
ranking in the top 10 percent of 35 sales offices nationwide.

Education   B.S. Marketing, 1977, Case Western Reserve University,
Cleveland, OH

Memberships   American Marketing Association

Community
Activities
1980-1982   Member, Big Brothers of Chicago

References   Available on request

The following résumé was prepared for a purchasing executive who, for
purposes of our discussion, I'll call Marshall Talbott. He sought a position
with a large manufacturer at least the size of his present employer. We
mentioned "*Fortune* 500" in the first line of the profile to communicate immediately the magnitude of his responsibilities, since high on the ESP list of
his prospective employers would be experience with a similar-size company.

Another ESP item was the ability to negotiate large national contracts—
hence it became our first strength. Managing a centralized purchasing function
for a major company requires the ability to interact effectively with geographically dispersed manufacturing plants; we, therefore, stressed this point
in the current job description. Since a purchasing manager is measured on
the ability to control/reduce costs while maintaining or enhancing product
quality, every accomplishment listed was intended to support this impression,
e.g., $1.1 million annual savings, $630K savings in carton costs. Even the
accomplishment in his present job that discusses converting the purchasing
system from a manual to computerized mode contributes to this objective,
since it implies greater control over purchasing costs.

Because one of the most common challenges facing a purchasing manager
is how to make transitions from one product or packaging to another, we
included an accomplishment under his prior job that supported his ability in
this area.

Marshall Talbott   7 Hiram Road, Denver, CO 80235   303/555-7729

Objective
: A position as head of purchasing for a leading manufacturer of consumer or industrial products.

Professional
Profile
: Accomplished purchasing executive for pulp and paper division of *Fortune* 500 company. Consistent record of excellence in devising and implementing more productive purchasing and inventory methods and procedures.

Strengths: Skilled at negotiating large national contracts. Proven ability to provide effective direction to manufacturing plants in ensuring the timely implementation of purchasing policies. Superior ability to plan and manage product and packaging changes in a cost-effective manner.

Professional
Experience
: Martinson Corporation, Columbus, OH
(A leading producer of consumer and industrial tissue products; annual volume exceeds $450 million.)
4/80-present

7/88-present
: *Purchasing Manager.* Manage staff of five in purchasing $55 million worth of folding cartons, corrugated boxes, polyethylene film, and artwork. Negotiate contracts with regional and national suppliers. Purchase office equipment, furniture, and supplies to support ten regional offices. Liaison between Marketing and four mills nationwide in implementing purchasing and inventory policies.

Key Accomplishments
- Initiated the incorporation of a previously independent West Coast tissue mill into the company's centralized system, achieving significant savings through resultant economies of scale.
- Coordinated the down-gauging of polyethylene film, realizing a $1.1 million annual savings.
- Managed the computerization of the purchasing department's vendor records and quality trend data.
- By initiating relationships with national suppliers having regional locations, 40 percent saved in freight costs, and, in one instance, $630K in folding-carton costs.

Marshall Talbott—Page 2

Martinson Corporation, cont.

4/83-7/88   *Assistant Manager*, Purchasing and Packaging. After completing assignments as Inventory Control Coordinator and as Administrative Assistant to the Manager of Purchasing and Packaging, was promoted in 9/86 to Assistant Manager. Contributed to the formulation and implementation of policies and procedures relating to tissue products. Researched suppliers and negotiated regional and national contracts.

Key Accomplishments
- Implemented the establishment of the company's own ink-color standard system, greatly enhancing it's ability to achieve a consistency of product nationwide.
- Managed the transition from one size facial tissue box to another, with an 85 percent reduction in the write-off usually associated with such a project.

Education   B.S. Business Administration, 1983, University of Arizona, Tucson, AZ

Professional   American Management Association—Seminar on Inventory Management and Control Techniques
Education   Xerox Professional Selling Skills
Dale Carnegie Effective Speaking Course

References   Available on request

The writing of the following ("Alan Bern") résumé presented a particular challenge, since my client was seeking entry into the public relations or communications area after having been a teacher for eight years. I stated in the profile that he was an English teacher, since a good command of the language is an ESP Must to the public relations and communications areas—as was knowledge of sports, since he was targeting sports organizations. I chose to present his responsibilities and accomplishments in the functional format, since it allowed me to highlight aspects of his background that are valuable to the fields in which he sought entry, whereas the chronological format would not. I emphasized such nonteaching skills as his experience managing the public relations activities of his school's sports teams and of a local boating organization, as well as his negotiating ability, budgeting know-how, and leadership skill; these were important Other Valuable Characteristics on the ESP list I prepared for him. Although his experience as membership chairman and community relations director for a local organization was on a part-time basis, we felt we could include it first since it was his most recent position.

Lastly, we ended the résumé with an honor. Although being voted Teacher of the Year does not appear relevant to the public relations or communications fields, the fact that this man's performance was superior to that of his colleagues should imply that he would similarly deliver outstanding results in his new field.

| **Alan Bern** | **7 Elm Street, Annapolis, MD 05677** | **301/555-3782** |

| Professional Profile | Individual with background as high school English teacher and as coach of two sports teams, with experience managing associated public relations activities. Currently serve as Membership Chairman and Public Relations Director of community organization. |

Strengths: Thoroughly familiar with all major national sports league activities and players. Demonstrated ability to establish and cultivate strong press relations. Work well under time-critical deadlines.

Key Responsibilities
and Accomplishments

COMMUNICATIONS/PUBLIC RELATIONS . . . Currently employed as English teacher at Torrance High School; design and deliver courses in creative writing and journalism. As coach of the school's tennis and soccer teams, handle all public relations, i.e., press releases, media coverage, fund-raising campaigns. As Membership Chairman and Public Relations Director of Annapolis Power Squadron, promote the organization through radio appearances and panel discussion participation; also designed and presented boating safety course for the public.

ADMINISTRATIVE . . . As coach at Torrance, develop and administer annual budgets, delivering presentations on financial needs to school board. Serve as liaison to Mid-Atlantic Sports Conference in negotiating tennis and soccer teams' inclusion in intercollegiate competitions. Establish and administer policies governing students' participation in sports. Compile and analyze statistics pertaining to teams' performance, as well as prepare reports for school administration.

PROJECT MANAGEMENT . . . As school's representative to Torrance Advisory Committee on Education, organized and led a task force aimed at planning long-range educational requirements for the city, e.g., conducted market research study to assess current and forecasted demographic composition; prepared report detailing findings and recommendations.

Professional Experience	
3/85-present	*Membership Chairman/Community Relations Director*, Annapolis Power Squadron, Annapolis, MD
9/78-present	*English Teacher*, Torrance High School, Annapolis, MD
9/80-present	*Coach*, Tennis and Soccer Teams, Torrance High School, Annapolis, MD
1/86-6/86	*Project Leader*, Strategic Planning Task Force, Torrance High School Advisory Committee on Education
Education	B.S. Education, 1978, University of Maryland, College Park, MD
Memberships	Maryland Teachers Association Annapolis Power Squadron
Honors	*Recipient*, 1986 Annapolis "Teacher of the Year" award

WRITING YOUR COVER LETTER

While some ads specifically request that applicants submit a letter as well as a résumé, many just ask for a résumé . . . and many applicants make the mistake of literally complying with this request. *Always* include a cover letter with your résumé. Harking back to our supermarket analogy, sending a cover letter can be likened to a salesperson explaining why the product being sold is right for the shopper.

Even if you are sending your résumé to an employment agency or recruiter, a cover letter can be advantageous, since, if the recipient feels it's a strong letter, he or she may forward it to the client along with your résumé. Similarly, if a friend offers to circulate your résumé in his or her company, including a letter with your résumé will enhance the impression you make.

A cover letter, unlike a personal letter, should include your telephone number, since it may get separated from your résumé during the review process.

The Components of the Letter

The Salutation

You should make every attempt to ascertain the name of the person to whom your letter is addressed, and the title (e.g., Mr., Dr., Ms.) by which he or she prefers to be addressed. If you are unable to obtain a name through the company—or if you are responding to a blind ad—use "Dear Sir or Madam."

The Opening Paragraph

If you are responding to an advertisement, use an opening similar to this:

> I read with interest your February 19th advertisement in *The Wall Street Journal* for a controller, and I believe there is a strong match between your requirements and my qualifications. Currently the Assistant Controller of a leading manufacturer of electronic equipment, I am seeking a controllership position that will present challenges consistent with my accomplishments in the field.

You can also refer to the advertisement to which you are responding in the following manner:

> Jonathan C. Sinclair
> 4896 Lancaster Boulevard
> Dallas, TX 75252
> 214/555-6132
>
> Mr. Robert F. Dixon, President
> Dixon Hotels
> 45 Montgomery Street　　　Re: Advertisement for Controller
> Dallas, TX 75211　　　　　*The Wall Street Journal*, 2/19/88
>
> Dear Mr. Dixon:

This approach can be helpful in ensuring that your letter fits on one page, since it saves the space usually devoted to communicating that information after the salutation.

If you are initiating contact with a company—as opposed to responding to an ad—use this approach:

> I am confident that I can make an immediate and significant contribution to Wilson Electric's profitability. Currently the Assistant Controller of a leading manufacturer of electronic equipment, I am seeking a position that will present challenges consistent with my considerable accomplishments in my field.

The Body

WHEN RESPONDING TO ADS: Advertisements always specify qualifications sought by employers, e.g., a Benefits Analyst position might ask for three years of experience in benefits administration, the M.B.A. degree, and knowledge of ERISA tax laws. Address yourself in the body of the letter to each, detailing the extent to which you are qualified. If you satisfactorily fulfill all of them, use a bulleted approach, indenting each item, like this:

> The attached résumé details my background, relevant highlights of which are:
> - five years' experience in benefits and compensation positions of increasingly higher responsibility for a *Fortune* 500 manufacturer,
> - experience designing and implementing computerized accounting systems to satisfy company and federal regulations, and
> - the M.B.A. in Human Resources.

If you have some, but not all, of the qualifications mentioned, do not use a bulleted approach because that will highlight the areas where you are not fully qualified. Instead, write the paragraph in one block to avoid calling attention to your weaknesses.

Always include some information in the body that shows your familiarity with the company's activities. This will counteract the impression that your letter may be part of a mass mailing.

WHEN INITIATING CONTACT: Use an approach similar to the above, highlighting those experiences and skills in bulleted format that you have determined are employer's scoring points (ESP).

The Closing Paragraph(s)

Use a strong and positive closing. Here is an example of one that could be used by someone targeting a high-level management position:

> May I have the opportunity to meet with you and learn about your needs in the areas in which I have experience—as well as to outline my approach to addressing them?

If the company is well-known as a leader in its field, here is a good closing to use for all levels of professional jobs:

> In summary, I am confident that my performance as Manager of Training and Development would be consistent with the high standards I know IBM to have. I look forward to the opportunity to present my qualifications to you in person.

If you feel that the tone of the letter thus far conveys sufficient courtesy, you can end it at this point. Otherwise, you may want to add a closing courtesy statement as a separate paragraph, such as "Thank you for your consideration."

Cover Letter Samples

We've looked at the components of a cover letter. Let's now see how these can be put together to generate a strong impression, favorably distinguishing you from other candidates. Here are two complete cover letters:

Marjorie L. Bashevsky
45-15 David Street
Summit, NJ 07741
201/555-3718

October 20, 1988

Mr. Allen Storm, Director of Personnel
Dugan Financial Services
5561 Whittier Street
Newark, NJ 07734

Dear Mr. Storm:

I read with interest your October 6th advertisement in the *Newark Star-Ledger* for a Manager of M.I.S. Currently the Director of Systems and Programming for a leading producer of tableware, I believe there is a strong match between your requirements and my qualifications. Dugan Financial Services' fast growth in the mortgage industry leads me to believe that your company offers a work environment that would present challenges consistent with my considerable accomplishments in M.I.S.

The attached résumé details my extensive background in M.I.S., relevant highlights of which are:

- experience managing the development and implementation of systems to support every function of a business generating $250 million sales annually;

- responsibility for implementing and supporting office automation, artificial intelligence, and end-user computing capabilities;

- the M.B.A. in Management Information Systems.

May I have the opportunity to meet with you and learn about your needs in the areas in which I have experience--as well as to outline my approach to addressing them?

Thank you for your consideration.

Sincerely,

Marjorie L. Bashevsky

Frank B. Prescott
82 Willow Way
St. Paul, MN 44396
602/555-1043

September 9, 1988

Mr. George L. Fallon, Group V.P.
Contempora, Inc.
4291 Commercial Drive
Minneapolis, MN 44388

Dear Mr. Fallon:

I am confident that I can make an immediate and significant con-
tribution to the management of one of your divisional marketing functions. Currently a product manager with a *Fortune* 500 health and beauty aids division, I am seeking a position whose challenges are consistent with my marketing accomplishments. I am familiar with Contempora's recent product launches targeting the upscale consumer segment and believe that my experience in marketing some highly successful premium product lines would prove especially valuable to you. My résumé is enclosed for your review.

Developing new products in the health and beauty aids industry requires the ability to identify fast-changing consumer trends and develop profitable products that capitalize on these. That I have successfully met this challenge is reflected in:

- the shampoo product line I launched for my current employer that carved a niche for the company in the premium-priced professional hair care segment;

- the packaging design innovations I developed that garnered two awards for excellence from industry trade associations, in addition to being credited with increasing our market share by 5 points;

- my successful launch of the company's first line of men's skin-care products, which generated first-year sales of $35 million, exceeding forecast by 28 percent.

May I have the opportunity to present my qualifications to you in person and learn about your marketing needs in the areas in which I am experienced, as well as to give you details regarding my potential contribution to Contempora's profitability?

Very truly yours,

Frank B. Prescott

WHEN TO SEND A LETTER WITHOUT A RÉSUMÉ

In some situations—specifically, when some information appearing on your résumé could negatively affect your candidacy—it may be advisable to send a letter only. For example:

- if the dates of your employment would betray the fact that you have not been continuously employed;
- if you have been demoted at some point in your career, and if this would be obvious to the reader of your résumé;
- if you are targeting a type of work that you have either not performed in the recent past or have never performed (you will recall that this situation is a basis for using a functional résumé; instead of using a résumé at all, only a letter could be sent);
- if you believe that the employer desires someone with a particular type of educational background which you lack.

There could be any number of other considerations that may justify your sending a letter without a résumé. If you do choose this approach, go into greater detail about your accomplishments than you would in a cover letter.

Naturally, the fact that you are sending a letter without a résumé may make the reader suspicious. And if you are asked to send a résumé but you send a letter only, you run the risk that the employer will not review your qualifications at all. You must weigh the pros and cons of the two approaches and choose the one that you believe offers the better opportunity to get you in the door.

PREPARING A SALARY HISTORY

Many advertisements today ask applicants to submit a salary history along with their résumés. While no set format exists for this document, I like to present the salary history on a separate sheet, for aesthetic considerations. I recommend this approach:

John Morgan—Salary History

Title	Beginning Salary	Ending Salary
Manager of MIS	$75,500	$92,600 (current)
Manager of Systems & Programming	52,000	66,700
Senior Systems Analyst	40,300	47,500
Systems Analyst	30,000	35,000

If the total compensation in any of your jobs has included anything more than a straight salary—for example, bonuses, company car, profit-sharing—replace "Salary" with "Compensation" and include the value of the total compensation. If you've been on a fast track, including the dates associated with the starting and ending salaries will reinforce that impression. Also, if you have held many jobs, you needn't include data going back to the beginning of your career. It's okay to list the four or five most recent positions only.

One school of thought advises against sending a salary history even when it's requested, especially if you're confident that your résumé will strongly support your candidacy for the position. The rationale is that if your stated salary requirement is too high or too low, you will not be called in for an interview. However, sometimes a favorable interview can result in the employer finding another, more compatible job for you—or raising the salary for the advertised job.

PREPARING YOUR REFERENCE LIST

Good references can tip the scales in your favor for a position, even offsetting liabilities or weaknesses in your background. The type of reference list that makes the best impression is one containing three references in each of two categories: professional and personal. Professional references should be people who were former supervisors; even if these individuals no longer work for the companies where you reported to them, you can still use them. In such a situation, add a parenthetical comment after you list the individual's name: for example, "(Former supervisor at Osborne Chemicals)." In some cases, using a supplier or customer might be advisable. Civic leaders are good candidates for personal references, but avoid using anyone who might be considered controversial.

It goes without saying that you will pick people who you feel have a favorable opinion of your work, but beyond that you can enhance the impact your references will make on the inquiring company. First of all, it's very important that you *ask* your potential references if they are willing to act as one for you. Do not *tell* them that you are doing it, since people feel more favorably inclined to do something if it's a request, as opposed to an announcement. And even if Charlie Spencer told you five years ago when you were leaving Osborne Chemicals that if you ever needed a reference you shouldn't hesitate to use him, you must contact Charlie now that you are leaving the position you started after you left Osborne. If the prospective employer calls Charlie without your having paved the way now, Charlie may have a case of amnesia on the telephone and not immediately be able to place your name with your face. This will not make a very favorable impression on the employer. It's much better if Charlie has his case of amnesia when *you* call him.

Sometimes people you use as references will ask you if there is anything they should mention specifically that would support your candidacy. Even if they do not take this initiative, you could suggest some points that may help seal the offer. What kinds of points are best?

If you are changing careers, we know that one concern of the employer will be your ability to master responsibilities quickly in a new environment. In such a case, your reference should mention that you have this quality— or something from your ESP list—in spades. In general, any information that will alleviate any concern the employer may have about your qualifications would be worth mentioning. Another point worth bringing up could be some requirement on the ESP list which you truly satisfy, but for which you have no substantiation.

USING RECOMMENDATIONS

A recommendation differs from a reference in that it is a letter, usually addressed "To Whom It May Concern," so that you can present it to anyone. The one negative associated with recommendation letters is that many employers give them to employees whom they fire. Often rather glowing, these letters are designed to assist the employee in getting placed, thereby alleviating the guilt the employer may feel about terminating the individual's employment. If you do use a recommendation letter, therefore, it's important that the writer encourage the reader to call her or him, and that during that phone conversation the writer speak just as glowingly of you. I have had situations where I've received very good recommendation letters for candidates and subsequently called the writer and probed extensively as to the candidate's qualifications, only to get a lukewarm opinion of the candidate. It's much easier to maintain a charade in a written document than in a telephone conversation; in the latter case the vocal tone and inflection will usually betray the person's true feelings.

PRESENTING REFERENCES AND RECOMMENDATIONS

In general, including references and recommendations when you send your résumé to a company is not a good idea, because it allows the employer to check up on you; for all you know the nature of the job and the terms of the offer could turn out later to be unacceptable to you. Why wear out your references? If the people who expressed a willingness to recommend you are called by many companies, they may object to it and express their annoyance in the form of cutting short later inquirers, thus defeating your objective in using them.

If an interview goes well, the interviewer may ask to see your references or you may decide to offer them. In either case, you could say something like:

> I have very favorable references that I would be glad to show you now, but I prefer that these people are not contacted until we both know there is a good match and all that is left is checking my references.

If you have any doubt about the care that the company will take to see that your request is honored, do not leave your references with the individual.

In some instances, a prospective employer may express interest in you as a candidate, but say that you must agree to let them contact your current employer before an offer can be made. If you have kept your job-hunting activities from your employer, you should definitely not yield to this request, regardless of how tempting the offer is. If, after the prospective employer calls your current company, the offer is not made to you, you could be a lame duck; it might take you many more months to find a bona fide offer. In the meantime your position in your present company could be very uncomfortable. Sometimes, however, an employee's status in his or her company is enhanced if the employer learns of the job-hunting activities.

If you believe there's a possibility that news of your job-hunting activities will get back to your employer, you can prepare your résumé without giving the name of your employer. (See page 118.) You could then reveal your employer only to those interviewers where the job offer appears attractive enough.

Notwithstanding the above, however, there are two instances when submitting references or recommendations with a résumé is advisable:

- if you have a recommendation letter from—or are using as a reference—an individual who is very well known and/or is an executive of a leading organization in your industry, or
- if there is some liability apparent in your résumé that will be offset by the contents of a recommendation letter.

HOW TO PRODUCE OUTSTANDING DOCUMENTS

Preparation of the Master Version of the Résumé

Once your résumé is composed, the next step is to prepare the original—or master—version; you will then reproduce this document, generating as many copies as you need. A résumé should always be presented in a typeface, as opposed to being handwritten. You have three options for producing the master résumé: a typewriter, a printer attached to a word processor or computer, or typesetting.

Typewriting
This is the method with which people are most familiar. The only kind of typewriter I find acceptable for producing the résumé is a self-correcting, electric machine, since the use of correction fluid or paper almost always results in the corrected character looking a bit different. In addition, it's important to have all letters strictly on the same level; in my experience, only office-size typewriters offer the assurance of consistent proper horizontal alignment.

Many typewriters today allow you to select either 10- or 12-pitch spacing for the letters. A 12-pitch typeface signifies that one inch equals 12 letters; a 10-pitch typeface means that one inch contains 10 letters. I favor 12-pitch typefaces for résumés because they allow considerably more information to be included on a page. Since résumés targeting business positions should be limited to two pages, this is an important consideration.

Computer or Word Processor
A computer or word processor (the latter is a special-purpose computer) can be used to compose the résumé, after which the machine activates its printer in which paper has been placed, just like a typewriter. Some computer printers are called dot-matrix printers—the image of the letter is formed by a series of dots; these are not suitable for preparation of a cover letter or the master version of a résumé. Only letter-quality printers, which produce lettering comparable to a fine typewriter, are appropriate. Most letter-quality printers offer boldface capability, the ability to make words stand out with heavier lettering.

Typesetting

Typesetting allows you to select a particular style of type from among many available to the typesetter, along with a size—or point—for the letters. The greater the point, the taller and wider the letter. You can choose a point smaller than 12—although, for readability, you wouldn't want to go lower than eight. The chief advantage of typesetting is its ability to mix typefaces to differentiate between various portions of the text, e.g., to set boldface headings, italicize very important phrases. On the other hand, typesetting is relatively expensive, unless you have access to a desktop publishing system. Despite the high cost, however, I would enthusiastically recommend typesetting if I felt it offered an advantage to you. The fact is that typesetting is not only unnecessary in most cases—I'll get to the exceptions shortly—but, in my opinion, can even be detrimental in some instances:

- First, many job applicants submit typeset résumés for jobs where the persons hiring for the position do not themselves use typeset résumés for their job campaigns. In this situation the typeset résumé may threaten the hiring manager in that it implies that the applicant can afford a fancier job-hunting package.
- Second, it is a well-known fact nowadays that some people pay professionals to compose their résumés. When my clients have been asked whether they wrote their résumés and responded that they did not, they were not penalized. However, I believe it is in the applicant's best interest if the perception is that he or she wrote the résumé. A typeset résumé, because it has the most professionally prepared look, will tend to make the reader feel that not only was the type set professionally, but the writing was probably done professionally as well.

There are some types of jobs where I do recommend a typeset résumé— for example, in the case of a creative director of an advertising agency, or for an executive in a stock brokerage firm. Also, if it's important to include an amount of information on the résumé that will exceed two pages, you may want to consider typesetting. This was the experience of one of my clients in the social services field. Since people in this field generally use very simple résumé presentations, she selected a typeface that looked exactly like a standard typewriter's typeface and decided against using the boldface capability. But typesetting allowed her to specify a letter size that enabled her two-and-a-half-page résumé to fit on two pages.

Reproduction Methods for the Résumé

Whether you use the typeset, typed, or word-processing approach, there are two ways to generate copies from your master: offset printing and photocopying. These considerations should guide your decision:

- *Turnaround Time*: Offset printing usually takes a few days, whereas photocopying can often be done while you wait.
- *Aesthetics*: Some commercial copying machines reproduce black marks on the copy, although it is possible to find large, sophisticated equipment that is mark-free. Also, cleaning the glass on which the original is placed on a photocopying machine can often eliminate any black marks. Offset printing should never show black marks.
- *Cost*: Offset printing usually requires an order of a minimum quantity of 100.

Résumé and Cover Letter—Paper Color/Quality

It is quite common and acceptable today for résumés to be presented on paper other than bright white. While all paper companies have unique names for their colors, I have found several other generic color categories to be acceptable: ivory (slightly yellow); natural white (slightly off-white or eggshell); pale gray. Since most résumés are prepared on bright white, natural white, or ivory, a gray résumé will tend to stand out a bit—an important consideration if you are responding to an ad and need any edge you can get. In some fields, tan and light blue, as well as other colors, may be acceptable. Check with people in your field if you have doubts, or, as an insurance policy, stick to one of the basic four colors.

It is a universal rule that applicants should dress well for a job interview. But before the actual interview in which the candidate meets with the employer, there is another equally, if not more important, interview; namely, when the employer "eyeballs" your résumé. With this in mind, it is imperative that your résumé be "dressed" in very good clothes, i.e., on a very fine quality paper. I've seen many instances where individuals seeking middle- and upper-management positions have used plain copy paper . . . which is analogous to wearing a potato sack to the interview.

Use a heavy, fine-quality paper with either a laid (textured) or wove (smooth) finish. Buy a top-quality 24-lb.-weight paper at a print shop or stationery store. It may cost a nickel or so more per sheet, but what a difference it will make in the impression created. Despite this recommendation, however, if you believe that the recipients of your mailing would themselves use a low-cost paper, you should choose the same quality for your résumé and letter.

It's a good idea to match the cover letter paper to that of the résumé. If you customarily use personalized stationery, you should use it for your cover letter only if you believe the recipient of your letter and any interviewers would themselves use personalized stationery; select a color for the résumé paper that will be fairly close.

PRESENTING YOUR RÉSUMÉ AND COVER LETTER

In most cases, I recommend that job hunters avoid using folder-type résumés because I feel it's pretentious. I say "most cases," because I do know of a few instances where individuals seeking top-management positions in leading companies successfully used folder-type presentations, both in the regular 8½″ x 11″ paper size and even in a smaller, pocket-size presentation. But I would not recommend this approach below a top-management level.

Leave a fair amount of white space. A substantial part of a résumé's impression relates to its aesthetic appeal. Crowding information together and using narrow left/right and top/bottom margins detracts considerably from the impact—this, by the way, is one consideration that bolsters the case for a second page. Staple the pages of a two-page résumé together and use a clip to attach the résumé to the letter.

In medium- and large-size companies the human resources representative will usually review the submittals, forwarding those that appear to satisfy the hiring criteria to the functional manager. If you send only one copy of your résumé, you will never know whether the functional manager saw your good-looking version or a cheap-looking copy made on the company's problematic copying machine. But this is easy to avoid: include a *second* copy of your résumé with your mailing. In addition to ensuring the quality of the résumé given to the functional manager, you may make the recruiter appreciative of the time your thoughtful action saved him or her.

As for the cover letter: some job hunters who send out many résumés (which I usually do not advise, as Chapter 5, page 160, explains) make a master version of a cover letter. They leave the addressee section blank, use "To Whom It May Concern" or "Dear Sir or Madam" as a salutation, and send copies of that letter. Other people make the same type of form letter, insert a recipient's name and address on each copy, and plug in the name after "Dear"—but the fact that the letter is a copy is still obvious. Both methods are poor, because they each send the clear message that the job hunter took a shortcut—leaving the recipient with the impression that perhaps the same habit will characterize the person's approach to his or her work. In addition, many executives resent receiving a depersonalized letter. If you are sending a large number of letters, use a commercial word-processing service. You can provide them with a master letter and your recipients' names and addresses, and they will produce individualized letters, but remember to include some statement in each letter that demonstrates your familiarity with the company's activities.

The Envelope

You would probably be inclined to put your résumé and cover letter into a standard number-10 envelope, but I suggest that you do not. Use a 9″ x 12″

manila envelope so that you don't have to fold the résumé and letter in thirds. Using an envelope large enough to accommodate your résumé without folding will enhance the impression made on the recipient. (*Note:* some publications specify that applicants responding to their box numbers must use a number-10 envelope, e.g., *The Wall Street Journal*, in order for it to fit in their boxes.)

BE CREATIVE

The guidelines I have presented here are just that: guidelines. Since everyone's situation is unique, you must decide whether some novel form of presentation is warranted to make your résumé stand out. Remember, only you know exactly whom you are addressing and what will turn them on. One of my clients gave this a lot of thought and came up with a creative approach to presenting her résumé. (See Figure 8 following.) This folder approach (even though I usually recommend against it) was designed to look like a page from a dictionary and capitalizes on the woman's complicated, long name that people usually have difficulty pronouncing.

Teresa received an excellent reception from many companies with this résumé, probably due somewhat to the fact that she was targeting a position within the creative area where innovative forms of presentation are constantly sought. A creative résumé might not be as effective in noncreative functions, but don't just assume so. If you think of an approach that's a bit out of the ordinary, test-market your idea with some people in your field.

CHECKLISTS FOR ENSURING QUALITY

Once your résumé and letter are completed, review their contents against these checklists, which include points frequently overlooked by job hunters:

The Résumé Checklist

1. Are your address and phone number on the résumé?
2. Does each job entry show the employer, your title, and the dates*?
3. Have you used all technical terms properly?
4. Have you used proper grammar?
5. Is every word spelled correctly?
6. Do the dates dovetail, i.e., does the beginning of each job follow the ending date of the previous one (if you have no gaps in employment)?

---

*Older job hunters sometimes omit dates from their résumés. (See page 274.)

K

Kwiatkowski, Teresa (k-fē-ät-*k*of-ski, te-*re*-sa) *n.* photographer with a long, often mispronounced last name.

Figure 8. An unconventional cover page of a résumé in a creative field.

7. Is the print dark enough to read, and will it be legible if the recipient makes a photocopy of it?
8. Are mistakes that have been corrected on the master version invisible on the reproduced copies also?
9. Have you left enough white space so that the résumé does not look squeezed onto the paper?
10. Is the format pleasing to the eye?
11. Is your name on the second page?
12. If you must split a position between pages 1 and 2, do you indicate at the top of page 2 that the second part relates to the job mentioned on the bottom of page 1?
13. Does the résumé end with a strong point, e.g., an honor or professional affiliation, as opposed to a low-level job performed a long time ago?
14. Does the résumé provide information on your promotions?
15. Do you have at least two accomplishments for your current (or most recent) job?

16. Have you quantified your accomplishments, where possible?

17. Have you included all items from the employer's scoring points (ESP) list that you satisfy?

The Letter Checklist

1. Are the addressee's name, title, and organization correct?

2. Have you put the date on the letter?

3. If you are not sure of the addressee's sex, have you used "Dear Sir or Madam" as your salutation?

4. If you are responding to an advertisement, have you indicated the date and publication in which it appeared, as well as the title of the position?

5. Do you have an opening, middle, and closing section?

6. If you are responding to an ad, have you provided substantiation of your having all qualifications (or as many as you have) sought by the employer?

7. If you satisfy all qualifications sought by the employer, have you set off those items with bullets or other symbols?

8. Is the letter centered on the page?

9. Is the grammar correct?

10. Are all words spelled correctly?

11. Is your telephone number on the letter?

12. Have you signed the letter?

13. Does the letter paper match the résumé paper (or closely resemble it if you are using personalized stationery)?

SUMMING UP

I have devoted many pages to advice on developing your résumé and cover letter. The lengthy treatment of these topics definitely reflects the importance of these job-hunting tools. Properly prepared, the résumé and cover letter can communicate your enthusiasm, competence, communication skills, motivation, and interpersonal skills. Badly prepared—with little thought to the reader's perspective, with little care given to accuracy, with no test-marketing feedback—they can impede your getting the interview you need to get the job you want. By spending a lot of time and effort on your only opportunity to make a first *visible* impression (your telephone contact may precede your résumé), you will facilitate the employer's comparison-shopping expedition, resulting in your being selected for the preliminary "purchase decision": the interview.

5

How to Get an
Interview Appointment

PREPARING TO MAKE YOUR INITIAL CONTACT

When you complete your research, you will be familiar with your targeted organizations' products and services, as well as with any major expansion or other activity reported in the regional or national press; you will also have compiled a list of executives in your targeted organizations. Always confirm the accuracy of executives' names and titles before contacting them, since changes may have occurred since publication of the information you gathered. This is best done by calling the main number of the company and asking the switchboard operator to verify your information.

DECIDING ON THE INFORMATION-INTERVIEW VS.
THE JOB-INTERVIEW APPROACH

Earlier I discussed an approach that can be used effectively by career changers to gather information about prospective fields. It can also be used to advantage by job hunters who are really seeking employment, but who use the information interview as a method of soliciting suggestions and job leads. The fact is that people feel less pressured when asked for information than when asked for a job. Thus requesting an information interview may open more doors for you. On the other hand, there are a couple of disadvantages inherent in the information interview:

- If you do get an interview appointment on the basis that it will be for information—and not a job—it is inappropriate for you to produce your résumé, since that would be violating the terms under which the executive agreed to talk to you.

- So many people have used information interviews as a way of getting in the door for a job interview that executives have become suspicious of the motivation; when you ask for an interview, they may feel manipulated by what they perceive as a ploy, and immediately respond with "I'm sorry, but I do not have a job available."

I favor the job-interview approach because it's more direct, but you may find that the other approach is just as productive. For this reason you may want to alternate your approach for the first twelve or so contacts. If you see little or no difference in the success rate of the two methods, use the job-interview approach, since it allows you to pull out all the stops in your presentation.

EVALUATING VARIOUS METHODS OF APPROACHING EXECUTIVES

Now you must consider whether to use the letter, the telephone call, or the personal visit to initiate contact. Let's address the visit first. If you're interested in a job within the headquarters operation of a business, it's doubtful that you'll actually meet with anyone from that function without an appointment. The most that will happen is that you'll be met by a human resources representative who will ask you to fill out an application.

The one type of job that I strongly recommend applicants solicit in person is sales representative. Surely high on the employer's scoring points (ESP) list (see page 102) of a sales executive would be the ability to make "cold" calls on prospective customers. By visiting a sales executive without having an appointment, an applicant would communicate clearly that he or she has that ability—which is especially important if the job hunter doesn't have sales experience.

Paying an unannounced visit is easiest if there is a regional field sales office nearby—or if the sales function operates out of a small company headquarters, since gaining access to a large headquarters facility is usually not feasible. Applicants should call the office on the day of the planned visit to confirm that the executive is in. The visit should be made about a half hour to an hour after business hours, since the executive is likely to still be there. Job hunters who use this approach should study the dialogue of a telephone call between an executive and a job hunter that begins on page 160.

Weighing the Letter vs. the Phone Call

I am strongly in favor of job hunters using a phone call to initiate contact, for these reasons:

- When you send a letter you have no control over whether the person to whom it was addressed actually received it—and whether he or she read it. It may have been thrown away, filed, or rerouted by a secretary. Job hunters often think that sending a letter to the president of the company will be effective. If you are targeting a medium- or large-size company, he or she will probably never see it, since his or her secretary will have been instructed to forward all résumés down the hall to the Human Resources Department.

• The best-written letter in the world cannot communicate what a personal conversation can about you and your qualities. An engaging voice and manner of speaking can be much more effective in winning over a prospective employer than a letter.

• Since the purpose of a letter and résumé is to present your qualifications in a succinct fashion, you may have omitted—or have given minimal treatment to—an aspect of your experience that may be exactly what your targeted employer needs. If you send a letter, you'll never know what the person's objections are to your qualifications. But, if you make a phone call, there is a good chance that the person will verbalize his or her objections. For example, if you're seeking a corporate advertising and sales promotion job and you call the executive in charge of this function, he may ask you if you've had trade show experience and you'll have an opportunity to respond to this question.

On the other hand, if you were to send your résumé with a letter, you may have omitted this aspect of your background, thinking that the employer would be more interested in your experience coordinating the design and production of direct-mail catalogs. And, in fact, you may have come to that conclusion after doing a proper amount of research, but the executive, in our example, may have recently decided that participating in trade shows might be more cost-effective than using direct-mail campaigns. If he or she were to receive your résumé and not see any indication of trade show experience, you might never have an opportunity to address that concern.

• Companies are deluged with letters. With the availability of directories and mailing lists covering every industry, everyone has access to data on executives. And generating hundreds of letters quickly and cost-effectively is made possible through the use of word-processing equipment. The result: mountains of résumés are sent to anyone with any authority in an organization. IBM, for example, receives 1.3 million employment applications per year. While this company is certainly one of the more prestigious and one we'd expect would receive a high number, the figure is still staggering, isn't it? The *Fortune* 500 executives with whom I've spoken told me that their companies typically receive about 200–400 unsolicited résumés weekly. What all this means is that your mailing will probably not get the kind of attention you need to be granted an interview.

With all this in mind we may well ask: why do so many people persist in sending letters? Because it's easier to drop a bunch of letters in the mailbox than it is to get past secretaries, make repeated phone calls in order to reach executives, and deal with objections that the companies are fully staffed—or that your experience is not relevant to the organization's needs. Making a telephone call certainly requires more work, but it's a much more effective approach than the letter.

Letter Writing—Ineffective for Career Changers

My analysis of the negatives associated with the letter-writing approach applies to *all* job hunters. For career changers looking for jobs, the letter-writing avenue is even gloomier. Let's say you're a career changer who wants to contact a busy public relations executive. You send him or her a letter explaining your interest in public relations, and you enclose a handsome résumé. It all looks very nice, and he or she will probably read it and see that you have achieved some degree of success in your present occupation. But, frankly, that executive really doesn't have time to spend on a long shot—which you are, because as a career changer you have no track record in public relations—when he or she has on file 15 résumés of seasoned, proven public relations specialists who could start being productive on day one of their employment. Thus, regardless of how accomplished you are in your current career, regardless of how intelligent you may be, your background is a liability because your experience will appear to have no relevance to the executive's needs, and he or she will not be interested in meeting you.

The implication of all this is that your objective should be to "walk" your résumé into an interview with the executive *after* you've arranged such an interview by using the telephone. This way, by the time all the liabilities are "on the table," if you succeed in impressing the executive with your character, intelligence, and drive, there is a good chance that he or she will overlook the liability of your previous experience. Yes, it's true that you may be asked over the phone about your public relations background, but in some cases you can negotiate an appointment by pointing out that your accomplishments in your current occupation reflect general skills (e.g., analytical, communication) and that based on the research you've done—in particular, your conversations with public relations people—you've determined that these very same skills are important to the public relations function. And if the executive asks to see your résumé before granting you an interview, he or she may be so favorably impressed by the directness of your telephone contact and by your presentation that your lack of experience will not be considered a liability. (Beginning on page 160, I go into considerable detail on techniques for negotiating interview appointments.)

Negatives of the Telephone Approach

As with most things in life, the telephone approach has drawbacks:

• A phone call may be an intrusion, whereas a letter can be read at any time.

This is absolutely true. However, you can very easily ask anyone you call if he or she is free to speak. It's far better to get a "no" than to try to engage in conversation someone who is frantically preparing a budget due in an hour.

- If you do use the telephone, you may have to deal with a major obstacle, the secretary.

From the perspective of the job hunter, the secretary is one of the most powerful people in any organization, for it is this person who literally stands between you and the executive you wish to contact. Anyone who has ever had to interact with an organization is all too familiar with the "third degree" the secretary gives a caller not known to him or her. I like to compare the secretarial "defense" to a huge wave in the ocean. You, as the swimmer, do not want to be washed away by the wave; you want to get past it. How can you accomplish this? By timing your attack so that you go under the wave when it is at its most threatening, you can get beyond it. Similarly, by timing your approach against the secretarial "wave," you can progress toward your targeted executive. In this case, you time your attack to take place when the secretary cannot possibly rebuff you: *when he or she is not there.*

How will you know when the secretary will not be around to defend the executive's turf? Here's how: most executives—because they have achieved their high positions—are people whose work habits are not governed by the usual business hours. These are people who frequently arrive at their offices anywhere from a half hour to an hour before the work day begins and stay at the office anywhere from a half hour to an hour and a half after the work day ends. So what you must do is this: during normal business hours call the company's main number and ask for the direct dial of your target. This is the number that you can dial directly to reach him or her without going through the switchboard operator. Then, after business hours that day—or the next morning—call the person; there is a very good chance that he or she will answer the telephone. If you are not able to obtain a direct dial, calling during a lunch hour would be a good alternative approach, since executives often work through lunch, while secretaries usually do not. Above all, avoid contact with the secretary.

When Letter Writing Is Recommended

Notwithstanding the disadvantages of sending letters, there are some situations when initially contacting an executive by letter is advisable (but I reiterate my belief that if you're changing fields, it is an ineffective method for getting a job). For example:

- *If you believe that your vocal presentation is not very effective*
This would be a good reason for using a letter. But if you're weak in

this area you won't be very effective in either the interview or on the job, so I recommend that you correct this before you undertake a job campaign, if possible. (For advice on how to address speech and voice problems, see page 250.)

- *If you have top educational and/or employment credentials*
  Graduating from a top school can open doors. If you're fortunate enough to have this kind of credential, you'll probably have a somewhat higher success rate in sending letters than your job-hunting competitors. Similarly, if you've been employed by a blue-chip company, that may imply to prospective employers that you are fairly well qualified, since that type of company is thought to have relatively stringent hiring criteria.

- *If you can use the name of a referral*
  Nothing paves the way as well as mentioning the name of a mutual friend or acquaintance who recommended that you speak to a prospective employer. While it often happens that the contact will not develop into a job offer, it usually ensures your obtaining an interview appointment, regardless of whether you write or phone the individual. In conjunction with this, enclosing glowing recommendation letters from people at very high levels in companies with which the prospective employer would be familiar may be very effective.

By now, you probably know which approach would be best for you. Even if you use the telephone approach, you'll need to prepare a résumé and letter, since the employer may ask to see your résumé before giving you an interview. Guidance on preparing and mailing these documents is presented in Chapter 4.

Using the Telephone Approach

If the organization is a relatively small operation—or if it has an old-fashioned telephone system—the operator or receptionist will tell you that you can reach the executive only by going through the main number. Therefore, you will be restricted to calling during normal business hours. If you encounter such an obstacle, try the lunch-hour approach.

Incidentally, it's unlikely that a small business will have a direct-dial capability. Call the main number of this type of business after or before hours just as you would call a large company using a direct dial. The proximity of the executives to the switchboard in a small office may result in one of them answering the phone during those periods when the receptionist/switchboard operator is not available; also, in some small offices, all incoming calls will ring on all telephones.

Where Should You Do Your Telephoning?

This question is not answered simply. If you are currently working and know that your company doesn't mind employees making personal calls from the office, you could use your office, if you have sufficient privacy. You may have to arrive a little earlier or stay a little later in order to catch your targets without their secretaries. As for which number to leave as a call-back, I am against your leaving a home number. Some people who change jobs do so because they have been fired. If you do not fall into this category, you should definitely leave your business number, since, by not doing so, you may arouse suspicion in the minds of those you contact that you have been fired.

If you have been fired—or have voluntarily left your previous organization—try to arrange with your former employer for you to continue to use the office number as a return number and pretend that you are still employed. Unless you have severed ties in an unpleasant fashion, this should be an easy thing to arrange; it's a very common practice at the largest companies when they lay off or fire employees. If you do succeed in arranging phone coverage, make sure that all people in the firm who could take a telephone message for you are made aware of such an agreement, and are coached as to how to respond to callers—for example, "he's at an off-site meeting," "she's out of town today." When using this technique, either you must call the office daily for your messages, or someone in the office must communicate them to you.

If you are very concerned about your company finding out about your job-hunting activities, don't use your office telephone for any of your inquiries or discussions with agency personnel or employers. Prospective employers are usually understanding about the need for confidentiality and, if they are interested enough, will make the extra effort to contact you at home in the evening.

The Telephone Dialogue Between You and the Prospective Employer

The strategy underlying the telephone dialogue is that, once you have the executive's attention, you should mention key points about your background or skills that will impress her or him. For guidance, use the employer's scoring points (ESP) list you developed in preparing your résumé.

The following dialogue is an example of how you could present yourself over the telephone to a business executive, regardless of whether you are changing jobs within your field or changing your career. In this example, let's assume that you, the job hunter, are a teacher who is seeking a sales position.

> YOU: Ms. Brown, my name is Tom Larson. We haven't met but are you free to speak now for a few moments?

(This is a very important part of the conversation. During the opening you must identify yourself first, then say you haven't met in order to preclude the executive from wondering whether he or she knows you. If he does focus on whether he knows you, he won't pay attention to what you say afterward. Also, if you don't ask the question, you run the risk of interrupting him in the midst of something pressing. If so, and you continue your presentation, you will probably elicit a negative reaction.)

> EXECUTIVE: As a matter of fact, I am right in the middle of something.
> YOU: When would be a good time for me to call you back?
> EXECUTIVE: Try sometime tomorrow.
> YOU: Thank you, I will.

Make any subsequent phone calls to the executive before or after hours, since this approach proved effective.

Assuming that the executive says:

> EXECUTIVE: Yes, I have some time.
> YOU: Ms. Brown, I've recently completed extensive research and determined that my skills could be best used in the sales area. I've studied Webster Luggage's activities and learned that you're involved in some innovative products. I'm confident I'd be able to make a significant contribution to your sales efforts. May I present my qualifications in person?

Be prepared for two possible responses:

> a) EXECUTIVE: If you're interested in a job with us you'll have to go through our Human Resources Department at headquarters. It's company policy.

If you get response *a*, ask for the name of the Human Resources person you should call. Then call that person, using the name of the executive who referred you, e.g., saying that you were just speaking to that individual about your interest in employment at Webster Luggage and she suggested that you contact him or her.

> b) EXECUTIVE: Have you had any sales experience?

If you get response *b*, then:

> YOU: While I haven't had actual sales experience, I have had considerable experience selling educational concepts to my students.

I've played a key role in selling my administration on implementing major new curricula and on approving budgetary requests
for extracurricular programs. Also, based on numerous conversations with sales executives, I've learned that capabilities I have
in abundance—excellent interpersonal skills, drive, communications abilities—are very important to the sales function. With
respect to the specifics of your sales operation, I'm a very fast
learner and could pick those up quickly.

At this point you'll probably get one of three responses:

a) EXECUTIVE: What you say sounds interesting but before I agree
   to get together with you I would like to see your résumé.
b) EXECUTIVE: What you say sounds interesting. How about
   stopping by next Wednesday at five?
c) EXECUTIVE: What you say sounds interesting but, frankly, I'm
   fully staffed now and don't foresee the need for any additional
   salespersons in the near future.

If *a*,

YOU: I'll mail it to you today and give you a call in a week.

You will then send your résumé with a cover letter, being sure to mention
this telephone conversation in the opening sentence. Otherwise, the secretary
will assume that yours is just another one of those unsolicited résumés, and
forward it to Human Resources.

If *b*,

YOU: That would be fine, thank you. In case anything comes up
on your end that interferes with our appointment, here's a number
where you can reach me, etc.

If *c*,

YOU: I can certainly appreciate that. However, I'd like to suggest
that in case you suddenly lost a member of your sales staff, your
operation could maintain its level of productivity if you knew of
someone who could quickly take that person's place. If, after we
met, you determined that I could be a backup candidate for one
of your people, I could immediately fill that gap. I realize that
my contacting you directly is a bit unconventional, but I thought

you'd be glad to avoid the costs and time associated with recruiting.

After giving your response to *c*, you'll probably get one of these responses:

  a) EXECUTIVE: Perhaps it would be worthwhile for us to meet
     now. Can you make it next Wednesday at five?
  b) EXECUTIVE: I'm sorry, but I'm still not interested in getting
     together.

If *b*,

    YOU: In that case, may I send you my résumé for future consid-
    eration?

Regardless of whether you are changing your career or just your job,
carefully think in advance of your call about the *conceptual* similarities that
exist between the job you are targeting and the job you now hold, or have
in the past. When you hear an objection raised about the differences between
your experience and what a company's requirements are, state what you
believe to be the similarities between them and acknowledge the differences.
Explain that you're a very quick learner and would be able to master the
details of the new position very quickly; give examples from your employment
experiences that support your assertion.

At whatever point in the conversation you get a "not interested" response
that cannot be reversed with your "backup candidate" attempt, ask if you
can send your résumé for future consideration. If you get no response in two
weeks, call the executive. If he or she expresses interest in you as a possible
candidate, but is reluctant to give you an interview because no opening exists,
remember that the situation could change at any time. Therefore, you must
plan on making periodic phone calls—approximately every three months—
to inquire about opportunities that may have arisen in the interim. In the
original conversation try to lead the discussion to some point that will make
it easy for the executive to remember you when you call again. For example,
if he or she gives you a suggestion for a lead to other employment opportunities, you could refer back to that discussion when you call again, thanking
him or her for the suggestion and describing what resulted from your following
through on it.

You may feel that making a telephone call directly to a targeted executive
is a brazen move in that it bypasses the Human Resources Department (unless
you have your sights set on a job in that function). Perhaps it is. But you
must realize that to be successful in many of life's endeavors, some degree
of aggressive behavior is necessary. Furthermore, if you are seeking entry
into a new field and observe all the traditional procedures for job hunting,

you won't get very far, since the normal business system does not accommodate changes as drastic as the one you wish to make. Therefore, you will have to bypass some of its unwritten rules. And even if you seek a job in the same field, the telephone approach affords the opportunity to deal directly with the prospective employer, considerably enhancing your chances of success.

Telephone calling is an effective means of getting in the door, and, contrary to what many people believe, some personnel executives fully endorse applicants contacting the managers of the functional areas they want to penetrate. They know that it is the functional managers who are most familiar with their human resource needs since they have firsthand knowledge of changes within their areas.

Why This Approach Works

To appreciate why the telephone approach can be effective, put yourself in the position of the person you are calling. Because you have identified the highest-ranking person within the function in which you hope to obtain employment, you can assume that you are talking to someone who has the authority to hire you. If you present yourself well over the telephone and demonstrate that you are familiar with the organization's activities, you will certainly impress this individual with your motivation and resourcefulness. Furthermore, the executive you've called knows from experience that:

- unbeknownst to him or her, an employee could be planning to leave the organization;
- to find a replacement could take months, and while the position remains unfilled the productivity of the department could be seriously hampered;
- he or she may have to resort to an agency or recruiter to conduct a proper search in filling an opening, which could mean an expenditure of $3,000 to $15,000 or more, in addition to the employee's salary, or, if the employer conducts the search himself, possibly several hundred dollars for an advertisement—not to mention the cost and time entailed in screening respondents. Since all executives are measured on the degree to which they control costs, they should be very interested in reviewing the qualifications of applicants who initiate contact with them.

Now I'm not suggesting that everyone you contact is going to respond positively, but remember—all you need is *one* person who has a job opening to react favorably to your telephone approach who is also sufficiently impressed in the interview, and your search is over. With this in mind, let's now consider how you should present yourself in an interview to ensure that *more* than one person will react positively to your presentation at that stage, giving you the delightful dilemma—which I'll guide you in resolving on page 197—of having to choose from among several offers.

6

Putting Your Best Foot Forward in the Interview

A young man who had just graduated from college went through every floor of a ten-story office building, introducing himself to executives in various companies and asking to be considered for a position. He obtained several interviews and, after one of them, the interviewer walked him to his car. This young man had been working throughout the summer mowing lawns and landscaping and, not having a truck, was in the habit of using the backseat of his car to transport his lawn mower. The backseat was full of grass clippings, and the man who escorted him to the car took a long, hard look at the mess in the back and was visibly turned off. The young man, of course, did not get the job. When I heard this story from a friend who knows the fellow's mother, I was very impressed by the fact that the young man went to the trouble to scour that office building for a job, and had worked all through college. Clearly, such a person will go far in whatever occupation he undertakes, and the man who allowed himself to be influenced by the grass clippings in the back of the car lost out on a potentially valuable employee.

However, while the man made a mistake by jumping to a conclusion about the applicant's habits, the young man also erred in not considering the possibility that a prospective employer might see—and draw an unfavorable inference from—the condition of his car. Naturally, you're probably well past the stage where you're likely to be having landscaping jobs. Your "grass clippings" could be baby bottles or other paraphernalia, tennis gear, sales brochures, or other items cluttering up your car. Since you may open your briefcase during the interview, be sure to have its contents presentable as well. (As for handbags, female job hunters should refer to Chapter 11 (page 267) for advice on this subject.) But cleaning your car is one small aspect of the preparation required for your interview. There are seven key rules of preparation necessary to ensure the success of your interview:

1. Know the organization.
2. Understand the interviewer's perspective.
3. Prepare responses to questions you are likely to be asked.
4. Conduct role-playing interview rehearsals.
5. Prepare your questions in advance.
6. Know your rights regarding a lawful interview.
7. Prepare logistically for the interview.

1. Know the Organization

I earlier mentioned the importance of researching the organization in order to understand its philosophy and operation, but it is worth emphasizing again. During the research phase your objective was to analyze potential employers to determine whether they offered environments compatible with your job needs and career objectives. Now reread any material you obtained about these employers so that you sound well-informed about the company when you are asked—as you may very well be—what you know about it. An applicant who demonstrates knowledge of the company's activities sends the message that he or she is resourceful and willing to work hard during the job-hunting process. The interviewer can safely assume that the individual, if hired, will behave similarly toward his or her assignments.

If the information you were able to obtain about the organization is rather limited, at the time the interview appointment is arranged ask your contact at the company to send you any descriptive material about its business.

2. Understand the Interviewer's Perspective

A friend of mine who is a partner in an employment agency tells this story of a job applicant, a woman, who had an interview scheduled for a particular day. Two nights before her interview was to take place she crept up to the outside of the company's building and peeked in the window to see the colors in which the office was decorated—they were orange and beige. For the interview she wore . . . you guessed it, orange and beige. She got the job.

What is interesting to me is that when people hear this story they marvel at how clever the woman was to think of dressing in the same colors as the decorating scheme of the company. Obviously, this woman believed that by dressing in the same colors she would appear attractive to the executive interviewing her, the assumption being that he had a hand in choosing the color scheme. Now, the way I view this story is this: if this woman went to the trouble to check up on the color scheme and dress accordingly, I am sure that she went to a comparable amount of trouble in the rest of her presentation. And it was the effect of her *whole* presentation—a tiny portion of which *may* have been the colors she wore—that resulted in her getting the job. For all we know, the executive not only didn't have a say in the office's colors, he may have hated the colors, and it was only because the woman's total impression was so superior that he overcame his revulsion toward orange and beige.

The point of this story is this: the woman is obviously an activist about her life. Rather than sit around and hope that everything would go well at her job interview, she set aside some time to think about the way she could appeal to a prospective employer. She realized that human psychology plays a significant role in the impressions we make on others, and she capitalized on it. In addition, by going to such lengths to ensure that her interview would be a success, this woman must have developed tremendous confidence in her ability to present herself well. And there is no doubt that the interviewer reacted favorably to such a self-assured applicant.

Those of you who will be having job interviews in high-rise office buildings with tight security, don't panic! You don't have to go to such extremes. But you do have to think long and hard about the psychology underlying the interview process. With this in mind, let's consider the interview from the interviewer's perspective.

In the job-selection process in a medium- to large-size organization, an applicant will usually be interviewed by at least three people:

1. a representative from the Human Resources department;
2. a functional manager to whom you, the candidate, if hired, would report (also called "reporting manager"); and
3. that manager's superior, who is a manager at the next higher level.

Let's look briefly at how their perspectives may differ. While the Human Resources interviewer is familiar with the requirements of the job, not being an engineer or computer programmer or financial analyst, for example, he or she may not be equipped to ask highly technical questions, although sometimes the functional manager provides the Human Resources representative with these. But, generally speaking, the Human Resources representative's objective at the interview will be to find out what kind of personality you have, whether you exercise good judgment in making decisions, whether you communicate the type of professionalism consistent with the level of the job. The reporting manager will be very interested in your technical skills. And the higher-level manager will have a perspective similar to the reporting manager's but, in addition, may be evaluating your promotion potential—possibly as a replacement for the reporting manager—or as a future candidate for positions in other areas under his or her direction.

While all three types of interviewers may question you about the responsibilities and accomplishments listed on your résumé, they must often take your word for the truthfulness of these points because the interview process does not always afford the kind of in-depth investigation necessary to assess your background accurately. The fact that you obtained the interview demonstrates that the information presented on your résumé or communicated in a telephone conversation impressed these people. Or, if a friend or colleague has sponsored you to the employer, he or she has surely extolled your virtues.

Thus, by the time the interview appointment has been set, the assumption on the part of the employer is that you have the technical skills to perform the job. But companies want to hire employees who fit well into the atmosphere of their organizations. If you have worked in several companies, I am sure you will agree that each has a special character and, furthermore, that the most successful people are those whose behavior is compatible with the organizational "personality." For all these reasons, therefore, the focus of the interviews will be on assessing your personality, character, judgment, leadership ability (or potential), communication skills, appearance, and your compatibility with the corporate culture.

Another point to consider is that the performance of a new employee will reflect on the individuals who participate in the hiring decision. If it's good, they'll look good. If it's bad, not only will it reflect negatively on them, they'll also have a problem on their hands: the burden of trying to improve the employee's performance, or, if that fails, of firing her or him . . . an even more unpleasant task. As such, the interviewer is often as nervous as the applicant, since, while you are hoping to make a great impression and get the job offer, he or she is hoping not to make a mistake and hire a lemon. Because of this, you should realize that the interviewer is looking for evidence that indicates that hiring you will be a wise decision, and will happily use that evidence to lobby for you to be chosen for the job.

Therefore, a good investment of your time is to focus on what the interviewer's orientation is and what his or her objectives are. Sometimes an interviewer will provide you with this information in remarks he or she may make at the outset, but in most cases you will have to rely on your analytical ability and draw your own conclusions.

I should mention that years ago a type of interview—called a "stress" interview—was somewhat fashionable in professional recruitment. For example, after a luncheon interview, an interviewer might deliberately put on the coat of the applicant and insist that it was his to see how the person would react. There were also stories of interviewers who chopped three inches from the legs of the chairs applicants would use during interviews to create an intimidating situation. This type of interview has been out of vogue for some time now, and it's unlikely that you will encounter such a situation.

A skillful interviewer will attempt to put you at ease, primarily to set the stage for you to reveal a lot about yourself, since the more you do, the more informed will be his or her decision. I will never forget a segment of a film on interviewing skills used by General Electric's Management Development Institute, where I served as a member of the adjunct faculty. The moderator advises managers that one way to put an applicant at ease and get him to be more open is to minimize any liabilities he might bring up, so that, for example, if a male applicant with several years' experience in business admits to having done poorly in high school, the interviewer could say, "Well, at that age, boys are more interested in girls and baseball than in school." On the other hand, the moderator cautions, if the applicant mentions that he served four years in Alcatraz for armed robbery, the interviewer should not say something like, "Well, sooner or later, we all get into trouble."

3. Prepare Responses to Questions You Are Likely to Be Asked

With the above as a backdrop, let's now consider some questions commonly asked by interviewers to arrive at well-informed hiring decisions—as well as my advice on how to formulate responses tailored to your particular situation:

WHAT ARE YOUR STRENGTHS AND WEAKNESSES?: How you answer this question will depend largely on what you will have learned thus far in the interview. Since your résumé already highlights your strengths as related to the job for which you are interviewing, referring to these (without looking at your résumé) and giving appropriate examples that support their validity would be a good way to proceed. But suppose that during the interview and after your résumé has already been reviewed, you learn that the employer considers you to have a particular weakness—in such a case it's important that you respond to this and any other question in a way that counteracts this impression. For example, you may be told during the interview that another sales candidate being interviewed is considered somewhat stronger than you in that she is already familiar with the territory that will be assigned to the individual hired, since she's managing it in her current job. If so, a good way to respond to this question, therefore, would be to talk about your being a "quick study," i.e., someone who can quickly master a new assignment, drawing from your experience to describe a situation where you did just that.

By the way, this "quick study" type of response is an excellent approach for any career changer to use, since the job in question will always be a new experience and the employer will be rightfully concerned about how much on-the-job training will be required before the individual can work with minimal supervision.

The "weaknesses" part of the question poses a thorny problem, for how do you answer the question without coming across either as lacking some important qualification or, if you say you have no weaknesses, as an egomaniac? One approach suggested in current career literature is to describe a weakness that could be interpreted as a strength. For example, saying that you have little patience when it comes to your subordinates' carelessness in preparing reports, while presented as a weakness, might be viewed as a strength in an organization where precision and accuracy in written communications are valued. Because this approach is so transparent—not to mention so widely used that it may be recognized as a ploy—I am not in favor of your using it.

There is a way to deal with this question effectively and, in addition, use it to your advantage. Refer back to your employer's scoring points (ESP) (page 102) for all those qualifications sought by the employer in the candidate for the job you want. Then think of one or two weaknesses you have that do not directly contradict the items on this list. Let's assume, for example, that you are now interviewing for a job in which knowledge of French is not an ESP item. But suppose you had a past job where you were required to interact with a French subsidiary and you could not speak French. Mentioning this liability will, of course, not be detrimental to your candidacy.

Furthermore, if you are able to respond to the weakness question with a shortcoming which you have taken action to correct, it will reflect favorably on you that you both acknowledged having the shortcoming and took action to eliminate it. Thus, in the "French" example, subsequent to discovering your shortcoming, having taken a series of French lessons was the proper course of action and should, therefore, be communicated to the interviewer.

I should tell you that the strengths-and-weaknesses question has been so widely used that many interviewers are keenly aware that candidates expect it. I've spoken to a number of personnel executives who have told me that they avoid using the question for this very reason. I know one who will instead ask applicants to describe a work situation that frustrates them, since that will get at the same information.

WHAT MAJOR PROBLEM HAVE YOU ENCOUNTERED AND HOW HAVE YOU DEALT WITH IT?: As with the strengths-and-weaknesses question, listen during the interview for any concerns stated or implied by the interviewer, and fashion your responses accordingly. Thus, in describing a major problem encountered in the past, use one that will demonstrate to the interviewer that his or her concern is not justified. If the question specifically asks about a problem related to your work, limit your response to that environment. Otherwise, you could mention a problem outside the work environment, e.g., from your experiences in community or professional organizations where you held a key office.

To prepare for responding to the "problem" question, jot down several problem situations in advance of the interview, thinking about which of your strengths they exemplify and, more important, which of your weaknesses they offset. When you hear the interviewer mention any concerns, scan this list in your mind and verbalize the one or ones that would best alleviate this concern.

WHAT SALARY ARE YOU SEEKING?: Generally speaking, it is to the applicant's advantage to have the subject of salary brought up as late in the interview process as possible—ideally, at the time of the job offer. (See pages 180 and 196 for exception situations.) But some people are eager to state their salary requirements at this point so they can determine as early as possible whether they and the employer are in the same ball park. If this applies to you, yet you want to leave open the possibility of negotiating a better salary later, give a salary range instead of an absolute figure. After stating your preferred range, add that you would like to know more about the position's requirements before giving a specific figure.

If you are not eager to answer this question—and if it is posed fairly early in the interview process—one approach is to say something like this:

> I would like to deal with the salary question after I have learned more about the opportunity, since the compensation should reflect the position's scope and responsibilities.

If you are asked the salary question late in the interview process—and are reluctant to respond—a good way to answer would be to say:

> I am sure that my salary requirement would be consistent with the company's policy.

In either case, if you are pressed for an answer, you could give a salary range which your research will have determined is consistent with salaries paid to people with your demonstrable qualifications.

TELL ME ABOUT YOUR WORK EXPERIENCES, BEGINNING WITH YOUR FIRST PROFESSIONAL JOB: While the résumé provides a snapshot of your employment experience, being asked this question gives you a wonderful opportunity to expand on those points that will be most impressive to the interviewer. While responding to the question, you should not look at your résumé. Jerry Buegler, Staffing Manager of 3M Corporation, once asked this question of an applicant, only to have the man read his résumé. In addition to showing a lack of originality and creativity, referring to the résumé implied that the man would similarly depend on crutches in performing his job's responsibilities. Since professional positions require creativity and independence, this man was sending the message that he was a poor candidate for the position. Furthermore, referring to his résumé to answer this question may mean that the man was lying about some aspect of his background and had to depend on his written story.

If you inherited a negative situation in any of your work experiences—for example, sales were down, data-processing production work was heavily back-logged, orders weren't getting shipped on time—that you addressed successfully, a good way to describe your responsibilities is in the form of a "before" and "after" situation, i.e., this is what the situation was when I came into the job; these are the actions I took to correct the situation; these are the results. If this kind of description is not appropriate because things were in pretty good shape before you took over the job, then describe your responsibilities and accomplishments in considerably more detail than your résumé does. One reason many interviewers ask this question is to see how well candidates express themselves. Since it is a well-known fact that many people hire professional résumé writers, interviewers want to determine for themselves the communications skills of the applicant. And even if the interviewer doesn't doubt that the candidate wrote the résumé, he or she will want to assess the oral communications capability of the individual, since some people are very good at writing, but weak in oral presentation.

WHY ARE YOU LEAVING YOUR JOB?: This question is virtually inevitable. If you have been fired, refer to Chapter 10, page 259, for guidance on dealing with this issue. Regardless of the reason you are leaving, never make disparaging comments about your employer. If you are leaving voluntarily, it's always better to explain your decision in terms of the positive attraction of an opportunity outside your present organization, rather than the negative aspects of your present situation.

WHY SHOULD I HIRE YOU?: In a role-playing session I once conducted with a client, I posed this question and she responded with "Because I'm the best person for the job." By now you know that I am all for people coming across as assertive, but I found this response to be cocky, not assertive. Its greatest weakness is that—assuming that the person had not been told that she was the only candidate—it reflects her jumping to a conclusion without having sufficient data, for how could she know whether she was the best candidate for the job unless she was privy to the other candidates' qualifications?

A better way to respond to the question is to itemize the requirements of the position as presented in the job description or outlined by the interviewer, pointing to information that supports your satisfying each of them, and summarize with: "Because I fully satisfy the position's requirements, I believe I am a strong candidate." If this sounds a little like a lawyer's summation to a jury, it shouldn't be surprising. After all, you must make your "case" by pointing to all the evidence in support of the "jury verdict" you want: the job offer.

Open-ended questions (such as the ones with which we've dealt thus far), as opposed to those that can be answered with a "yes" or "no" or other brief answer, are the kind likely to be posed by deft interviewers. "Tell me about your current responsibilities" or "Which job listed on your résumé did you like least, and why?" certainly will reveal more to the interviewer than "Did you complete the design of the order entry system on schedule?" or "Have you consistently met the budgetary guidelines your department manager set for you in your current job?"

Bill Byrnes, President of TeleSearch, Inc., a nationwide recruiting firm owned by Fidelity Investments, asks candidates to describe different people who demonstrate skills they would like to have. Says Bill, "I use this question because it allows people to comfortably project their shortcomings, which helps me determine if the candidate is a good match for the job. For example, in the case of a sales position, if the candidate responds by describing someone who is an excellent public speaker, I might be concerned about his qualifications for the job, since a sales position requires the ability to communicate with customers, both in informal sessions and in structured sales presentations." Other open-ended questions Bill will ask are: "What would I find out about you in six months that I wouldn't know from today's interview?" and "What expectations about your present job did you have and how did the reality differ from those?"

Applicants often fail to provide the interviewer with a complete response to each question, due to their not listening carefully. Beware of this pitfall and, as you are asked a question, note how many responses are sought. Examples of questions that ask for more than one response:

> What were the least enjoyable tasks associated with your last job and why?
>
> Why did you choose the training and development field and what are your three most rewarding accomplishments to date?

A well-known survey of employers determined the fifty most common questions asked during their interviews with college seniors. Here are some questions from this survey that candidates for higher than entry-level jobs are likely to be asked.

1. What are your long-range and short-range goals and objectives, when and why did you establish these goals, and how are you preparing yourself to achieve them?
2. What specific goals, other than those related to your occupation, have you established for yourself for the next ten years?
3. Which is more important to you, the money or the type of job?
4. How do you determine or evaluate success?
5. In what ways do you think you can make a contribution to our company?
6. In what kind of a work environment are you most comfortable?
7. Why did you decide to seek a position with this company?
8. What criteria are you using to evaluate the company for which you hope to work?

9. What have you learned from your mistakes?
10. How would you describe yourself?*

Here are a number of other questions commonly asked in professional interviews:

1. How did you happen to get into this line of work?
2. What has been your biggest disappointment?
3. Who has had the greatest influence on you and why?
4. Describe a situation in which your work was criticized.
5. What kind of supervisor gets the best performance from you?
6. What decisions are the most difficult for you to make?
7. What did you like least/best about your last job?
8. What books have you read recently?
9. Why do you want to work in this industry?
10. What are the disadvantages of your chosen field?
11. Why do you prefer a small/large company?

Dealing with Shortcomings and Liabilities

Since the interviewer must try to formulate an opinion as to your value to the organization, he or she will undoubtedly explore any weaknesses or negatives in your background. Let's consider some common shortcomings in applicants' backgrounds, as well as how to address them with minimal negative impact.

NOT OBTAINING A BACHELOR'S DEGREE: While it has become more common for people to go to college today than, say, 20 years ago, there are many successful people who have not. If you are one of them, you have probably found that your performance on the job is in no way inferior to that of a college graduate. Still, many employers prefer to hire college graduates. This is most common among *Fortune*-listed companies, since they are deluged with applications from individuals with advanced as well as undergraduate degrees.

There are a number of possible reasons for dropping out of college, including lack of money, a change in career objective, illness, a business opportunity, boredom with school, and poor grades. Some of these reasons, or variations on them, will apply to individuals who never begin college or who don't pursue their studies beyond an associate's degree. Furthermore, several reasons may apply in the case of one individual. Just which one or ones that pertain to your situation would be the most appropriate to mention if the subject is raised will depend somewhat on the organization. For example,

---

*Victor R. Lindquist, *The Northwestern Lindquist-Endicott Report.* © 1988 Northwestern University, Evanston, IL. Reprinted by permission.

certain companies place a high premium on ambition; this would suggest that if you didn't find college challenging enough and left to pursue an opportunity, that would be a satisfactory explanation. In many instances the primary reason for not finishing college is lack of—or an urgent need for—money, either of which would require your being employed on a full-time basis. Regardless of the reasons that apply in your situation, if you have already achieved more than most people of your age, you could easily justify why you didn't finish college by pointing to your accomplishments.

BEING A JOB HOPPER: Before addressing this issue, let's define "job hopper." Having five or more positions, each lasting two years or less, would tend to classify someone as a job hopper—especially if there isn't one long-term (six or more years) position in his or her work history. The assumption on the part of most people is that everyone is entitled to one, and possibly two, short-term employments. Three or four will raise eyebrows and prompt a question about the duration of the positions. Five or more is a closed case, i.e., the person is definitely thought of as a job hopper. Sometimes people have a run of bad luck through no fault of their own. I have seen situations where people worked in a series of companies that were poorly financed, resulting in their being laid off consistently—which underscores the importance of doing research on the company before you accept an offer.

If the company's poor financial health resulted in your losing your job, say so. If, on the other hand, you lost a couple of jobs because of friction with your supervisor or poor performance, you've got a problem. If you know that your employer will give you a good reference despite the cause of your leaving, you might talk about the work not being challenging enough. However, if you believe your former employer will state the real reason, you have no choice but to tell the truth and defend yourself as best you can. In doing so, try not to make the employer appear the bad guy. Instead, talk in terms of differences between your work style and his or hers. You should know, however, that nowadays companies are extremely careful about divulging information to employers or investigators.

LACK OF SUBSTANTIAL ACCOMPLISHMENTS: Some types of jobs seem not to present the opportunity for accomplishments as tangible as, for example, sales and marketing do. Yet these positions—which are continuous functions, as opposed to being project-oriented—do, in fact, offer the opportunity for achievements in the areas of productivity improvements, cost-saving measures, incorporating new technology, and training others. For example, accountants perform routine tasks that are very important to the functioning of an organization, yet their accomplishments are rarely measurable or innovative. If your current job is such a continuous function, it may be a little harder for you to think of accomplishments—since you may feel that you were just doing your job—but a rereading of pages 114–116 where I present a list of accomplishments representative of many functional areas may help you do so.

If you really do not have any accomplishments, and if any of the positions in question were of relatively short duration (up to nine months), then a possible explanation could be that they weren't long enough to allow you time to accomplish your goals. You might also talk about having to spend a lot of time initially in restructuring the poorly performing organization you inherited and positioning it for improved productivity.

If you have had positions of more than nine months' duration where you cannot point to bona fide accomplishments, but there are other assignments of comparable duration where you have had accomplishments, it might have been because the entire organization was managed in a way that did not foster achievements—which may have been the reason you decided to leave that company.

4. Conduct Role-Playing Interview Rehearsals

The only difference between a theatrical audition and a job interview is that in the former case you can usually see how your competition does. Some people resent this analogy because they don't like to think of a job interview as playing a role, but the fact is that every day of our lives we play various roles; the interview process is just one example.

With this in mind, it's important that you rehearse for your interview just as an actor would for a part. "Rehearsing" in the interview process is called by another name: role playing. What it means is that you play the part of the job applicant and you get a friend to play the part of the interviewer. His or her job is to ask you questions that will put you on the spot, thereby making you think about how you can respond more skillfully to them at the real interview. Your "interviewer" should scrutinize your résumé and try to find liabilities and weaknesses in your background, asking questions accordingly. While you may feel you've reached the stage in life where you can forgo such exercises, remember that candidates applying for the position of President of the United States have mock debates with their aides in order to prepare for nationwide TV debates (job interviews) before election day.

Be Sensitive to Nonverbal Cues

The interviewer's words are, of course, only part of the story, since posture, body movements, and facial expressions can communicate impressions as powerfully as can words. Job candidates can benefit from the analysis of nonverbal signals in the book *Body Language*, by Julius Fast. Mr. Fast cites a study showing that if a person looks away from us while speaking, it means that he does not want to be interrupted. One nonverbal cue indicating that it is okay to interrupt, according to the study, is the speaker's locking his gaze with yours. Here are several other points Mr. Fast makes that I suggest you consider during your interview:

If you look away from the person who is speaking to you while you are listening, it is a signal, "I am not completely satisfied with what you are saying. I have some qualifications."

If you look away while you are speaking it may mean, "I am not certain of what I am saying."

If, while you are listening, you look at the speaker, you signal, "I agree with you," or "I am interested in what you are saying."

If, while you are speaking, you look at the listener, you may be signaling, "I am certain of what I am saying."*

Mr. Fast says further that looking away while someone is speaking to you may imply that you are concealing something.

You might wonder whether there is anything you can do to counteract what you perceive as some negative body language on the part of the interviewer. Let me give you an example: Suppose you, as a marketing manager, had just described how, under your management, your company increased its share of the market for a particular product line by 16 percentage points. If you then see a reaction that would indicate that the interviewer doubted that statement, you could add that you know that increase to be correct, since a syndicated research company conducted a study that analyzed the market share of your company versus the other leading participants in the industry.

5. Prepare Your Questions in Advance

If there is one inevitability characterizing the job interview, it is that at a certain point you will be asked, "Do you have any questions?" Many applicants do not prepare for this by thinking of questions before the interview and writing them down so they can refer to them at the right moment. This serves two purposes:

- It reduces the risk of your leaving the interview and forgetting to ask a crucial question, the answer to which may influence your decision to accept.
- It enables you to communicate an important message to the interviewer: that you planned ahead for this important meeting by thoughtfully preparing pertinent questions. The interviewer will infer from your action

*From BODY LANGUAGE by Julius Fast. Copyright © 1970 by Julius Fast. Reprinted by permission of the publisher, M. Evans and Co., Inc., 216 East 49th Street, New York, NY 10017.

what your work style is; namely, that you are well organized and possess good planning abilities.

Therefore, before your interview, write down four to seven questions to ask at the point where you are given the opportunity to do so. Here are some suggested ones:

MAY I SEE AN ORGANIZATION CHART OF THE COMPANY (DIVISION, DEPARTMENT, ETC.)?: By examining an organization chart you may see a box for the job for which you are interviewing, as well as for lateral and higher-level positions. This should give you some insight into how stiff the competition will be for advancement. You should also be able to develop a sense of the types of functional areas with which you will be working, enabling you to ask further questions that will demonstrate both your interest in and understanding of these other areas.

MAY I SEE A JOB DESCRIPTION?: Although sometimes the reality of a job bears little resemblance to the job description, reading this document is still the best way for you to find out exactly what will be expected of you. If you are shown a job description, ask if you can keep a copy to study. In case you are told that no written description exists, ask the interviewer to list the job's responsibilities orally while you write them down. If what you hear verbalized by the interviewer—or read in the description, for that matter— sounds hazy or ambiguous, say so. If the job requirements are not clarified at that point, you should be suspicious that the description is vague in the interviewer's mind. Hazy job descriptions sometimes reflect poorly defined jobs and/or jobs that require people to be "gofers" (also known as errand runners). Being a gofer in an organization is known to lead nowhere except to the Land of Regret and Disappointment. One possible exception to this would be a position as administrative assistant, where the job description specifies responsibility for running errands and gathering information from various people in the organization.

HOW WOULD MY PERFORMANCE BE MEASURED?: Assuming that you are given a job description, whether written or oral, implicit in its itemized responsibilities is the requirement that you carry them out in a satisfactory manner. But the term "satisfactory" is rather nebulous, and what one person views as satisfactory may be another's less-than-satisfactory.

Thus, the importance of asking how your performance would be measured . . . which should prompt the interviewer to provide you with information about the performance-appraisal process, giving you a better idea of what is expected of you and within what period of time. For example, a sales representative's job description would probably state that the individual would be assigned a territory and be responsible for satisfactorily meeting sales quotas. By inquiring about how your performance would be measured, you may be told that after two weeks of training you would be assigned a territory and expected to meet your quota within two quarters (six months); if you had not met it, you'd be put on probation for one quarter, after which, if you still hadn't, you would be fired.

Your asking this question about a market research position may prompt the interviewer to tell you that to be considered performing satisfactorily, the market research studies under your responsibility would have to be completed within budget. This may, in turn, prompt you to inquire about the track record attained by other individuals in this position. If you are told that it has not been that good, explore what obstacles might exist in the organization that would make it difficult for you to achieve this goal, resulting in your performance being rated less than satisfactory.

A second, and very important, reason for posing this question is to prompt the interviewer to show you the form that will be used to appraise your performance. If you are lucky enough to see that document, you'll be able to use it as a guide in carrying out your responsibilities. Since employees usually don't see the performance appraisal form until they receive their first appraisal, you will have a distinct advantage, since you will know exactly what criteria are being used to evaluate your performance.

WHAT CREATED THE JOB OPENING?: This is an important question because you may be interviewing for a job that is being newly created. If the position was created because of the department's growth, that would be a good sign. On the other hand, the job may have been created as part of a new department the company is trying out. Upon finding this out, your antennae should go up, since a company sometimes decides to try out a new functional area, only to find out six months later that it didn't work. The BIG QUESTION for you as the holder of this ephemeral position is: whither go you when the experiment is over?

On the other hand, you may get an answer that the previous job holder left the company. If so, determine whether that person was fired and, if so, what the reasons were. They should sound acceptable to you. If they do not, it's possible that the person was fired for irrational (otherwise known as political) reasons. Perhaps the same flimsy reason will be used to justify firing you.

In response to this question you may be told that the previous job holder was promoted—in fact, the hiring manager may be replacing herself or himself. If so, this would signal that the company has a practice of promoting from within, indicating that any promises about future opportunities might not be idle.

HOW DO THE COMPANY'S PRODUCTS/SERVICES COMPARE TO THOSE OF ITS CHIEF COMPETITORS?: The interviewer will probably respond by describing the company's strengths and weaknesses relative to its competition, and may discuss plans the company has to address its shortcomings. The response to this question, coupled with your independent research into the company's offerings, should help you assess the company's position in its industry . . . which would have implications for its ability to offer a secure work environment over the long term.

SALARY QUESTION?—THE GREAT DEBATE: Whether an applicant should ask about salary early in the interview process is controversial. It's my opinion that in most cases it is in the applicant's best interest to have salary brought up as late in the hiring process as possible—ideally, at the time of the job offer.

By the time the interview is held, you may not have to ask about salary, since you may have seen the range specified in an ad, or have been told it by your agency or recruiter contact. If not, you may fall into one of two categories of applicants for whom asking about salary early in the hiring process is very important. If, for example, you're interviewing for a sales position, it's advisable for you to ask about compensation, since employers assume that money motivates salespeople to perform at their best. Not asking the question could knock you out of the competition early.

Or, if the time you spend in interviewing is an overriding consideration, it may be very important for you to know as early as possible whether the employer's and your salary objectives are in the same ball park. In either of these cases, you could say something like the following in the telephone conversation during which the interview arrangements are made:

> My total compensation in my present job is $48,000 and, of course,
> to make a change I would want a reasonable increase. If I'm the
> winning candidate, can I expect the kind of compensation I seek?

Some experts believe that interviewers resent applicants inquiring about salary, and, in fact, that may be true in some cases, for example, where the hiring of an employee represents a favor to someone. If you are unsure as to whether to pose the question, you could bring up the subject when making the interview arrangements by saying something like:

> Because I know how busy you are, I thought I'd ask whether you'd
> like to discuss the salary now, since it may save you some time if
> we knew now whether we weren't thinking within the same range.

This will help give the impression that the reason you're bringing up the salary issue is out of consideration for the interviewer. If you haven't learned the salary by the time of the interview, you can certainly ask about it, but make it the last question on your list.

One problem associated with being given an absolute salary figure early in the screening process is that it would prevent you from negotiating a higher salary later. It would be wrong to allow the employer to continue to expend resources in screening you for the job and then, when an offer is made, express dissatisfaction with the figure you have known all along. Being given either a salary range or no salary information leaves the door open best for future negotiation. If you are given an absolute figure and you wish to reserve the right to negotiate a higher salary later, respond with something like "I would like to think about the money aspect of the job later after I've learned more about its scope and responsibilities." Realize, too, that making this comment could eliminate you from consideration if the employer has other candidates with comparable qualifications who don't make statements implying that the salary may be negotiated. In deciding whether to avoid showing acceptance of any absolute salary mentioned, you must gauge how strong a candidate you are for the job and the degree of flexibility on the part of the employer. For advice on how to negotiate higher compensation than offered, see page 195 in Chapter 7.

To sum up, it is generally better to have salary brought up as late as possible in the hiring process, but you may decide that your situation falls into the exception categories I've described.

While we're on the subject of salary, I would like to suggest that you not bring up the subject of benefits in an initial interview. While benefits represent a form of compensation because they can be translated into dollars, some people might think it petty for a professional applicant to inquire about them so early in the hiring process. And if you do bring the subject up at a later interview, do so during a part of the interview that is not a spotlighted segment, namely, when the atmosphere is more easygoing—for example, while you're en route to lunch, or at the tail end of the interview as you're getting up to leave. Another approach is to raise the subject of benefits when the company is being discussed, so that it will be presented as an aspect of the company's way of doing business, as opposed to being a response to a question about your needs.

Why Asking Questions Is Important

You may feel that it's a bit aggressive of you to pose these questions, so I would like to assure you that in my talks with personnel executives of leading corporations, these people consistently expressed the view that candidates should have questions to ask. These questions can very well be probing questions, say personnel executives, since the candidate would be taking a big step in accepting an offer and deserves to make an informed choice.

Bear in mind that an interview is a meeting at which both parties will be deciding whether they want to work together. You have every right, as well as an obligation to yourself, to ask questions. The fact that the employment situation is tight may mean that it's a buyer's market, but employers hiring professionals want them to be confident and assertive, since this quality will be important in their effectiveness on the job.

A Postscript

Medium- and large-size organizations generally have formal structures for interviews that provide the opportunity for you to gather information in the manner I've described in the preceding pages. But there are many smaller organizations where you might be interviewed by the principal of a firm who developed it from nothing and who is unknowledgeable about management theory and professional recruitment approaches. I know of cases where five-minute interviews were conducted during which the applicant was not encouraged to ask questions, and learned nothing about the organization, but was offered the job and accepted it on a hunch. Sometimes these jobs turned out to be challenging stepping-stones to extremely high-paying positions. Whether or not you should accept an offer following such an interview is a choice only you can make. There certainly is a risk associated with it, and the decision has to be weighed very carefully.

6. Know Your Rights Regarding a Lawful Interview

Title VII, the law to which I referred in the résumé section, prohibits most employers* from discriminating in hiring practices on the basis of race, sex, color, religion, or national origin. Some states have gone a step further by including marital status as a discriminatory category.

As for how to deal with being asked a discriminatory question, I suggest that you respond by asking, "Is that information relevant to the position's requirements?" Responding in this manner may eliminate you from the competition, but that would be no loss—the fact that an interviewer would ask a discriminatory question in this day and age of widespread awareness about the law governing equal employment reflects one of two possibilities:

- the organization is not aware of the law, in which case I question how they can conduct their business successfully—the law has been publicized hundreds of times in the media; or
- the organization is aware of the law but has chosen not to implement changes in hiring practices to conform to its requirements.

Regardless of which of these applies, if this is the kind of treatment the candidate gets during the hiring process, it would not be any better once the

---

*To learn which kinds of organizations are covered by this law, and for detailed information on the law, see Chapter 10, page 254.

candidate becomes an employee—it would probably be worse. For this reason I recommend that you remove from consideration any company that shows evidence of discriminatory policies during the hiring process.

Furthermore, if you believe you have been discriminated against, you may want to file a discrimination complaint with the Equal Employment Opportunity Commission. See page 255 for information on the process of filing a complaint and the legal remedies available.

7. Prepare Logistically for the Interview

Many factors contribute to the outcome of an interview process. One that may affect the decision is the timing of your interview relative to the other candidates'. It is usually a strategic advantage to be interviewed toward the end of the sequence. One reason for this is that, as candidates are reviewed, the interviewer may modify his or her notion of just what kind of person is being sought. Another is that the interviewer may subconsciously believe that later candidates are more qualified.

For example, given ten candidates, the interviewer knows, as he or she is interviewing the first five, that five more will be screened, and may subconsciously allow himself to be more critical of the earlier ones—since there are a good number left, and the assumption is that one of them will probably be better qualified than the first five. As the sequence of interviews progresses beyond the first five—and since the interviewer will already have evaluated the earlier candidates as less than fully qualified—he or she may be more lenient in evaluating the later candidates, rather than be forced to reverse the earlier judgments.

So while you may be very eager to have an early interview, try to arrange one toward the end of the process. If you have no idea how long that will be, a safe approach would be to try to schedule the appointment a week after the date sought by the organization.

Well in advance of the interview, carefully check your directions or review the location of the office on a map. Leave yourself enough time to arrive at the interview 20–30 minutes ahead of the appointed time to take into account the possibility of getting lost or stuck in traffic. Bring with you to the interview

- an appointment book for scheduling a future interview if this one goes well;
- a pad of paper on which you can take notes (I will go into more detail on this later);
- your list of questions to pose to the interviewer;
- as many copies of your résumé as the number of people who will interview you (if you do not know that number, bring five copies);
- copies of your references and any recommendation letters, even if you sent these with your initial mailing to the company; and

- examples or copies of material supporting your candidacy for the position, e.g., portfolio of advertisements for which you wrote the copy; promotional brochures you designed and/or wrote; documentation of any manual/computerized system in whose design and/or implementation you played a major role; documentation of any patents you authored; newspaper/magazine articles praising some aspect of your company's performance for which you were responsible; glowing performance appraisals; documentation of awards for outstanding performance; letters from customers that suggest that you are Superman or Superwoman. These should be produced only if the discussion turns to any of these aspects of your qualifications.

Since the interview will be the first time you will be face-to-face with the prospective employer's representatives, make sure that you look the part of the job. Aspects of your appearance that will surely influence the impression you make include the appropriateness of your clothing for the job, the degree to which you appear to be physically fit and energetic, and your personal grooming and overall cleanliness. Refer to Chapter 10, page 251, for more detailed suggestions on your appearance and guidance on getting assistance to improve it.

With the preparation as prologue, let's now turn to a discussion of the interview process.

SETTING THE STAGE IN THE FIRST FIVE MINUTES

You would probably be shocked if you traveled an hour or more to get to an interview, only to have it last for just five minutes, wouldn't you? And yet, one study has indicated that the impression the interviewer had most often of the applicant after a lengthy interview was the same as the impression at the end of the first five minutes. While most job interviews are a half hour to an hour in duration, the results of the study underscore the importance of making an outstanding impression in the first five minutes.

If you have had some free time before the interview and gone shopping, do not bring your packages to the interview. Since the employer considers the interview an important meeting, you should similarly convey the impression that the interview is the focal point of your day; bringing packages to the meeting implies that it is not. Also, try to hang up your coat before greeting the interviewer so that you will be unencumbered when greeting him or her.

I have observed that some people tend to treat executives with greater consideration than they treat secretaries. This is extremely inappropriate behavior, since a person's worth isn't established by the office he or she holds. Furthermore, the secretary for the executive conducting the interview may tell him or her about a negative aspect of the candidate, thereby influencing the hiring decision. Assume that the interview has begun as soon as you are greeted by the first person in the company.

A firm handshake and smile will certainly contribute to your engaging the interviewer in the first five minutes. In order to accomplish the handshake gracefully, always carry your briefcase in your left hand, leaving your right hand free for the greeting.

If you are asked to fill out an application form, be sure to write your answers legibly. If there is not enough space for a response, continue it on a blank sheet of paper. Number each extended answer on the blank sheet to correspond to the question to which it relates on the form. Provide a pointer to the extended answer, e.g., "See item number four on attached sheet."

If the interviewer has been trained properly, he or she will probably begin the interview with some small talk, asking you a question similar to these:

Did you have difficulty finding the office (or parking)?
How was the plane trip?
Would you like some coffee/tea?

Regardless of whether your interviewer does "warm up" the interview with these pleasantries, you can certainly contribute to a convivial beginning. After you shake hands you might mention something similar to one of the following:

I was admiring the landscaping around the building; is it permanent or does it change with the seasons?

The artwork in the reception area is very interesting; was it done by a local artist?

Your directions were perfect; I didn't make one wrong turn, although the route from the airport was fairly complicated.

Obviously, you must use something that will be relevant to the situation. One of the best interviews I ever had was the day after a bad snowstorm. I had a ninety-minute drive from an airport on very icy roads in bitterly cold weather. When I met the man who would interview me, I said, "Well, do I get a handicap for the bad weather?" He laughed and I knew that my comment helped set the stage for a successful interview . . . which it must have been, since I got a job offer from the organization. A humorous ice-breaker is fine to use in some situations. The key point is that you must be sensitive to the interviewer's degree of formality and the particular situation.

CONDUCT YOURSELF AS YOU WOULD IN ANY IMPORTANT BUSINESS MEETING

Since an interview is an important meeting and since it's customary for people to take notes in such activities, bring a pad of paper with you, but before taking it out of your briefcase ask the interviewer if it would be okay if you took some notes. It is assumed that the interviewer will say yes to this request, but your asking will create an impression of a courteous person. During the interview, jot down important points without taking copious notes; balance the note-taking with sufficient eye contact and attentiveness. We earlier discussed the limitations of many interviews in providing in-depth insights into the applicant's potential to perform on the job. By taking notes you will be sending the message that you don't rely solely on your memory and you consider the information discussed in the interview to be important enough to reflect upon after the meeting is over. This will help project an image of carefulness and attention to detail—qualities important in *any* job.

Have your questions listed somewhere on the pad of paper so that you can refer to them at the appropriate time. They can be handwritten or typed, but leave spaces between them so that you can note the interviewer's responses under each.

IF YOU ARE INVITED TO LUNCH

Applicants are sometimes invited to lunch, where the interview is continued. If you are, it's better if you do not order an alcoholic beverage, since it will affect your alertness at a time when you sorely need it. Also, you may already know that there is a trend toward drinking nonalcoholic beverages, due to the awareness of the dangers of drinking while driving, and an increased emphasis on physical fitness. A good compromise to adopt if you feel you must order a drink is to ask for a mild one or take just one sip of the drink.

Also, avoid ordering sloppy or hard-to-handle foods. My own list of foods to avoid includes onion soup (which may have rubbery cheese in it); fish, since it may not have been boned sufficiently (you wouldn't want the highlight of the day to be your having the Heimlich Maneuver performed on you for the first time, would you?); a sandwich with filling that's likely to fall out as you're eating it; steak or other meat that could be so tough that you'll never be able to stop chewing long enough to answer any questions.

As far as I'm concerned the food that is guaranteed to be safest is any kind of omelet. But, by the way, even if after all your precautions something does happen at lunch that is embarrassing, don't be concerned about it. Lorna Joselson, Employee Relations Manager of Champion International Corporation's Retail Packaging Division, tells the story of a man who had accidentally gotten salad dressing all over his tie and still got the job, because he was the best candidate. The fact is that a skillful interviewer will be sensible enough to discount such incidents and focus on the important issue: the candidate's professional qualifications.

THE SMOKING ISSUE

The issue of smoking in the workplace has received a lot of attention in the past few years. Many companies have formulated no-smoking rules and some have even refused to hire people who smoke *off* the premises. It is not my objective here to take a stand on the issue, but rather to provide you with guidance on obtaining the job you want. There are more nonsmokers in this country today than smokers, and applicants who smoke during interviews run a serious risk of undermining their candidacy. And if you are a smoker who refrains from smoking during an interview and if you then get the job and smoke at work, you may hinder your chances for promotion. I know of no law that protects smokers from being fired, so you must assess the risks to your career, and make a decision on the issue.

INTERVIEW TURNOFFS

Through my conversations with personnel executives and my own experiences, I've compiled a list of aspects of candidates' presentations that leave negative impressions:

- being too casual or too friendly;
- trying to take over the interview right from the beginning, i.e., making sure the interviewer knows how wonderful you are;
- being overdressed for the job/being dressed in a sloppy manner;
- not being able to articulate accomplishments;
- putting one's feet up on the interviewer's desk (this really happens!);
- displaying a lack of enthusiasm (through a monotone voice or no smiling);
- swiveling in one's chair;
- lack of eye contact;
- expressing a negative attitude about one's present employer;
- not being prepared sufficiently with knowledge about the company;
- not having any questions to ask the interviewer;
- being late;
- trying to read papers upside down on the interviewer's desk;
- not bringing a copy of your résumé, especially if requested during the telephone arrangements;
- saying that you have only X minutes available for the interview.

ENDING THE INTERVIEW SUCCESSFULLY

How you come across at the end of an interview is just as important as your impression during the beginning and middle, especially since people tend to remember last words and actions in any type of encounter. Try to be sensitive throughout the interview as to when it should end. There are certain statements an interviewer could use to signal that he or she is ready to wrap up the session. For example, if you have just finished asking several questions after the interviewer has presented an overview of the job and questioned you, the interviewer might say, "Are there any other questions you have?" This statement implies that, if there are not, the interview is over, since each of you has "had the floor." At that point, in response to the question, you could initiate the close of the interview by saying, "No, all my questions have been fully answered. I'd like to thank you for taking the time to meet with me today."

At this point the interviewer will probably respond with some comment about having enjoyed meeting you. You may also be told that you will be notified regarding the decision, with or without a date being mentioned. If the interviewer does not offer information about the decision-making time-table, you should inquire by saying "What would be the next step in your selection process?" In either case, if the interviewer says that a decision will be made within some specified period, do not say that you will call him or her at the end of that time if you have not heard, for two reasons:

- you would be implying that the interviewer may not live up to his or her statement to have a decision by that time, which would be tantamount either to calling him or her a liar or insinuating that he or she is incapable of coordinating the organizational resources necessary to generate a decision by that time; and
- the statement can make the interviewer feel pressured.

In either case, the result will be that the interviewer feels uncomfortable. Bear in mind that even if you do not say that you will call, if you haven't heard by the given date, you still can.

I had an interesting experience in applying for my first professional job, at IBM. After a series of interviews, I was told that I would hear within two weeks whether I was being offered the job. When that period ended I called my personnel contact and learned that no decision had been made yet, but that they would definitely let me know by two weeks hence. Well, this went on for two more two-week periods and I called at the end of each, since I was told each time that I would hear by the end of the periods. When I called for the third time I was told that a telegram was being sent to me that day that would formally make me a job offer.

While I have no proof, I have always believed that the postponement of these dates was part of the screening process, that the company was seeking people who would be persistent in following through to obtain their job offers. And it makes sense, doesn't it? After all, if you were the employer, you would want someone who demonstrated motivation and persistence, since these are important qualities in any professional job. If you haven't heard from the employer by the date you were told you would, you should call.

SUMMING UP

If you prepare for your interviews by following the guidelines I've presented, you will greatly enhance your chances of success over those applicants who will decide—as millions do—to "wing" it. Remember, interviewers are eager to find evidence that convinces them that a particular candidate is the right one for the job. Make it easy for them to conclude that you're the one!

7

After the Interview

AN EFFECTIVE POST-INTERVIEW TOOL

The most productive way to spend your time after an interview for a desirable job is to think long and hard about what happened in the meeting, and how you came across to the interviewer. You may conclude that you made a couple of mistakes, either in what you said—or what you did not say but should have. Welcome to the club—it happens to everyone! Some mistakes—especially missed opportunities for bringing up certain points—can, however, be rectified in the thank-you letter that you should send within a few days after the interview.

Sometimes when I have suggested to a client that he or she send a thank-you letter I have been met with a look of surprise (one man even said it was a "sissyish" idea). I like to explain the importance of the thank-you letter by hypothesizing two applicants who are identical in every way—appearance, credentials, responses to interview questions—except that one of the two follows up the interview with a thank-you letter. If you were the employer, which applicant would you hire? The key point is that your objective should always be to create an impression that distinguishes you favorably from your competitors. Because it is a relatively uncommon gesture, a thank-you letter will accomplish this objective. It will also allow you to state formally why you believe you are the best candidate, as well as mention important information supporting your candidacy—information you may have omitted during the interview.

Unlike thanking someone for a social occasion, the business thank-you letter should be typed. If you were interviewed by more than one person in the organization, each should receive thanks. You can accomplish this by addressing one letter to the two or three individuals and sending it to one of the addressees. That person will then forward it to the others. Or, if you prefer, you can send a letter to each individual you wish to thank. Always use the thank-you letter as an opportunity to reinforce your desirability as a candidate. Remember, there may have been a number of candidates interviewed over a period of time by several people—none of whom has a perfect memory—so it's perfectly okay for you to restate the points you made during your interviews with them.

Examples of Thank-You Letters

Two sample thank-you letters are illustrated on pages 192–193. Notice that the first one uses the opportunity to bring up a piece of information that the candidate forgot to mention in the interview; the second addresses more thoroughly a concern voiced by the interviewer.

You will notice that the senders of these letters have used the recipients' last names in the salutation. By all means, use the addressee's first name, if appropriate, i.e., if in your prior contact with him or her first names were used. And remember to sign your letter in accordance with how you addressed the recipient—if you used his or her first name, then sign yours that way, too. If not, sign your full name.

After you have sent your thank-you letter, there is really nothing more you can do until the end of the company's decision-making period as stipulated by the interviewer. If you have not heard from the employer by that time, call, explaining that you're touching base to see if there are any developments in the selection process. Meanwhile, make productive use of the time while you are waiting for a response from a desirable employer by continuing to conduct your job hunt aggressively. This way, you're likely to have some more irons in the fire by the time you may be told that you were not selected. Any disappointment you may feel at not being the finalist may be offset by some positive results from other avenues.

GETTING WORD

Sometimes employers let candidates know the job has been filled by sending them a fairly complimentary letter which states that another candidate's background more closely matched the position's requirements. These letters are written in a general way and do not specify why the recipient was not considered the strongest candidate. Often they state that the applicant's résumé will be kept in an active file for X months, receiving consideration for any opportunities that arise within that period.

People often wonder whether these form letters really mean anything, whether the company will let you know of any opportunities that may arise. Human resource executives with whom I have spoken told me that they do

Donna F. Hagstrom
44A Ashley Road
St. Louis, MO 63129
314/555-8123

August 7, 1988

Mr. Edward A. Sanderson, President
Sanderson Market Research, Inc.
5612 Lionel Drive
St. Louis, MO 63102

Dear Mr. Sanderson:

I would like to thank you for the time you spent with me on Wednesday, explaining the requirements of the position of Senior Project Leader at Sanderson Market Research. I have studied the job description very carefully since our meeting and feel even more strongly that I am the person for the job.

Specifically, as I mentioned to you in our meeting, my demonstrated ability to manage client projects within budget means that I can similarly keep Sanderson's costs under control—I know that you are concerned with that objective. In addition, while it did not occur to me in our meeting, I just recalled that the director of market research at Playtime International, one of your most important clients, is Bob MacKintosh, a client of mine when he was with Allen Toys and I was employed by Omega Surveys—and with whom I had an excellent working relationship.

Lastly, with my background working with personal computers I would be able to assist you in achieving your year-end goal of computerizing your project-management and client-reporting functions.

In summary, I am confident that my performance in the position of Senior Project Leader would be consistent with the high standards I know your company to have. I look forward to the opportunity to demonstrate this.

Sincerely,

Donna F. Hagstrom

Alan P. Tremaine
1892 So. Wallace Boulevard
Baltimore, MD 21206
301/555-6412

October 14, 1988

Ms. Marilyn S. Cummings, National Sales Manager
Richfield Technology, Inc.
1127 Fourth Avenue
New York, NY 11534

Dear Ms. Cummings:

I very much appreciate your taking the time on Monday to outline the requirements of the Eastern Region Manager position.

I was glad you were candid about your concern that I haven't worked in your industry before. However, as I pointed out, in my assignments with Grayson Manufacturing and International Electronics I sold their products to the same market as Richfield targets, i.e., design engineers. I know their technical needs, and am sure that my performance as branch manager would be characterized by accomplishments comparable to those I described in our meeting.

Because of your concern, however, I would like to add to the list of references I provided you the name of Leonard Michaelson, my regional manager during the first six months I was Philadelphia Branch Manager for Grayson Manufacturing. I assumed this position with no prior experience in Grayson's business. I would like you to hear from Len just how long it took me to master that business and generate results. He can be reached at Phillips Brothers Manufacturing, 8825 Maxwell Road, Pittsburgh, PA 15234, 412/555-1186.

I believe that the most significant requirement of the job you described is the need to turn around the poorly performing territories. Since in three of my positions I quickly transformed unprofitable areas into top-producing territories, I know I can deliver the same results for Richfield.

Lastly, since I try to practice what I preach to my sales staff—namely, never closing a sales presentation without asking for the order—when can I start?

Very truly yours,

Alan P. Tremaine

take a serious look at a candidate's qualifications and, if the letter so states, will keep the résumé on file for a particular period. After about six months, most organizations assume that you have found suitable employment, and for this reason, if you have not, you should reregister your interest with the company.

Chemistry—the Deciding Factor

If you are told that the company has made a decision in favor of another candidate, you may want to inquire about the reasons you were not felt to be the strongest. How worthwhile the response is depends on whether or not you are told the truth. If the reason you did not get the offer has to do with a factor unrelated to the job's requirements, you will probably not be told the truth. People will only offer reasons that sound valid, most of which boil down to your being overqualified or underqualified. Yet in many of these cases it's something else—it's probably chemistry. Organizations seek employees whose personalities will mesh with their culture. Since the interviewer will usually reflect the "personality" of the organization, he or she will resonate to candidates who seem to offer the best match. As the interview progresses, you will probably get a sense of whether there is that chemistry between you and the interviewer. If, after an honest evaluation, you believe it is there, that doesn't necessarily mean that you've got the job, but it is a positive sign. If you feel that the chemistry definitely is not there, it is highly unlikely that you will receive an offer.

But since you yourself have experienced the chemistry factor in your encounters with people, try to accept the fact that not everybody is going to love you. Most important, don't take it personally, for if you dwell on the rejections, that will surely have a negative effect on your future encounters. Just move on to the next interview with a positive attitude.

If you do learn that some other candidate is offered the job, it's to your advantage to view the decision as a learning experience. After all, you probably fine-tuned your interviewing skills through the process, made a few contacts at the company that might come in handy someday, and, if you were told the real reason you were not made the offer, you may be able to take action to preclude that factor from applying in a future situation.

In addition, since all organizations experience turnover, there is always the possibility that you will be considered for an opening that materializes in the future. I have always believed that applicants who've gotten as far as the interview process, but did not get the offer, could capitalize on their exposure and revivify the company's interest in the future. This belief has been supported by many personnel executives with whom I've talked, including Lorna Joselson of Champion International, who has said, "If an applicant we interviewed, but did not select, responded to our rejection letter with a note expressing appreciation for the consideration we showed them, as well as expressing a continued interest in opportunities within our company, it would leave us with a positive impression. It could enhance their candidacy for future positions." So, you see, while you might have thought that receiving a rejection letter was equivalent to a closed door, you *can* do something that sets the stage for a "welcome mat" in the future.

If You Get an Offer

Learning that the employer wants to hire you should rightfully please you, since competition in the job market is very stiff today. It is most common for offers for professional employment to be communicated by telephone after the interview process has been completed; however, sometimes it may be presented during a second or third interview. In either case, never accept the offer on the spot. Instead, thank the individual and ask when the organization needs to have an answer, assuring the person that you will respond before that time.

A small digression is called for here: I have heard of several instances where recipients of job offers were told that the company had to have an answer by the end of the day. I find it hard to believe that an organization cannot give a candidate one night to sleep on the decision. However, companies may be prompted to ask for an immediate decision when they fear that the applicant may accept a better offer. If you have another, more attractive, offer pending that you believe there is a high probability of getting, try to stall. That's a better approach than accepting an offer and resigning shortly after you begin your employment because the other offer came through.

Negotiating Your Compensation

Once an oral offer has been made, you can do one of three things: accept it, reject it, or try to modify it to make it more attractive. As discussed earlier (on page 181), though, if you were told initially that the offer was an absolute figure, e.g., $45,000, and you stated or implied acceptance of that figure, you really cannot try to negotiate a more favorable salary. It would be unethical to lead an employer to believe that a salary figure was satisfactory, and—after all the time spent on interviewing by the employer—express dissatisfaction with it.

Very few people try to negotiate a higher salary, stemming probably from an uneasiness they feel in discussing the value of their services, as well as a limited understanding of the process by which salaries are established. This is unfortunate, since a higher salary is often achievable. By the time an offer is extended to you, usually two or three people in the organization have decided that you are the most desirable candidate. Also, job titles usually have salary *ranges*, not specific single figures, and companies try to hire applicants in the bottom third of the range. So employers do have the latitude to raise compensation offers and will often do just that if it will induce you to accept. As to the mechanics of negotiating a higher salary—as I suggested earlier, always ask for some time to think over the initial offer. Before the date by which your answer is required, call the individual who made you the offer and say:

> I've been thinking over the offer you made me. I'm very enthusiastic about the opportunity and the people I've met in the company, but I feel that I am worth more money than the salary offered. Can anything be done to increase it?

Notice that I am not suggesting that you make a higher salary a condition of your accepting the offer. What will probably happen is that the individual will say that he or she will have to get back to you, since this kind of decision usually requires a consultation with others in the company. When you do get a response, it will probably fall into one of three categories:

- The organization does not feel it can increase the salary offer, but hopes you will join it nonetheless, since the employer feels that the opportunity is a good one for you.
- The salary cannot be increased, but instead of the usual one-year period before a first salary review is given, the company will give you a review after six months, at which time if your performance is fully satisfactory you will receive an increase.
- The organization is willing to increase the salary offer by X dollars.

In my experience, this technique has never resulted in an offer being withdrawn. In addition, personnel executives with whom I have spoken have said unanimously that they would not rescind an offer if a candidate they selected tried to negotiate a higher salary. In some instances they said that the initial salary offer is one that reflects a lot of thought on the organization's part, so they weren't optimistic about a higher salary being negotiated, but they did say that the request for a higher salary would be given consideration.

My point is that you have nothing to lose—and you may make a significant gain. And whether or not you are successful in making the offer more attractive, you will benefit from an interesting phenomenon: people will judge you according to the way you show you value yourself. By asking for an improvement in the salary, you will be showing that you place a high value on yourself. This will validate the company's good judgment in making you the offer in the first place, and will often make them even more eager to win you as an employee.

There is another strategy you can use if you are a long-term employee of your present company, and if your tenure at any prior employer would not be viewed as too short. If the sole reason that you are leaving is money, then state this during your initial interview when asked why—but be sure to explain that you love everything else about your job, or the interviewer may think that your only interest is money. This will communicate clearly that the offer would have to be very attractive relative to your current compensation. Hearing this—and realizing that your current employer may make you a counter offer—the prospective employer may be motivated to offer a highly favorable compensation package. This technique is most effective if you are confident that you are a strong candidate for the position.

Get the Offer in Writing

If the offer was an oral one, you must receive a written offer before resigning your current position. In many companies it's standard practice to send the winning candidate a letter confirming the position title, starting date, and beginning salary and requesting the candidate's written acceptance of these terms. If you have negotiated a date for your first performance and/or salary review, that should be included as well.

If you are told that the oral offer should be sufficient, insist politely on a written confirmation. While a contract does not have to be in writing to be binding, having a written offer gives you added protection, enhancing your chances of collecting damages for having given up a satisfactory job if the new employment falls through. I know of a number of instances where an offer was withdrawn or the original salary quoted the candidate was reduced. I would be extremely suspicious of any company that refused to give a written offer, even if "the secretary's all tied up on important projects." If the employer is not willing to take a half hour to set forth in writing the terms of the offer, what kind of consideration will you receive once you are in the organization? After all, people always put their best foot forward initially.

Another advantage of a written offer is that you can use it to negotiate a more favorable counter offer from your present employer or a better, quicker offer from another employer considering your qualifications. You should not, however, undertake a job hunt as a tactic to get a counter offer from your present employer. That would be taking advantage of employers considering hiring you, since they would be spending a great deal of time and money on interviewing you. But if, when you explain your reasons for leaving, your employer is motivated to make your present situation at least as attractive as the outside offer, then you may want to consider seriously the option of staying.

EVALUATING THE FINAL JOB OFFER(S)

Whether you are evaluating one or four offers, the process should be the same—namely, analytical and thorough. While I am not discounting "gut" decisions, a decision based on intuition often is proven to be mistaken. The first step toward making an objective evaluation of your offers is to formulate your personal job criteria. To aid in developing your own criteria, scan this list:

- Job Content
  Do you think you will enjoy the daily tasks of the position? To what extent does the job present challenges?

- Compensation
  Consider the total compensation, i.e., the sum of salary and benefits such as dental plan, medical insurance, tuition reimbursement, stock option plans, company car. If a move from another city is involved, will the employer pay your relocation expenses?

- Soundness of the Company
  What has been its recent financial performance? What are its projected results? Is it in a growing industry? (The last consideration will be meaningful if you perform a job function that is not industry-dependent, e.g., data processing.)

- Quality of the Organization's Products/Services
  How does the quality of the organization's products/services rank relative to that of its competitors'?

- Reputation of the Organization in Its Industry
  While the reputation may sometimes be consistent with the quality of the organization's products/services, this is not always the case, i.e., sometimes a company's reputation was gained from a product or service it launched many years ago, and its current offerings are of lesser quality.

- People
  Do you think you will get along with your supervisor and co-workers?

- Time Requirements
  What is the commutation time? Out-of-town travel time? Overtime? Does the company's business have seasonal peaks?

- Culture
  Is the corporate culture (for example, informal/formal, liberal/conservative, high pressure/low pressure) consistent with your personality and needs?

- Quality of Organizational Management
  Does the organization appear to be well-managed? Is there relatively little turnover at the middle- and upper-management levels? (Low turnover is very often an indication of a well-managed company; on the other hand, there are fewer opportunities for advancement in such an organization.)

- Physical Environment
  Will you have your necessary level of office privacy? Is the working environment safe and secure beyond a minimal level?

- Long-Range Benefits
  What long-range job opportunities exist in the organization? How consistent with your long-range career goals is the position? How transferable to another employer will the skills be that you'll gain? What technical knowledge will you acquire that will enhance your stature and value in your profession? What is the long-term outlook for job security in the organization?

- Geographic Location
  Is it in a part of the country in which you want to work? If this job doesn't prove satisfactory, how difficult will it be for you to conduct a successful job hunt from that location? While the geographic location is usually a consideration before you pursue employment with an organization, the position offered will sometimes entail relocation—either immediately or after a year or so—to a remote location.

You will probably think of some other items that are important to you. Certainly, some criteria will be more important to you than others. For example, your total compensation may carry greater weight than the job's demands on your time; the opportunity for advancement may be more important to you than the amount of travel, etc. To take into account the relative importance of each of these factors, assign a numerical value (weighting factor) to each item, using a scale of one to ten, with ten being the most important and one being the least important.

Now construct a matrix (if you read Chapter 2, you will recall that I suggested a similar technique in evaluating alternative careers), with each row containing a job criterion important to you. Use the columns to list each option: Offer One, Offer Two, Offer Three, etc. If you are considering staying at your present job, it should also be an option. As you evaluate each option, assign a value—again from one to ten—to reflect the degree to which you believe the job meets each criterion. After every box has been assigned a value, multiply this by the weighting factor you assigned to each criterion to arrive at the weighted score. To obtain a weighted total for each option, add all weighted scores pertaining to that option. You will then have an absolute number that quantifies the attractiveness of each option.

Let's consider the case of a California client of mine who was the Los Angeles branch sales manager for a computer company, and who had to decide between two opportunities. The first was with a large and well-managed conservative company that has an excellent reputation; the job entailed managing the California district for the company. If he were successful in this position, he would be in line for a regional manager's job within two years. The office was convenient to his home and luxuriously furnished; he liked the supervisor and staff with whom he would be working.

The other opportunity was a sales management position for a well-financed small company with no reputation to speak of, although an article in a trade publication praised the innovative computer it had just started marketing. As the national sales manager for the company, my client was expected to travel extensively throughout the United States to work with manufacturers' representatives who'd be selling the product. This fellow liked the people in this company, too. The company's office, although convenient to his home, was in the basement of a building in an industrial neighborhood. The immediate compensation, although adequate, was not very attractive, but the appeal of the offer was that it included a fair amount of stock in the company: if the marketing effort were successful, the fellow knew he'd be rich. In addition, as a member of the start-up company's first management team, his future opportunities seemed excellent.

Figure 9 shows how the application of the analytical technique I described can be helpful in evaluating these two options.

ACCEPTING THE OFFER

Once you decide to accept an offer, you will probably communicate your decision by telephone to your contact in the organization. Some companies will ask you to put your decision in writing to them. If this is not a requirement, you'll make a very nice impression if you prepare a letter anyway. It doesn't have to be elaborate; in addition to including your acceptance, say something about how you are looking forward to joining such a fine organization.

HOW NOT TO BURN YOUR BRIDGES

After you have accepted a written offer, you can resign your current position. Traditionally, giving two weeks' notice has been viewed as the very minimum length. If you have worked in the organization for five years or more—or if transferring your responsibilities and knowledge will take longer—try to give three-to-five weeks' notice. Prospective employers are generally sympathetic to this need, since they can then feel secure in the knowledge that you would behave similarly when you end your employment with them. If there is an urgency to begin the new job, try to work out an arrangement with your current employer that you will wrap up any unfinished business over several weekends or evenings after you leave. The main thing to keep in mind is that you should leave your employer on good terms, since you will probably want to use the company as a reference in the future—or, as sometimes happens, resume employment with them if you find out that the new

Criterion	Weighting Factor	OFFER 1: Blue Chip Co.		OFFER 2: Start-up Co.	
		Score	Weighted Score	Score	Weighted Score
Compensation Now	6	7	42	4	24
Compensation in 5 years	10	7	70	10	100
Job Content	10	7	70	10	100
Physical Environment	8	9	72	6	48
Company Reputation	6	9	54	3	18
Quality of Products	8	6	48	7	56
Financial Soundness	7	9	63	7	49
Quality of Management	8	8	64	8	64
Corporate Culture and People	6	7	42	10	60
Not Excessive Time Demands	6	4	24	3	18
Long-Range Benefits	10	6	60	10	100
Geographic Location	4	6	24	6	24
Total Weighted Score:			633		661*

*More attractive option

Figure 9. An example of a comparative analysis of two job offers.

employer's "grass" *looked* greener from afar, but once you got close enough you could see all the "weeds."

TYING LOOSE ENDS—AND PLANNING AHEAD

Another type of bridge not to burn relates to all those people who assisted you in any way during your job hunt. Send a letter to any people in companies where you are under consideration for employment, thanking them for their time and interest in you. Next, there will probably be a number of friends and colleagues who extended themselves on your behalf. They, too, deserve a note thanking them for their assistance and informing them of your promising new opportunity.

While the rationale for these notes is common courtesy, the consequence of your contacting these people will be that, should the need for their assistance arise in the future, you will find them especially receptive because of the considerate way you treated them.

TIME AND COSTS
ASSOCIATED WITH A JOB SEARCH

You may wonder how much time and expense will be involved in your job search, assuming that you already know which field you are targeting. It's difficult for me to give a reliable figure for your particular situation, since I have no way of knowing whether you are looking for a job during a recession, whether you are aiming for a job in a glutted field, whether your salary requirement is very high, or whether you will have to travel some distance to interviews at your own expense. But to give you some food for thought, I would like to tell you about a client of mine who was looking for a job as an advertising manager for a medium-size company. She spent about thirty hours conducting research—through personal contacts, studying mailing lists, and library work. Costs for this component of the job search were approximately $350, incurred through long-distance calls, networking lunches, and the purchase of a mailing list.

An additional thirty hours were spent in developing five drafts for her résumé and letter, and in test-marketing them with colleagues. Using a commercial word-processing service for preparation of the final version of her résumé and for 50 copies cost her $42. She also purchased 100 sheets of letterhead stationery, matching envelopes (for thank-you letters), and 50 large envelopes (for mailing résumés); the total cost of these items was $95.

One hour was spent in making telephone calls to her references to ask for their approval of her using their names and to discuss points she hoped they would emphasize to prospective employers. My client spent a total of eight hours on composing her list of references, a salary history, and initial and follow-up letters to four executives who were unavailable by telephone; it cost her $72 to have these materials prepared by a word-processing service. Using a combination of telephone calls and letters (the latter only when executives were consistently unavailable), my client spent about 28 hours in obtaining and participating in eight local interviews. She also spent about $215 on transportation, parking, and telephone calls associated with nego- tiating, participating in, and following up on her interviews, as well as on eight thank-you letters prepared by a word-processing service, and trips to the word-processing service.

This woman spent a total of $774 and 97 hours on her job search. This represents a fairly typical amount for someone at a middle-management level. If you are seeking a top-management position, your job search will probably require more research and more interviews. For a more junior position you won't need letterhead stationery, and your résumé and letter-preparation time will probably be less, but you may still incur comparable costs in the other areas.

TAKING STOCK

At the beginning of this book I asked you to take a quiz in which you were asked to rate your confidence level in a number of areas. Without looking at your answers, take the quiz again. (See page 2.)

Afterwards, compare your answers now to those you wrote earlier. If I have done my job properly, your scores in all these areas will have risen. If they are not at a very high level yet, though, do not be concerned. Two factors will play a significant role in increasing your confidence level to a nine or ten:

- the information you will gain through your research that will close the gap between what you know about what you are targeting and what there is to know about what you are going after; and
- the degree to which you actually get out there and contact executives in your targeted area of employment, to develop skill and confidence in presenting yourself.

Whether or not you are under a lot of time pressure (self- or externally imposed) to find a new work environment, the success of your campaign will depend strongly on your ability to *keep the momentum going*. Closing the cover of this book should signal your opening the cover of your notebook to make a list of what steps you must take to implement your plan successfully. The most effective way to manage a project as major as this is to divide it into manageable segments of work. I find that when clients set only a *final* date by which they will have effected a change, they are not as successful as clients who make a commitment to work a minimum number of hours per day or per week on the project, with interim steps to accomplish. In the latter case, the lack of a deadline removes any anxiety associated with missing it, while the weekly time commitment and effort ensure a successful outcome.

One problem many people have in conducting a job-hunting or career-change program is the "advice" given by friends, relatives, and colleagues. There are apparently a lot of people in this world who—whether they are projecting their own insecurities or are jealous of your goals (probably the same situation)—are ready to deflate the optimism of others pursuing ambitious career goals. You have two options in dealing with this: you can follow such "advice" and tone down your aspirations, or you can decide to pursue your dream—regardless of what others may say.

I'm tempted to wish you good luck, but I think we both know that luck won't be the reason you achieve your goal. Luck is more appropriately applied to playing roulette, or, to be more relevant, responding to advertisements that attract hundreds of other applicants, making the probability of your résumé being "drawn" a comparable gamble. No, it definitely is not luck that will get you your outcome. Once you have read this book and have the information you need to achieve your objective, the success of your project will depend on your own hard work and persistence—and on your belief in yourself.

8

The Workplace— A Guide for Newcomers

FINDING THE WORKPLACE THAT BEST MATCHES YOUR NEEDS

Selecting a new career from the many options available can at first seem an overwhelming task, since so many possibilities exist. But there are very distinct characteristics of the various subdivisions of the workplace, and you will probably find some types of work environments appealing to you more than others, enabling you to home in on your targeted field more quickly.

The Business, Not-for-Profit, and Government Sectors

One way to consider the work world is in terms of three sectors: the private (business) sector, the not-for-profit sector, and the public (governmental) sector. The chief characteristics of each are:

Private Sector

- objective is to make a profit
- greatest opportunity for participants (employees and employers) to make the most money
- lowest job security of the three sectors in the sense that frequent organizational changes must be implemented to react to competitive and consumer/customer changes, resulting in layoffs and outright firings
- highest job mobility in the sense that, should you lose a job in a business organization, there are many more job opportunities in the business sector than in the public and not-for-profit sectors

Not-for-Profit Sector

- includes such organizations as educational and cultural institutions, foundations, social service agencies, charities, most hospitals
- compensation in this segment is relatively low
- offers lower job security in that many of these organizations receive their financial support from the government and/or contributions from the private sector, and it is sometimes difficult to predict their financial health
- offers somewhat less mobility than the business sector, since there are many fewer not-for-profit organizations than businesses

Public Sector

- offers the highest job security, i.e., it is extremely difficult to fire an employee
- offers moderate salaries
- offers less mobility than the private sector, in terms of absolute number of jobs
- tends to be characterized by highly structured work environments, career paths, and promotion procedures

The Functions of Organizations in the Workplace

Organizations, regardless of whether they are within the private, not-for-profit, or public sector, typically encompass certain activities:

- the design of a product or service;
- the presentation of the product or service to its targeted segment, whether it be businesses, consumers, the poor/sick, or taxpayers;
- the manufacture of the product (services, because they are intangible, are not manufactured);
- the delivery of the product or service;
- the planning of the future direction of the organization;
- the management of the organization's financial and accounting functions, e.g., payroll, tax filings, accounts payable, accounts receivable, financial planning;
- the general administration of the organization, which may include such functions as facilities management and real estate;
- the representation of the organization to the public;
- the staffing of the organization, development of compensation and benefit plans, and the training and development of its employees; and
- the management of the organization's legal affairs.

The greatest similarities among the private, public, and not-for-profit sectors lie in the last five areas—namely, the financial/accounting, administrative, public relations, human resources, and legal functions. Although not-for-profit organizations have traditionally not engaged in the same kind of marketing and sales as have business organizations, many are involved in fund-raising and membership drives. A term designating the function within a not-for-profit organization responsible for these activities is "development." In addition, there has been a significant trend in the past five years toward private and not-for-profit voluntary hospitals establishing formal marketing functions. This is due largely to a reduction in the demand for hospital services, resulting from a federal government-sponsored cost-containment system known as the "diagnosis-related groups," or "DRG," system.

Generally speaking, public-sector organizations do not engage in marketing. Notable exceptions are the semigovernmental U.S. Postal Service, which competes with private mail delivery services for business, and the armed forces, whose recruiting campaigns constitute a marketing effort.

The Advantages of a Career in Business

Several considerations prompt me to recommend the business sector as the one you should target:

• Financial Rewards

No one will dispute the strong financial advantage of working for a business organization over a not-for-profit or governmental organization. Total compensation—consisting of salaries, benefits, and perquisites—in the business world tends to be significantly higher. The reason is that a business must generate profits in order to remain viable in a highly competitive marketplace . . . which, in turn, enables it to reward its employees with higher compensation than do other types of organizations.

• Mobility

The number of jobs in each of the three sectors—16 million total federal, state, and local jobs; 2.3 million jobs in the not-for-profit sector; 75 million in the private sector—clearly implies that there are significantly more opportunities in the business sector. By now, most people in this country have correctly come to the realization that they will change their jobs—either voluntarily or through termination—at least several times in their career. With this in mind, the private sector certainly presents many more opportunities for job seekers.

• Stepping-stone to Opportunities for Future Self-Employment

Although right now your concern is to obtain a good job working for someone else, people change their goals as they go through life. While starting your own business may be the furthest thing from your mind, at some future date you may be very interested in doing so. Therefore, I would like to point out that the greatest opportunities for self-employment are in serving the needs of businesses and consumers. Through your employment in a business or-

MARKETING & SALES

- Develops new products/sevices and new features for existing ones
- Develops pricing strategies
- Conducts market research
- Designs advertising and promotional programs.
- Devises and implements sales campaigns
- Manages administrative aspects of sales, e.g., forecasting, inventory management, field communications, sales meetings
- Plans and coordinates distribution of products
- Processes orders

ENGINEERING & MANUFACTURING

- Designs new products and new features to existing products according to Marketing's specifications
- Purchases raw materials and components
- Develops safety standards for products
- Designs and purchases tooling and equipment to manufacture products
- Develops quality-control systems and procedures
- Manufactures all products
- Continually analyzes products for cost improvement opportunities and recommends these to Marketing
- Researches and develops new and improved products for consideration by Marketing
- Formulates short- and long-range manufacturing capacity requirements and develops plans for meeting them
- Designs plant layouts
- Manages all plant activities, e.g., inventory control, materials handling, production planning

FINANCE

- Forecasts the organization's expenditures and working capital requirements

- Manages tax planning and filings

- Manages accounts payable, accounts receivable, payroll, credit and collections functions

- Analyzes and reports on financial performance of all functional areas

- Develops and implements data-processing systems for entire company

- Manages strategic planning function: analyzes near- and long-term impact of environmental factors (social, legal, economic) on company's business; manages mergers and acquisitions function

HUMAN RESOURCES

- Ensures that all functions are properly staffed and develops succession plans

- Designs and administers benefits and compensation programs

- Manages EEO/Affirmative Action activities.

- Develops new approaches to structuring the organization to meet its changing objectives and needs

- Administers training and development function

- Handles union relations and contract negotiations

- Ensures that the company complies with environmental and worker-safety regulations

ADMINISTRATION

- Develops and implements public relations and communications programs

- Handles relations with investors, charities, community organizations

- Handles corporate secretarial function and legal affairs

- Manages government affairs function

- Manages physical facility

- Purchases real estate and manages properties

- Provides administrative services, e.g., records retention, printing, travel arrangements

Figure 10. Chart illustrating selected principal functions typically performed by each major corporate organizational area.

ganization you may have the opportunity to gain considerable skill in important business functions, enabling you to sell your ability for a handsome price some day.

For these reasons the focus of the remaining portion of this chapter and of Chapter 9 will be on business careers, but in the discussion of those fields I will point out instances where they can be pursued in the other sectors.

To begin, let's take a look at the structure of a business enterprise. The organization of a typical manufacturing company might look like Figure 10. The product-development cycle in this kind of company could look like Figure 11. It is important to realize that product-development cycles can range from as little as three months to as much as twenty years. The timetable indicated in Figure 11 is typical of many household appliances.

Subgroups Within the Private Sector

The word "business" applies to many different types of companies, each having the following objectives: survival, growth, and profitability. While the U.S. economy comprises hundreds of industries—for example, retail, health care, publishing, brokerage—each with a unique way of operating, there are certain ways of categorizing companies other than by industry, with significant implications for job hunters. These are:

Services vs. Manufacturing Companies

The word "services" refers to intangibles such as brokerage, insurance, financial planning, career counseling, banking, health care, and detective work. "Products" companies are manufacturing companies. To adapt our manufacturing company organization chart (Figure 10) to conform to the structure of a services company, we could replace the manufacturing and engineering functions with something called "operations." The particular nature of an operations function will vary from one type of service organization to another—and the names for these operations functions will vary, too. For example, in an insurance company, operations would include such functions as underwriting and claims processing; examples of operations functions in a bank would be mortgage processing and statement processing.

Businesses market products and/or services, which they sell to consumers and/or other businesses and/or institutions (e.g., hospitals, schools). Forty years ago, about two-thirds of the workers in this country were employed in manufacturing industries, with one-third in services jobs. Today, that proportion is just about reversed—70 percent of all jobs are in services industries. Services companies tend to be somewhat more receptive to hiring individuals changing careers, perhaps because they deal with intangibles in their business, and it's easier for them to appreciate someone's ability to make the transition from one field to another.

Long vs. Short Product-Development Cycles

There is an interesting pattern among manufacturing companies. Because product-development cycles are always on tight schedules, it's advantageous to companies to have the same group of individuals work on the development of the product, since disruptions in staffing usually mean delays in the completion of the project. As such, those companies that manufacture products requiring long product-development periods tend to also offer somewhat more secure work environments than do companies with shorter ones. The pharmaceutical, munitions, and aircraft engine industries are a few examples of those with very long product-development cycles—with the food, health/beauty aids, and apparel industries, to name a few, having relatively short cycles.

Small vs. Large Organizations

Many people who have not worked in business believe that a large company is overwhelming because of its many employees. Having worked in both small (five people) and large (IBM and General Electric) companies, as well as in several within this range in size, I can tell you that this is not the case. In order to manage their businesses efficiently, large organizations establish many suborganizations in which small groups of people function. My experience working in a number of jobs within large companies is that the typical number of people with whom any one individual will interact on a daily basis usually won't exceed ten. However, if someone is in a sales support job, he or she may interact with dozens of customers in one day, but this situation could apply equally to small and large organizations.

Notwithstanding the above, there are certain differences between small and large companies that may hold implications for your next career move.

- Opportunities for Advancement

Obviously, the larger the company, the greater the opportunity for advancement, in terms of sheer numbers of positions. The paths to achieving these opportunities are more clearly defined in a larger company, with formal promotion procedures usually in place. Furthermore, since smaller companies are generally family-owned businesses, it's very common for relatives of the owner to be promoted over others who may be more qualified. While some nepotism does exist in larger companies, it's far less pervasive. In fact, a number of major companies have policies against it.

- Exposure to Broader Responsibilities in Smaller Companies

People who work in smaller organizations often find themselves performing responsibilities pertaining to several functional areas, since the company usually cannot justify hiring a full-time employee to perform those additional duties. Employees who are asked to wear many hats are the beneficiaries of this situation, since they gain experience that would not otherwise be available

Figure 11. An example of a product-development cycle for a consumer product.

Inception of Idea/Concept	Feasibility Evaluation	Product Development
Develop concept for new product or for new feature to existing product	(2–3 months)	(6–9 months)
	Determine customer/consumer acceptance through market research.	Build prototypes for engineering testing
Obtain management approval to proceed		Complete engineering drawings and specifications
	Determine whether product feasible from engineering and manufacturing standpoint.	Develop final product cost and implementation expenses
	Evalute whether total program feasible financially	Develop long-range forecasts of sales and profitability
	Determine whether another company or individual has patents or proprietary status which would prevent launch of the product	Develop detailed description of product, costs and pricing, i.e., design guide
		Develop program schedule and establish multifunctional product team
		Establish engineering design direction and industrial design appearance

to them at this stage in their careers. This experience augments their capabilities and enhances their attractiveness to other companies. On the other hand, the size of a large organization usually precludes it from offering this kind of opportunity. Therefore, if you are interested in fast exposure to several functions of a business, you should seriously consider getting a start in a small company.

• Benefits Generally Better in Larger Organizations
While this is certainly not a universal rule, it's safe to make a generalization that large organizations do, in fact, offer more comprehensive benefit plans. Since you may require use of certain benefits (e.g., day care, dental plan), this should be a consideration when you research potential employers (although, as explained on page 181, do not ask about benefits in an initial

Implementation Phase	Production and Distribution Phase	Post-Production
(9 months)	(1 month)	(ongoing for the life of the product)
Obtain company approval of product program budgets	Analyze pilot-run test results	Implement periodic cost improvements in packaging and design, as feasible without negatively affecting sales
Purchase tooling and equipment	Conduct final safety review, cost update and quality plan	
Prepare sales and promotional materials	Staff manufacturing facility (equipment and assembly lines)	Conduct periodic market research to get feedback on consumer satisfaction and suggestions for product improvements
Conduct pre-pilot and pilot run of product using production tooling and equipment	Manufacture and ship product	

interview). But don't assume that just because a company is small it won't offer generous benefits. And be sure to consider the *total* compensation—the value of your salary plus benefits and perquisites—in evaluating the attractiveness of any offer.

• Termination Arrangements Usually Better in Larger Organizations
While termination arrangements do constitute a kind of benefit, they are usually not spelled out at the time of hiring, as are health and disability insurance, for example. In many instances they are negotiable, depending on a combination of factors, including the length of one's tenure with the organization, the level attained, and the relationship with one's manager.

Perhaps because larger companies' actions have a greater impact, they widely offer generous early-retirement packages, as well as outplacement services for fired employees—unless an individual is fired for certain causes. Some companies also give fired employees a week's severance pay for each year of employment with them. Even though you are looking for a long-term position, I'm sure you realize that in today's climate of mergers and cost-cutting programs there is some probability that you will have to be concerned in the future with how favorable your employer's termination benefits will be.

• Large Companies Look Better on Résumés
Here again, since nothing is forever in today's work world, you should consider that the immediately recognizable stature of a major company as a previous employer can enhance the impression you make on a prospective employer. In planning your career always think about the impact that your current job will have when viewed by your next potential employer . . . which can translate into a higher-than-customary salary offer.

Significant Differences Within Organizations

Just as organizations within the work world have unique characteristics that contribute to distinct types of working environments, so, too, do functional areas within one organization. One way to distinguish the differences among an organization's subfunctions is through the use of the terms "line" and "staff" (in this situation, "staff" has a special meaning). Line functions are those activities within a business organization that are directly responsible for producing the products or services that generate sales and profits. Thus in a manufacturing company, line functions are:

Manufacturing
Engineering
Sales
Marketing

Staff functions, on the other hand, exist to provide services to the line areas. They are not responsible for producing the product or service, but their activities are necessary for the smooth functioning of the line areas of the organization. Some staff functions are:

Finance/Accounting
Human resources
Public relations
Strategic planning (sometimes called "corporate planning")
Research and development
Facilities management
Legal

In general, line functions are thought to be more high-pressure areas in that they have direct responsibility for the development and marketing of the organization's products or services. Because of their more critical contribution to the success of the company, fewer marketing and sales jobs will be terminated in an economic downturn than, for example, those in public relations and strategic planning.

The End-User Environment vs. the Consultant/Contractor/Supplier Environment

It is important to realize that one can perform virtually all the business functions listed on the chart in Figure 10 either as an employee of the corporation which is the end user of the function or within a firm that provides services to end-user organizations, which can range in size from small companies to the largest ones in the country. For example, you can write advertising copy for Company A while working in its advertising department, or you can write advertising copy for Company A while working for an advertising agency (service company) that has been hired by Company A. The companies that provide business services are called by many different names—agencies, suppliers, consultants, free-lancers, contractors. And these companies are also end users since they, too, purchase services from agencies, suppliers, consultants, etc. IBM, for instance, is a computer hardware and software supplier to other end users. But, at the same time, it functions as an end user because it purchases real estate and advertising services, and writes software for its own purposes.

The following table describes some types of companies providing services to a number of end-user business functions:

Companies Providing Business Services	*Commonly Provided Services*
Marketing Consultants	Provide assistance in determining what kinds of products or services the company should develop, in formulating pricing and promotional strategies, and in analyzing competitive strengths and weaknesses
Market research suppliers	Design and conduct market research studies to support new products/services/features and the ongoing evaluation of existing ones
Advertising agencies	Design and implement advertising campaigns; some agencies also provide public relations, sales promotion, and market research services

Sales promotion agencies	Design and produce sales promotion programs, e.g., sweepstakes and couponing programs, premium giveaways
Public relations counselors	Design and manage campaigns aimed at enhancing their clients' images. Advise clients on how to counteract negative publicity. Counsel executives on how to present themselves to the media; write speeches delivered by top management
Purchasing consulting companies	Help companies develop systems and procedures to improve their purchasing performance; may advise on negotiating with vendors and suppliers
Computer counsulting firms	Develop specialized software systems on a project basis; many also hire programming personnel to work on projects for clients at client locations
Training and development consulting firms	Design, conduct, and administer specialized training programs addressing the needs of an organization's salaried and hourly employees; some examples of programs are sales training, effective presentation skills for managers, interpersonal communication skills, managerial skills for supervisors of white-collar workers, managerial skills for supervisors of blue-collar workers, time management
Pension consultants	Provide guidance to corporations in establishing pension plans and in managing them for optimum profitability
Organizational development consultants	Provide direction to human resources management in structuring the organization to adapt to changing environmental (economic, legislative, competitive, consumer) factors, while meeting its business objectives
Employment agencies, executive recruiters, manpower services	Act as the organization's agent in researching and interviewing candidates for jobs at client companies. Agencies and recruiters find candidates who are hired by client companies for permanent positions. Agencies and manpower services hire personnel (secretarial, technical, administrative, accounting, etc.) for short- and long-term temporary assignments at client companies, assuming responsibility for payroll and benefits aspects.

Although the work performed by these business service companies is similar to the duties performed within their counterpart functions in the client companies, there are significant differences between the two environments. For example, if the clients of a business service company are geographically dispersed, its professional employees who provide client services should expect to travel 50–80 percent of the time. Also, because of the exposure to a number of clients in a broad array of industries, working for a company providing business services to end users often provides a variety in job content rarely matched by the comparable position within an end user. This kind of work experience can broaden your skills and at the same time enable you to develop excellent contacts in various industries that can be used as a springboard to a better job, or as a client base when you start your own company.

9

More Information on
Best Bets—
for Career Changers New to
the Corporate World

THE BEST FIELDS FOR
CAREER CHANGERS . . . AND WHY

As a rule, professional positions in the following functional areas in any organization tend to require specialized education:

Finance/accounting—requires business administration education, usually with emphasis on financial or accounting procedures

Manufacturing and engineering—requires a degree in one of a number of engineering disciplines

Data processing—usually requires a computer science or information systems degree, but career changers can penetrate this area with relatively little training, as Chapter 2 (pages 6–71) explains

Legal—requires a law degree

Strategic/corporate planning—generally requires financial training in order to perform mergers and acquisitions analyses

By eliminating the above, we can see that those functional areas offering the best opportunities for career changers who seek to enter a new field without formal education are marketing, sales, public relations, and human resources. These areas draw primarily on general skills—communication, negotiating, project management, creative and analytical abilities—as opposed to those requiring specialized education. One other function relatively easy to enter is purchasing, which, in a manufacturing company, will be found in the manufacturing department. In nonmanufacturing companies, purchasing is usually under the management of the controller or vice president of Administration.

What follows is an overview of these "best bet" areas, with descriptions of widely found job titles within them. It is important to understand that the names I will be using for these functional areas and the subdivisions within them are not uniform throughout the work world. For example, what is called "human resources" in one company may be called "employee relations" in another and "personnel" in still another, although the activities of all three of these departments will be comparable. One company may give the title "marketing" to the function responsible for advertising and sales promotion, while another may have a marketing department that includes several subfunctional areas, including "product planning" and "advertising and sales promotion." And the marketing function within a not-for-profit organization is sometimes called "development" or "fund-raising." The implication of these variations is that you should always learn the names and functions of the various departments within the companies you target, as well as the subdivisions within those areas.

Marketing

Marketing is justifiably mentioned first since it provides the direction of any company. This is the functional area that makes decisions as to which products or services will be offered; if a manufacturing company, how many of each product will be made; the pricing for the products or services; the method of advertising and promotion. But marketing is a broad category that is composed of several subfunctions, each of which makes a significant contribution to the profitability of the organization. Let's take a look at the roles of each of the primary marketing subfunctions.

Product Planning (or Product Management)

To illustrate the marketing process in its most traditional and common form, let's begin by considering the job of a product planner at a consumer products manufacturer—specifically, a household appliance manufacturer. "Product planner" is a job title found in most medium- and large-size companies' marketing functions. It can be an entry-level position, and entails responsibility for a logical group of products, e.g., all smoke alarms, all hair dryers, all products of a particular cosmetics brand. The product planner is responsible for developing new products within his or her product line, as well as for adding new features to existing products.

Suppose that a product planner responsible for electric coffeemakers comes to the conclusion that it would be nice to have a coffeemaker that includes an electronic digital clock that the consumer can set before going to bed, in order to wake up to freshly brewed coffee. He or she requests preliminary cost figures from the Engineering and Manufacturing departments for the unit cost of the product (how much it will cost to produce each coffeemaker) and the cost of the equipment and tooling required to manufacture the product. With the unit (individual product) cost in mind, the product planner, knowing the amount of profit the company must realize on a product in order to justify its manufacture, calculates the retail price of the proposed coffeemaker. It is important to realize that at some steps in this process the product planner would require approval from his or her manager to proceed in the direction he or she feels would be best for the project.

At this point a significant piece of information is missing, namely, an answer to the question "Will enough consumers be willing to buy this new product— at the required retail price—to provide the company with a sufficient return on its investment in the project?"

To determine the answer to this question, the product planner must now ask the Market Research (sometimes called "Marketing Research") department to conduct a study that will provide a reading on the proposed product's potential reception in the marketplace. A critical component of the product-planning process, market research is what I call business's "insurance policy," since it helps reduce the risk of implementing unprofitable product programs—and at a relatively low cost. It is far less expensive to spend $50,000 to find out that the consumer is not willing to buy a product at the price at which the company must sell it than it is to spend $3 million on engineering activities and tooling and equipment and *then* find out the same thing. (Costs of market research studies and of implementing new-product programs will vary from industry to industry; I've just presented a typical example.)

In the case of a service, as opposed to a manufactured product, engineering and manufacturing costs aren't incurred, but there may be significant costs associated with the development of the service, e.g., for advertising and promotion, legal counsel, public relations. Market research is therefore just as important in a services environment.

Most market research studies are conducted by specialized companies hired on a contractual basis, rather than by the employees of the company marketing the product or service in question. Typically ranging in size from five to fifty people, market research suppliers design and conduct studies for companies marketing consumer and industrial products and services. As a liaison to the product planner, a market research analyst in the market research department of the end-user company will request proposals from several competing suppliers detailing their approaches to conducting the study, a schedule for the project, and estimated costs. The market research manager, with the input of the market research analyst, will decide which supplier will be engaged to perform the study. It is the research analyst's job to coordinate the study with the supplier company to ensure completion on schedule.

If the study results are favorable, the product planner will prepare a request for the funds necessary for the product program. This document, often called an "appropriation request," will:

- contain the rationale for the program;
- outline what, if any, competition exists;
- describe the market research results; and
- detail the costs of designing and manufacturing the product or of developing the service, as well as the expected financial results over the first few years of the project.

Assuming that the new product program is approved, the product planner must establish a development schedule by working closely with personnel in Manufacturing, Engineering, Home Economics, Industrial Design, Advertising and Sales Promotion in, for example, the case of a household appliance. This schedule will contain completion dates for such activities as design of the physical product and its engineered functions, development of the tooling and equipment, testing by home economics, design of packaging, and advertising and promotion activities. The product planner will also issue a design guide that will contain all the preliminary specifications for the coffeemaker— its estimated cost, pricing, physical appearance, type of packaging, scheduled production date, etc.

Close monitoring of the schedule by the product planner is necessary to ensure completion on time. For example, in the case of a consumer product such as a coffeemaker, it is important that the product be introduced at one of the semiannual housewares trade shows in Chicago, with shipment promised within a specified period after these shows. All industries have trade shows at which producers of new products display their offerings to buyers who purchase merchandise for their companies. Buyers in our coffeemaker example would include those representing department stores, mass merchandisers, wholesalers, catalog showrooms, drugstore chains, and mail-order houses.

Suppose the item being marketed is a service, not a product. In this case a "product-development" schedule is still necessary, but no engineering and manufacturing would be involved.

Each industry has its own unique team of technical personnel working on new-product programs. In a company that manufactures cosmetics, this team would include a chemist instead of an engineer; in a food company, a food technologist would be a team member. Regardless of the type of industry, the introduction of a product or service will always entail some kind of promotion of the new offering, since the targeted segment—whether consumers or businesses—must be enticed to purchase the product or service. The function responsible for this activity, often called "Advertising and Sales Promotion," represents another "best bet" for those seeking new careers. I will go into more detail about the advertising and sales promotion function a little later, but first let's consider a *Typical Workday of a Product Planner* responsible for electric coffeemakers in an appliance manufacturing company:

8:30–9:30	Phone calls: to Art Abrams, Design Engineer on the Smart Coffeemaker, to determine whether temperature tests were successful; to Arlene Spencer, Manufacturing Engineer, to find out earliest date when tooling can be completed; to Howard Myers, Financial Analyst, to determine whether cost analysis on clock component of coffeemaker is ready; to Peter Whitman, Industrial Designer, to determine whether he has talked to the manufacturing engineer about proposed new type of plastic to be used for the housing
9:30–10:00	Meeting with Barbara Watson of Product Service to review excessively high number of returns of D14 drip coffeemaker and develop plan to address the most serious causes
10:00–10:30	Meeting with Carl Wilson of Advertising and Sales Promotion Department to outline plans for lower-cost packaging for the P12A percolator; phone call to manufacturing plant to obtain stock levels on current packaging and estimate of date when stock will be depleted; reviews schedule for completion of package artwork with Wilson and agrees on date that finished product will be shipped to the manufacturing plant
10:30–11:00	Meeting with product-planning staff on new form for monthly report on product-development schedule changes and problems
11:00–11:30	Reviews monthly syndicated market research data on sales of 36 brands of coffeemakers in selected group of department stores, catalog showrooms, and discount stores; makes note to purchase two recently introduced competitive models having fairly strong sales
12:30–1:30	Phone call to Hal Richardson, Production Engineer, to discuss plant's recommendation that P14 percolator cap be redesigned because of quality problems; call to Margaret Dunlop, Production Engineer, regarding her recommendation that On/Off switch on D12A combination drip coffeemaker/grinder be replaced by On/Off switch used on D14, so that the plant can buy in greater quantities and reduce costs of each switch, with annual savings estimated at $9,000; call to Peter Whitman, Industrial Designer, to get his opinion on whether proposed changes will have any negative human engineering or design implications
1:30–2:00	Meeting with product-management staff on upcoming presentation to Steve Miller, Division General Manager, on all new product programs; reviews presentation schedule and format, and agrees on points to emphasize for each product program

2:00–3:00   Meeting with Alice Maynard, Market Research Analyst, on methodology and schedule for study aimed at assessing market for proposed new espresso coffeemaker; reviews Alice's proposed questionnaire for use with one-on-one consumer interviews to be conducted by the market research supplier; makes suggestions for modifications to some questions, and for additional questions

3:00–4:30   Returns phone calls from manufacturing plant on some problems with preliminary production schedule for the Smart Coffeemaker; reviews three complaint letters on model D12A combination drip coffeemaker/grinder sent by consumers to the chairman of the board; prepares memo to Jennifer Walter, Marketing Manager, describing design modifications implemented in October that should have eliminated two of the problems cited and informing her that the third problem has been known for a while, but is too expensive to fix

4:30–4:45   Responds to phone call from Peter Whitman, Industrial Designer, regarding impossibility of having prototypes of GX coffee grinder ready for Housewares Show, due to Industrial Design's already large backlog of work; determines that cost of hiring outside modelmaker to do the work will be $12,000; authorizes expenditure of money in order to meet trade show date.

4:45–5:30   Reviews Home Economics report detailing results of proposed lower-cost coating for heating element of drip coffeemakers, to replace current coating; prepares memo to Mark Reid, Product Manager, recommending that coating not be used because it reduces coffee temperature to an unacceptable level

The above represents a fairly typical day in the life of a product planner. Other activities that someone in this position might engage in are

- semiannual travel to an industry trade show to promote new products to buyers from various retailers;
- a one-day overnight trip, approximately once a month, to the manufacturing plant responsible for the product planner's products for meetings with engineering and manufacturing personnel;
- travel to participate in a group session on using creative techniques to generate new product ideas; and
- writing an appropriation request (request for funds) for new product programs.

Market Research

As I said before, market research provides marketers of products and services with a cost-effective way to measure the potential for proposed new-product or feature introductions, and to enhance their success. The methodology used to conduct the market research for a particular type of product or service can vary widely, depending on the type of information required.

For instance, to determine how well a proposed new product will fare against existing competition, the leading competitive products and the proposed new product are displayed to prescreened potential consumers who are asked to make a "purchase" and explain the reasoning behind their selection. If, for example, 24 of 100 consumers choose a particular model coffeemaker from among those included in the simulated sales test, the manufacturer can project this to the real marketplace and assume that its product has the potential to garner 24 percent market share.

While there are many other types of market research methodologies, a few commonly used ones are:

- Owner surveys: Questionnaires are sent to purchasers of a product to get feedback on their dislikes and likes.
- Focus groups: Under the guidance of a moderator, six to eight people discuss their opinions on a particular subject of interest to the company commissioning the study—for example, their toasters, coffeemakers, how they feel about cleaning their houses.
- One-on-one in-depth interviews of consumers: This methodology is often used to test a completely new product concept.

As I mentioned earlier, the product planner enlists the assistance of the market research department in designing and administering the study. Once such a request is received, a market research analyst is assigned to the project. The larger the company, the greater the likelihood that it will not be conducted by the company, but rather contracted to a market research supplier.

Once a firm is selected, the market research analyst acts as the liaison between the product planner in his or her company and a project leader (sometimes called "project director" or "study manager") in the market research supplier company, with responsibility for ensuring that the supplier lives up to the commitments it made in its proposal. The market research analyst concurrently handles a number of studies at various stages of completion.

The supplier is responsible for hiring survey companies to conduct interviews of consumers, writing proposals to get new business, managing the study within budget and on schedule, and analyzing and reporting on the study findings. Now let's look at a *Typical Workday of a Project Leader* in a market research supplier:

8:30–9:30   Reviews requirements for market research study needed by Allure Cosmetics; calls survey companies in Atlanta, New York City, and San Francisco to get cost figures and possible schedules

9:30–10:30   Conference call with Global Foods' Jane Drummond, Market Research Analyst, and Mark Cornwall, Product Planner, to review questionnaire to be used with study aimed at developing new coffee blends

10:30–12:00   Prepares field kit for Clean-Mates paper towel study, i.e., questionnaire, instructions to interviewers, forms to summarize responses; calls Dick Weldon at Clean-Mates and gives him addresses of three survey companies to which Clean-Mates towels and those of three competitors should be shipped

12:45–2:30   With John Nash, Summertime Barbecue Grill Product Planner, visits local survey site at shopping mall, where study aimed at assessing consumer reaction to self-cleaning grill is being conducted, to observe consumers being interviewed through one-way mirror

2:30–3:30   Meeting with Karen White, company President, regarding approach for one-on-one in-depth interviews to be conducted for National Bank study aimed at developing new mortgage products and financial planning service

3:30–4:00   Compiles results to date of Summertime Barbecue Grill study, using a desktop computer system to analyze preliminary data; telephone call to John Nash to give him preliminary results and tell him that final data due tomorrow is not likely to change preliminary conclusions discussed yesterday

4:00–5:15   Prepares portion of first draft of final report on Summertime study results, including six charts detailing consumers' responses to the most important questions; writes four pages of prose commentary for report

5:15–6:00   Prepares expense account form for three trips to clients last week; prepares memo recommending methodology of study to be conducted for Smartoys' new educational toy

Advertising and Sales Promotion

I have already told you that the advertising and sales promotion function is an important contributor to the successful marketing of a product or service. Let's now look more closely at what each of these two activities—advertising and sales promotion—entails. Advertising is the process of persuading the targeted customer (which can be a business) to buy a product or service. Examples of advertising media are newspapers, magazines, television, radio, and the great blue sky, in the case of sky writing. Sales promotion refers to any other method of promoting the product, some examples of which are sweepstakes and other contests, coupons, gift with purchase (very big in the cosmetics industry), and rebates.

Sales promotion is used extensively by manufacturers to sell their products to retailers, who, in turn, sell them to consumers. There are always a lot of manufacturers vying for the retailer's purchase decision, but the retailer is concerned with stocking only those items he or she believes will sell . . . and quickly. Because of this, manufacturers spend a great deal of money to try to sell their customer, the retailer, on the advantages of buying their products. Sales promotion methods used by the manufacturer to accomplish this objective include catalogs depicting their products, full-page sheets displaying a product photograph and listing its features, contests, and industry trade show exhibits where retail buyers place large orders for their stores.

Here again, one can be employed within the advertising and sales promotion function of an end-user company—for example, General Electric, Apple, Rubbermaid, Procter & Gamble—or within an advertising or sales promotion agency that provides services to end users. In general, it is easier to break into the field by getting a job in an end-user company, and therefore I will now describe a *Typical Workday of an Advertising and Sales Promotion Specialist* in a medium-size manufacturer of personal care appliances (e.g., hair dryers, manicure kits, electric shavers):

8:30–9:30	Meeting with Steve Ogden, Luxe Shampoo Advertising and Sales Promotion Specialist, and Jan Ward, Product Planner on Hair Dryers, to discuss joint promotional program whereby buyers of Luxe Shampoo will get a three-dollar coupon good toward the purchase of the HX13 hair dryer; reviews financial arrangements, preliminary coupon artwork and size; determines required quantity; establishes schedule for shipment of coupons to Luxe plant
9:30–10:15	Coordinates photography session for spring catalog; supervises free-lance hairdresser and photographer in shooting photos of female model using H9 hair dryer
10:15–11:00	Meeting with Jan Ward, Product Planner on Hair Dryers, and Sam Lawrence, Account Executive from Morrison Advertising, to review media plan developed by the agency for advertising campaign for the new model H15 hair dryer
11:00–11:30	Phone call to Rick Conlin, Graphic Designer, to confirm status of artwork for H15 hair dryer package; phone call to Ann Mitchell, Attorney in Legal Department, to coordinate meeting with Mitchell and Dave Allen, Product Planner on M16 manicure kit, to review claims planned for advertising campaign and package; phone call to United Boxes plant to find out if they have received package artwork for M11 manicure kit

11:30–12:00	Meeting with Carol Soule, Electric Shavers Product Planner, to review her proposal for coupon promotion with deodorant manufacturer for S16 ladies' shaver
1:00–2:00	Meeting with Carol Soule, Product Planner, and Sam Lawrence of Morrison Advertising to review Morrison's proposal for campaign to promote MS1 shaver/manicure combination appliance
2:00–2:30	Meeting with Frank Wallace, Advertising and Sales Promotion Manager, to review new departmental hiring and payment policies with respect to suppliers (free-lance artists, typographers, printers, etc.)
2:30–3:30	Meeting with Carl Rodman, Manager of Meetings and Special Events, and Marge Hopkins, Graphic Designer, to discuss creative approach for slide show displaying new products to sales force at upcoming national sales meeting in Orlando, Florida
3:30–4:30	Calculates cost estimates of audiovisual and other creative presentations required by Sales Department for national sales meeting, for presentation to Susan Marshall, Vice President of Sales
4:30–4:45	Responds to phone call from Carol Soule, Electric Shavers Product Planner, regarding typographical error she found on artwork for model S15 men's shaver; discusses schedule for implementing correction
4:45–5:30	Phone call to Art Eagleton at Reflections, Inc., to negotiate more favorable price for personal-size mirrors to be included with new H25 hair dryer; prepares memo to Jan Ward, Product Planner on Hair Dryers, detailing slightly better prices for each of six quantity levels
5:30–6:00	Meeting with Marge Hopkins, Graphic Designer, Joe Evans, V.P. of Marketing, and Susan Marshall, V.P. of Sales, to review creative proposals for spring catalog cover

Other activities of advertising and sales promotion personnel include

- evaluating presentations of advertising agencies that wish to "steal" the account;
- performing statistical analyses and evaluations of ad effectiveness;
- studying market and census data to aid in identifying best regional markets for advertising;
- designing trade show exhibits, as well as coordinating on-site trade show activities, e.g., product demonstrations, meetings with key customers; and

- meeting with suppliers of creative/production services to review their capabilities and fees.

Purchasing

All organizations must control the costs of their operations, regardless of whether they are business, not-for-profit, or governmental. Although not-for-profit and governmental organizations do not have to make a profit as do businesses, they would not be able to survive if they did not keep a careful eye on their expenditures. A key factor in keeping costs down is the skill of the purchasing department in researching products and services, and in negotiating prices and terms with vendors and suppliers.

About half of all purchasing jobs are in manufacturing companies, with the rest in services companies, governmental organizations, educational institutions, hospitals, etc. Within a manufacturing company, a purchasing agent will buy raw materials, parts, and components from which the company will make its finished products. He or she will also buy machinery to manufacture products, trucks and fuel to transport them, office equipment and various services, e.g., air freight, commercial cleaning. Governmental organizations—particularly the military—buy billions of dollars' worth of products from industry each year. Hospitals and educational institutions purchase food, linen services, maintenance services, etc.

Within the business sector, the purchasing agent's skill is crucial to the company being able to manufacture its products at costs that enable it to meet its profit objectives. But getting the best quality parts, supplies, raw materials, and prices isn't the only concern of the purchasing manager; timely arrival of shipments—and in the right quantities—is necessary to satisfy production requirements. Purchasing professionals must also find several suppliers of the same item, so that if one discontinues offering the particular merchandise, or raises its price, the company has alternate sources of supply it can draw upon quickly, avoiding production delays.

A purchasing agent will coordinate the testing of any item its company is considering, and will work with suppliers to upgrade quality to conform to the company's standards.

Study this *Typical Workday of a Purchasing Agent* for a company manufacturing health and beauty aids to see if the position involves tasks you would enjoy:

8:30–9:00	Meets with Jane Ryan, Sales Representative for Deluxe Packaging, to review samples of their proposed design for the new family-size combination plastic shampoo/conditioner packaging; discusses product specifications, availability, prices, and quantity discounts

9:00–9:30   Gives a Deluxe package sample to Susan Wood, Packaging Engineer, for testing and evaluation; telephone call to Russ Martin, Adult Shampoo Product Planner, to give him Deluxe's costs so that he can evaluate effect on profitability of shampoo product line

9:30–10:00   Call to Larry Cook, Dover Manufacturing's Sales Representative, to request that one dozen samples of proposed new cap for baby shampoo bottle be sent to Home Economics for testing; call to Alan Whyte, Baby Shampoo Product Planner, to notify him of samples being sent, so that he can prepare memo to Home Economics detailing test objectives

10:00–11:00   Meeting with Joe Dunnigan of Reliable Plastics and Susan Wood, Packaging Engineer, to review quality problem with heart-shaped shampoo bottle for Loveshampoo; reviews possible modifications to address problem; agrees on date for shipment of samples of modified bottle for testing; calls Russ Martin, Adult Shampoo Product Planner, to tell him about quality problems and inform him of probable two-week delay in production of Loveshampoo

11:00–12:00   Meeting with Lou Stanton of Production Planning Department and conference call with Alan Whyte, Baby Shampoo Product Planner, to plan phase-out of production of 8-ounce baby shampoo; calls Sally Harris of Royal Products to reduce order from 10,000 bottles to 3,500 to conform with reduced production requirements of phase-out

1:00–1:30   Meeting with Ralph Adams, Packaging Engineer, to discuss possibility of eliminating inner plastic wrap around Teen Dream combination package of shampoo, conditioner, and hand cream as a cost-reduction step; checks computer printout to confirm annual savings of this proposed step

1:30–2:00   Reviews family-size shampoo bottle caps rejected by Quality Control; calls Larry Cook at Dover Manufacturing to report defects in cap fit on shampoo bottle and cancel order unless company can provide 20,000 caps up to standard by next Wednesday; calls Hal Steiner at International Packaging to see if they can deliver 20,000 caps in time—and at what cost

2:00–3:00   Meeting with Purchasing staff and Ann Mackintosh of Software Solutions to discuss design of new computerized purchasing system, i.e., reporting requirements, implementation schedule, training needs

3:00–3:15   Phone call to Lois Campelli at Contemporary Products to negotiate better price on new furniture for Personnel Department

3:15–3:30	Takes call from Dave Roberts of Maxwell Products regarding tomorrow's scheduled shipment of 125,000 caps for 16-ounce hand cream dispenser; shipment will not be made unless check for last shipment is received today; calls Doris White in Accounts Payable to find out status of payment; calls Dave Roberts at Maxwell to tell him that messenger will deliver check this afternoon
3:30–4:00	Prepares orders for 500 yards of polyethylene film, 10,000 corrugated boxes, 162,500 shampoo pump dispensers
4:00–4:30	Takes call from Russ Martin, Adult Shampoo Product Planner, regarding proposed purchase of combs to be used as giveaways in upcoming promotion of Tressa shampoo line; calls Continental Combs to expedite their price quotation and get earliest delivery date
4:30–5:30	Sits in on presentation by Worldwide Computer on features and pricing of their new desktop computer being considered for installation in all engineers' offices

Other responsibilities of a purchasing agent include

- acting as a liaison to outside testing labs;
- preparing written requests for proposals, bids, and quotations;
- monitoring inventory levels to determine when to reorder; and
- participating in a company task force on some special manufacturing need, e.g., workers' right to know, hazardous waste removal programs.

Sales

The focus in this discussion will be on "outside," as opposed to "retail," sales. Retail is a specialized kind of sales, and I do not consider it an attractive enough option to suggest it, primarily because the pay is usually lower than comparable positions within outside sales functions.

Also, I would like to point out that there are positions—other than Sales Promotion—with the word "sales" in their title that do not entail actual selling. Such jobs are within the "Sales Administration" (also called "Headquarters Sales") function. I will be describing jobs in that area in detail a little later, but for now will deal only with positions that directly entail selling.

As a career changer, one of your biggest concerns is whether you will be able to make a transition to a new field without experiencing a setback in earnings. Sales is one area where this concern should be minimal since beginning sales positions often offer the opportunity for better compensation than do other fields, with significant increases possible in subsequent years.

The impression most people have of sales is that it is a high-pressure work environment and that you have to expend a lot of energy to convince people to buy your products or services. While this is true to a great extent, there are also many exceptions. Some products have such strong brand-name recognition among consumers—along with manufacturers backing them with substantial advertising campaigns—that selling them is not that difficult, since retailers know that shoppers will ask for them. Examples of brands that evoke strong positive reactions are General Electric, Farberware, and Rubbermaid. To sell these companies' products to retailers does not require high-pressure sales tactics. The key responsibilities of sales people promoting these products are to negotiate retailer participation in special programs and cooperative advertising support, to service their accounts with timely shipments to meet promotional programs and sales demand, and to process returned merchandise quickly.

This is an important point to bear in mind. You may have been deterred from entering the sales field because of anticipating anxiety associated with convincing people to buy your company's product. But you can probably find a more relaxed selling situation if you target a consumer products manufacturer with an excellent reputation.

The Operation of a Sales Organization

In a typical sales organization, each branch manager is responsible for generating sales in his or her geographical territory only. The branch manager is given a quota—or sales volume objective—each quarter (three-month period) by his or her manager.

Reporting to the branch manager are generally three to ten salespeople, each of whom has an exclusive territory to manage and a quarterly sales quota to meet. Usually each sales representative is assigned responsibility for selling to all companies within a specified geographical region. However, depending on the sales strategies of the company, one representative may be assigned responsibility for selling to one type of business within a geographical area, with another representative handling another type of business. For example, a paper manufacturer selling to both institutional (e.g., hotels, schools, nursing homes) and retail (e.g., supermarkets, grocery stores, drug stores) accounts may assign each segment to a representative, and both will sell within the same geographical area. An example of another variation would be a computer company that assigns one representative to sell to all educational institutions, another to sell to all hospitals, and another to sell to all utilities, etc.—all within the same geographic area.

All companies train their sales personnel to sell their products or services. However, depending on the size of the company and the sophistication of its products or services, the training period can range from a day of going on sales calls with an experienced salesperson to several months of full-time study at an off-site school. Sales positions in high-technology industries generally require more extensive training periods than others, with additional training necessary when a new product is introduced.

Being in sales comes closest to self-employment of all the positions we will cover in this book. Because you are responsible for developing and managing your territory, it's a lot like running your own business. Here's a *Typical Workday of a Salesperson* in the word-processing equipment industry:

8:30–10:00	Telephone calls to six prospects to try to set up appointments for presentations—three people not in, the others are happy with the equipment they currently use; researches the billing error claimed by Archer Steel with Accounts Receivable Department; prepares Weekly Significant Activity Report detailing new prospects contacted, probability of closing orders and anticipated dates, major problems with existing accounts, contracts signed this week; prepares handouts for distribution to Hamilton Motors personnel at presentation later this morning
10:00–11:00	Travels to Hamilton Motors, a prospective customer
11:00–12:00	Delivers sales presentation to Hamilton Motors personnel, including Purchasing Manager, Office Manager, and V.P.-Administration; conducts demonstration of word-processing equipment
12:00–1:00	Lunches with Hamilton Motors personnel in company cafeteria; calls office for messages; calls three prospects to confirm appointments for tomorrow
1:00–2:15	Starts drive back to office; en route to office, stops at Ridgeley Corporate Office Park for "cold calls" to four companies (two are using competitors' equipment and are very satisfied; one is considering buying equipment for the first time); arranges appointment for formal presentation with the Purchasing Manager (one is using a competitor's product and not happy, but budget is all spent for this year); makes note in appointment book to put prospect in "tickler" file for contact before end of year
2:15–2:45	Completes the trip back to the office
2:45–3:00	Reliable Secretarial Service has called about urgent problem with equipment that's holding up their work for clients; checks with Service Department to find out if problem has been corrected yet; calls Ms. Smith at Reliable to find out if she was satisfied with service provided on problem
3:00–3:30	Reviews weekly competitive newsletter sent by headquarters; notes price increases of several competitors and price reduction of one; re announcement of new machine by Patterson Automation: calls Charlie Miller in headquarters to ask about availability of specification sheet detailing its features

3:30–4:00	Allied Cleaning calls—wrong system delivered; issues correction notice to expedite delivery of correct machine; calls Tom Rich at Allied to give him delivery date and invite him to lunch next week
4:00–6:00	Branch sales meeting: discussion of new sales contest targeting *Fortune* 500 companies; Linda Brown, Manager, reports on branch quota realization to date for quarter—forecast is 5 percent under quota; she asks each sales representative to review status of accounts and develop plan to help branch exceed quota, for presentation to her by 10:00 A.M. tomorrow

While the above represents a fairly routine day in the life of a salesperson, other typical duties include

- travel to another city twice yearly to represent the company at an industry trade show;
- travel to a resort twice yearly to attend a three-day national sales meeting on new products, sales strategies, and competitive developments;
- travel to the corporate headquarters to participate in a task force aimed at improving some aspect of the sales process, e.g., faster processing of orders, better customer service; and
- training other sales personnel.

Manufacturers' Representatives

Sales consulting companies, called "manufacturers' representatives" or "independent agents," are hired by companies to serve either as a sole sales force or to augment a small sales force by providing coverage of geographically remote territories. Many independent agents represent product lines of several noncompeting manufacturers that can be promoted to the same customer segment. For their efforts, manufacturers' representatives will earn a commission on the sales of the products they represent. From a manufacturer's perspective, independent representatives, as they are also known, represent a cost-effective alternative or supplement to an internal sales force.

One can be hired as a manufacturers' representative either directly by a manufacturer or as an employee of a manufacturers' representative company. The primary advantage in being a manufacturers' representative on your own is that it is essentially self-employment. For further information on the activities of manufacturers' representatives, contact the Manufacturers' Agents National Association. (See page 33.)

Headquarters Sales

In the sample workday described earlier, you saw references to interactions between our mythical salesperson and people in the headquarters of the company. These people, known as "headquarters sales" personnel, provide assistance that enables field sales personnel to do their jobs effectively. Typical headquarters sales activities may be organized along the following divisions:

SALES ADMINISTRATION: This function:

• analyzes sales of various products and models within product lines on a national and regional basis. These analyses provide management with information that they use to
> evaluate the performance of sales offices;
> identify products whose sales are deviating significantly (either up or down) from forecasts and increase/decrease production levels accordingly; and
> identify competitive strengths and weaknesses that are often implied by the company's sales results.
• researches, compiles, and distributes information about competitive product/service offerings to field sales offices.
• prepares contracts for special pricing.
• organizes and manages the company's participation in trade shows, including exhibits, new product demonstrations, customer meetings; also plans and organizes national and regional sales meetings. (In some companies this activity will be handled jointly with, or exclusively by, the marketing function.)

INVENTORY MANAGEMENT: In a manufacturing company, occasionally there are orders for greater quantities of products than the available inventory can support. As such, headquarters sales personnel must

• research how much of each product is available for shipment;
• make decisions as to which customers will be allocated products for which there is a greater demand than availability; and
• work with marketing and manufacturing personnel to increase production.

NATIONAL ACCOUNTS: Because of the structure of a field sales organization (described on page 231), sales representatives who have the headquarters of a large company in their territories have the burden of trying to service the customer's geographically dispersed locations properly—not to mention handling other accounts as well. In addition, if other field representatives are required to service remote locations of that person's major customer, it would create inequities. These problems, coupled with the need to ensure a consistency of service throughout all customer locations, have provided the impetus for companies to establish national account groups. Located at the headquarters of the company, national account staff coordinate the activities of the company's branch personnel calling on nationwide locations of the account. In some companies, they handle all sales negotiations with personnel at the customer's headquarters; in others, field personnel conduct negotiations with local customer personnel, while national accounts people coordinate and monitor their activities. Other typical duties of national accounts personnel include

- instructing sales personnel in an account's organizational structure and purchasing practices;
- devising marketing strategies to generate additional sales from the account;
- preparing special reports for the account on its nationwide billing activity with the company; and
- organizing and leading meetings during industry trade shows.

SALES (CUSTOMER) SUPPORT: Depending on how a company is organized and what kinds of products or services it offers, it may also have a headquarters and/or field function called "Sales Support" or "Customer Support." For example, a company that manufactures stationery products will not need a formal customer support function since its products are not technically complex. While there may be defects in some of its products, the products will be returned and replaced rather than being repaired. On the other hand, a company that manufactures ultrasonic cleaning equipment will require sales support personnel to respond to customers' questions about equipment operation, and maintenance and troubleshooting procedures.

Since this type of company is likely to receive requests for all sizes and shapes of equipment to serve the needs of businesses from jewelers to heavy-equipment manufacturers, it will need people in headquarters who can gather information about customers' technical needs and act as liaisons to the Engineering department in developing price quotations and providing product technical specifications.

It is important to bear in mind that sales support is usually distinct from the customer service function. The latter is responsible for responding to customers' inquiries regarding pricing, order status, etc., and in some companies sales support personnel may also accept and process orders.

Note: it is quite common for field sales personnel to be transferred to the headquarters sales function of the company, assuming either lateral or higher-level responsibilities, and then move out to the field again. Headquarters sales people who want to move into field sales jobs may similarly have opportunities to do so.

A *Typical Workday of a Headquarters Sales Specialist* in a company manufacturing audio equipment could look like this:

8:00–9:30	Modifies report-generating software program to add a new column of information, percentage increase in sales from last month to current month, to monthly national sales report; enters last week's sales data into computer system, and issues electronic mail message to all branches informing them that report can be printed at their terminals
9:30–10:30	Meeting with Al Lansing, Sales Administration Manager, to develop faster procedures for arranging special pricing for customers
10:30–11:30	Reviews material regarding company's participation in industry trade show; writes memo to Al Lansing outlining recommendations regarding exhibit size, location, costs, etc.
11:30–11:45	Conference call with Jay Allen, Audio Buyer for Goodbuys, and Ann Shuster, Production Planner at manufacturing plant, to discuss increase in production of model R45 radio to meet the forecasted demand for the product, and changes in quantities to be shipped to two of their distribution centers
12:45–1:45	Attends presentation given by Compuconcepts on data-base software package being considered for department's planned customer data base
1:45–2:00	Prepares electronic mail message for distribution to all branch offices on price increases/decreases announced by three competitors
2:00–3:30	Reviews and edits weekly sales data for 24 radios; inputs data into computer system; prints weekly report and analyzes it for significant sales increases/decreases in each of eight regions around the country; calls managers of two of the regions to inquire about the probable reasons for unusually low sales for several models; writes memo to Al Lansing, Manager of Sales Administration, detailing the reasons given
3:30–4:00	Reviews telex message from manufacturing plant regarding their receipt of shipment of 15,000 defective knobs for model R48 radio for Sunshine Stores order; conference call with Marketing, Purchasing, and Manufacturing to discuss feasibility of getting knobs up to quality standard from same or alternate supplier in time to meet production schedule

4:00–4:30	Call from Barbara Nelson, Atlanta Branch Administrator, regarding incorrect branch sales data reported for models R38 and R25 clock radios in last week's report; prepares electronic mail memo noting error for distribution to all recipients of weekly sales report
4:30–5:00	Calls hotel where national sales meeting will be held to discuss audiovisual equipment requirements with Lou Como, Meetings Manager; prepares letter confirming details of telephone discussion, to be sent to Lou
5:00–5:30	Orders stationery and computer supplies; reads memo from Joan Wilcox, Sales Representative in New York Branch, regarding suggestion to add co-op* ad expenditures by product to monthly sales report

Other duties that a headquarters sales specialist may perform include

- participation in one or two trade shows yearly, with responsibility for representing the company at its exhibit and at meetings with key customers;
- participation in semiannual three-day sales meetings held at a resort, with responsibility for coordinating on-site logistics;
- working with a computer programmer or systems analyst to design a sales analysis/forecasting or inventory allocation system; and
- meeting with marketing personnel to provide feedback from field sales representatives on customers' opinions of current and proposed new products.

Human Resources

Of all the functional areas in a business organization, the human resources department is the one with which most people are familiar, since job hunters almost always have contact with representatives of an employer's personnel department. But the recruiting function is only one of a number assigned to this department. Others are Benefits and Compensation Administration, Equal Employment Opportunity/Affirmative Action, Training and Development, and Industrial (Labor) Relations. The larger the organization, the greater the likelihood that each of these functions will be handled by staff dedicated to the function. In a small company, one individual may be responsible for all these areas.

The best ways for career changers to enter the field are through personnel generalist, recruiter/manpower (succession) planner, and training and development positions.

---

*Co-op ads are jointly paid for by manufacturers and retailers.

Recruiting/Manpower (or "Succession") Planning

In a large company, recruiting responsibility is usually divided into two functions, exempt recruiting and nonexempt recruiting. "Nonexempt" means not exempt from overtime pay, and applies to hourly workers—laborers, clerks, secretaries. "Exempt," on the other hand, means exempt from overtime pay, and applies to professional (salaried) employees. (Occasionally, salaried employees are paid for overtime on special projects; this is called "scheduled" overtime.)

A typical progression would be from a position entailing recruiting of nonexempt personnel to exempt recruiting, since nonexempt positions are not as complex as exempt, and are easier for an entry-level recruiter to learn. After proving oneself as a nonexempt recruiter, one could be promoted to exempt recruiter. In some companies, one might be able to start as a recruiter of professional employees. Depending on the size of the company, one person may be responsible for handling professional recruitment for all functional areas, i.e., Sales, Engineering, Marketing, Public Relations, etc., or for only two or three. It's the recruiter's responsibility to understand fully the requirements for positions within his or her assigned areas; this implies a lot of interaction with managers in those departments. Thus a recruiter assigned to the Engineering Department would meet with the various engineering managers to determine what openings must be filled, and the necessary educational and professional qualifications sought in the candidates. A recruiter's job would likely entail these additional responsibilities:

- engaging and interacting with employment agencies and executive recruiters;
- planning and coordinating on-campus recruitment programs;
- writing and placing advertisements for personnel;
- conducting initial screenings of résumés forwarded in response to ads or from employment agencies, and determining which applicants appear to be best qualified for the job;
- administering employment tests;
- interviewing applicants; and
- checking candidates' references and credentials.

Usually, both the recruiter and the hiring manager will interview each candidate privately, later comparing notes on their evaluations. Although the recruiter's opinion is valued, if the functional manager and recruiter disagree on the attractiveness of the candidate, the hiring manager's opinion will prevail, since he or she is the one to whom the individual would be reporting. Once the decision is made to make an offer to a candidate, the recruiter will assist the hiring manager in arriving at a fair salary, and will deliver an oral offer to the candidate, representing the company in any negotiations about the terms of the offer. This individual would also be responsible for preparing a letter formalizing the terms of the employment agreement.

Manpower (or "succession") planning refers to the planning of the organization's exempt personnel needs and is often an integral part of a recruiter's job. Thus a recruiter/manpower planner would also work with the managers in his or her assigned departments to forecast personnel needs, identify those individuals currently in the organization who can be expected to fill positions at higher levels, and assist functional managers in developing plans to upgrade all employees' skills through training programs and on-the-job experiences.

In addition to handling recruiting and succession planning responsibilities, this individual will also act as an adviser to the functional managers within his or her jurisdiction on

- handling employee grievances and identifying potential legal implications;
- assisting with periodic performance and salary reviews;
- developing corrective action plans for poorly performing employees and, when necessary, terminating them; and
- helping the functional managers deal with personal problems that impede their employees' performance, e.g., substance abuse, marital problems.

What follows is a *Typical Workday of a Recruiter/Manpower Planner* in a medium-size company:

8:00–8:30	Meeting with Ann Wilcox, Design Engineering Manager, to determine how many electronics engineers are authorized for new Smart Radio project, and to agree on salary ranges and job specifications
8:30–10:00	Interviews two candidates for Sales Administration job opening.
10:00–10:30	Meeting with Bill Wigdon, Manager of Sales Forecasting, regarding poor performance of Alex Collingswood, one of his reports; outlines to Bill the steps that company policy requires before Alex can be fired
10:30–11:30	Participates in meeting with Bill Wigdon and Alex Collingswood to give Collingswood a warning on his poor performance during the past three months, and to determine why his performance has deteriorated; prepares written confirmation of warning and obtains Collingswood's signature
11:30–12:30	Joint presentation with Gail Preston, Attorney, and Alan Dunbar, Personnel Manager, to all managers on procedures for conducting a lawful employment interview

12:30–1:45	Luncheon interview with George Freemont, candidate for Electronics Engineering position; at conclusion of lunch, escorts him to interview with Ann Wilcox, Design Engineering Manager
1:45–2:30	Paperwork: prepares reports for hiring managers on interviews with Engineering and Sales Administration candidates
2:30–3:00	Meeting with Ann Wilcox, Design Engineering Manager, regarding Jim Callahan, top-performing electronics engineer, offering his resignation; recommends setting up meeting with Jim and matching offer he accepted with promise of managerial job within one year
3:00–4:00	Meeting with Dick Miller, Manager of Systems and Programming Department, Ned Fanton, Systems Analyst, and other company recruiters to outline specifications for company's first computerized data bank on employee skills, and to establish schedule for completion of project
4:00–4:30	Meeting with Susan Morgan, Advertising and Sales Promotion Specialist, and her manager, Elaine Cooper, to outline reasons she is being terminated; explains the severance package she is being given and her rights to continue her health insurance
4:30–5:00	Prepares report on termination meeting with Susan Morgan for file
5:00–6:00	Meeting with Gail Preston, Attorney, Wayne Simpson, EEO/Affirmative Action Manager, and George Larrimore, Quality Control Manager, regarding age discrimination suit being filed by Martin Eagleton, who reports to Larrimore; reviews documentation supporting company's position that the function Eagleton performed is no longer needed by the company; agrees to meet with Eagleton and his attorney to try to have suit withdrawn

Personnel Administration

This job function is most commonly found in a small-to-medium-size company and provides exposure to all personnel functions. The personnel generalist may be responsible for:

- acting as liaison to union officials;
- planning a company outing;
- mediating grievances between managers and their subordinates;
- developing personnel policies on absenteeism, vacation days, tuition refunds, etc.;
- designing and administering an employee-recognition program;

- writing job descriptions and establishing salary ranges;
- writing and placing recruitment advertisements;
- interviewing and evaluating job candidates;
- evaluating the costs and benefits of various health insurance plans; and
- conducting orientation programs for new employees.

Following is a *Typical Workday of a Personnel Generalist* in a medium-size company:

8:30–9:30	Meets with Dan Wood, Sales Representative for Worldwide Insurance, to review Worldwide's proposal for adding dental insurance coverage to the company's current medical plan
9:30–11:00	Meeting with Alice Dixon, Shop Steward of company union, to review grievance filed by Marjorie Ainsley regarding a recent disciplinary action
11:00–12:00	Prepares revisions to employee benefits handbook; submits revisions to John Wallace, Human Resources Manager, for his approval prior to printing
12:00–1:00	Luncheon interview in company cafeteria with Dan Riccio, candidate for plant engineering position
1:00–2:00	Participates in meeting aimed at improving plant security, following significant shortages of some inventory items and the theft of one typewriter
2:00–2:30	Meeting with Susan Miller, Account Representative for Superior Insurance, to review their proposed major medical insurance plan, which is expected to save the company 5 percent over current plan costs
2:30–3:00	Reviews David Pinckney's worker's compensation insurance application for accuracy prior to submittal to insurance company
3:00–3:15	Reviews and approves three employee requests for tuition reimbursement for courses completed this past semester
3:15–4:15	Studies fifteen résumés received in response to ad for industrial engineer job in last Sunday's paper; forwards the seven best to Jack Riley, Industrial Engineering Manager; calls newspaper to kill ad for this weekend

| 4:15–4:30 | Phone call to Commemorative Plaques to arrange for three plaques for employees with 25 years of service; phone call to employment agency to arrange for temporary word-processing operator to work in Accounts Receivable next week |
| 4:30–5:30 | Meeting with Carol Stern, company attorney, regarding design of new performance appraisal form for exempt employees |

Training and Development

This function, which has grown dramatically in the past ten years, is responsible for ensuring that employees develop the skills necessary to perform their present jobs, as well as for preparing them for higher levels of responsibility. Small and medium-size companies, i.e., under $200 million annual sales, usually don't have in-house training staffs (high-technology companies are notable exceptions). However, they may be just as active in developing their employees' skills as are large companies, making extensive use of training consulting companies.

In a large company, the training and development department will design, conduct, and administer training programs. It will also hire training consulting firms to conduct courses that the company has evaluated as meeting its standards. The types of courses companies offer their employees range from highly technical subjects related to engineering and manufacturing to training in general professional and interpersonal skills, and in personal growth. While the teaching of highly technical subjects is left to experts in these areas, learning how to lead a course in those other areas is a fairly easy task. Subjects addressed in these courses include

- managerial training—supervisory skills, budgeting, and decision making;
- management problems—counseling poorly performing employees, dealing with requests for higher salaries by valued employees, conducting termination interviews, etc.;
- effective written/oral presentation;
- time management;
- sales training;
- applied creativity; and
- interpersonal communication skills.

If the proper materials are available, an articulate, intelligent person with no training experience can rapidly become proficient in leading a business training program. Most training programs conducted in industry range from one to five days, with some as long as two to three weeks or more. Also, courses in the business world are unlike most college courses in that, in addition to oral presentations by the trainer, they make extensive use of

- films and audio tapes;
- case studies that simulate situations that class participants can expect to encounter on the job; and
- role-playing interactions within teams of two participants that simulate on-the-job situations.

What follows is a *Typical Work Week for a Training Specialist* in a consulting company that sells a sales training course to industry:

Sunday

3:00–5:00   Arrives at hotel in Chicago where three-day sales training program will be conducted for Wyman Company; confirms main meeting room and smaller meeting room arrangements with Assistant Manager; sets up classroom for 20 participants, placing required materials at each seat; sets up 35 mm movie projector and audiocassette player; prepares smaller meeting rooms with flip charts, chalk, pencils, writing pads

5:00–6:00   Greets participants in reception room during social hour

6:00–7:00   Dinner in hotel dining room with class

7:00–9:00   Introductory session; outlines program objectives; has participants introduce themselves to the group and explain what they hope to gain from the course

Monday

8:30–10:30   Delivers talk on importance of the sales function to the operation of any business; assigns case study designed to have participants analyze the sales process; participants move to smaller meeting rooms in assigned groups to work on case study; calls office for messages while participants work on case study

10:30–10:45   Coffee break; checks with main desk for telephone messages for class participants; distributes them to recipients

10:45–12:30   Presentation of case study analyses by representatives of small groups; summarizes conclusions of presentations; presents talk on results of study analyzing most frequent mistakes made by salespersons in presenting their products or services

12:30–1:30   Lunch in hotel dining room with class

1:30–3:30	Presents film on sales strategies; leads class discussion on film's contents and asks participants to describe personal sales experiences that support or refute film's points; assigns case study to small class groups; small groups move to assigned rooms; upon their return, reviews case study analyses by presenters
3:30–3:45	Coffee break; collects/distributes telephone messages for class participants
3:45–5:00	Plays audio tape of discussion between salesman and prospect; asks class to comment on strategies salesman implemented that were presented in film shown earlier; assigns new case study to class subgroups; groups return after half hour; reviews case study analyses by group representatives
5:00–6:00	Social hour in private room with class
6:00–7:00	Dinner in hotel dining room with class
7:00–9:00	Each participant outlines to class a sales problem facing him or her; assigns teammate to each person to assist in resolving sales problem by employing techniques studied thus far

Tuesday

8:30–10:30	While participants work with teammates privately to develop solutions to individual sales problems, reviews drafts of three proposed case studies being considered for upcoming customized sales course for Dolen Construction
10:30–10:45	Coffee break; confirms that limousines will be waiting at 2:00 tomorrow to take class participants to airport; collects/distributes telephone messages
10:45–12:30	Each person presents his or her solution to teammate's problem to class, with class members evaluating effectiveness of solutions
12:30–1:30	Lunch in hotel dining room with class
1:30–3:30	Assigns individual sales problems to each of five groups of four participants; explains videotaping procedure; introduces Bill Lathrop, the video technician who will circulate through the meeting rooms to assist in use of equipment; explains videotape assignment and procedure for each group to critique its members' performance; participants go to rooms to conduct videotape sales presentation exercises; while participants are videotaping, calls Hank Stanton, Human Resources Manager at Dolen Construction, to discuss case studies for their forthcoming customized training program

3:30–3:45	Coffee break during afternoon video exercise; collects and distributes phone messages
3:45–5:00	Videotape presentations continue; visits meeting rooms to check on progress
5:00–6:00	Social hour in private room with class
6:00–7:00	Dinner in hotel dining room with class
7:00–9:00	No class; takes swim in hotel pool

Wednesday

8:30–10:30	Shows film on techniques for closing a sale; assigns role-playing exercise to participants; selects four people to participate in two role-playing sessions on closing the sale; conducts role-playing sessions; leads class discussion of strengths and weaknesses of role-playing interactions
10:30–10:45	Coffee break; gathers participants for class photo session; collects telephone messages for participants; calls office for messages
10:45–12:30	Shows film on importance of record keeping for sales personnel and on benefits of computer software packages that allow development of customer and prospect data bases; conducts discussion about the film, and has participants talk about information management techniques they currently use; shows film on legal aspects of sales activities, including how to reduce liability risks for company and how to legally gather competitive information; conducts class discussion; has participants complete course-evaluation forms and collects them; distributes certificates of completion to class participants; dismisses class after announcements about limousine location, etc.
12:30–1:30	Lunch in hotel dining room with class
1:30–2:00	Packs belongings and checks out
2:00–5:00	Limousine to airport; flight back to Denver; checks in with office for messages; returns calls to two clients; goes home

Thursday

| 8:30–10:00 | Arrives in office; prepares report on Chicago class, including details on incorrect quantities of materials, problems with hotel facilities, etc.; prepares expense account form for trip to Chicago |

10:00–11:00	Reviews registrations for three upcoming sales courses; calls client contacts to get titles of two participants, which are missing from roster; calls Production Department to arrange for shipment of appropriate quantities of materials for the three courses
11:00–12:30	Meeting with Jane Hickham, Manager, on proposed modifications to sales training course; discusses areas needing changes; establishes schedule for their implementation
1:30–2:00	Returns calls from Production Department and several accounts
2:00–4:00	Starts work on modifications to sales training program
4:00–5:30	Analyzes brochures on competitive offerings and prepares memo evaluating the apparent strengths and lackings of those programs for Jane Hickham

Friday

8:30–10:00	Participates in staff meeting on organizational changes, anticipated new business, competitive developments, new procedures for filling out expense account forms, and new procedures for producing course materials
10:00–1:00	Works on development of new sales course specifically for telecommunications industry
2:00–3:00	Reviews evaluations of this week's course; prepares memo addressing three complaints
3:00–4:00	Telephone call to Ann Easton, Human Resources Manager of Ralston Bearings, to discuss tailoring the company's sales training program to Ralston's needs
4:00–4:30	Phone calls to Houston hotel to arrange for meeting rooms and audiovisual equipment for Conyers Air course in two months; confirms prices and availability of local limousine service and photographer
4:30–5:30	Examines shipment from printer for next week's Harper Foods class; notifies Production Department that modification to first case study was not included in this shipment, but should be corrected for next printing; reproduces twenty copies of corrected version for next week's course in Seattle

Public Relations

The complexity of many companies' operations today makes it virtually inevitable—even if they manage their businesses honestly—that some of their actions will not be viewed favorably by one or more groups with which they interact, i.e., consumers, employees, shareholders. And, too, a few companies commit illegal acts—cheating on government contracts, illegal banking practices, knowingly marketing dangerous pharmaceutical products—that are guaranteed to generate bad publicity. Counteracting the image problems that result from a company's actions is the task of the public relations staff. But even without any negative publicity, a company may have the desire to enhance its image as an organization that is community service–minded, innovative in its industry, or concerned about its employees. Regardless of whether the objective is to minimize negative publicity or enhance an image, similar tasks are involved: arranging for speaking engagements for top executives, as well as writing their speeches; establishing and cultivating relations with the media; planning and conducting press conferences; writing an employee newsletter and other communications.

Two areas that fall under the umbrella of public relations, but which entail somewhat different duties, are investor relations and community relations. If a company is publicly held, it is important to promote it as an attractive investment to the financial community. Investor relations staff coordinate communications with stockholders and financial analysts in brokerage and investment banking firms; their job is to emphasize the company's positive financial results and minimize negative performance. Community relations people may calm the nerves of the residents of a small town where a major manufacturing plant is planned, represent the company on the boards of charities and civic organizations, and review requests for donations from these organizations. Some very large companies have an educational relations function as well, which prepares communications for distribution to students.

Companies usually have to be of substantial size before they establish in-house public relations functions. But that does not mean that small- and medium-size companies do not engage in PR activities. Companies of all sizes hire public relations consulting firms, known as public relations agencies or counselors, to provide either all the PR services they need or, in the case of a large company, to augment the company's PR capabilities during times of special need—for example, when a crisis receiving a lot of public attention strains the company's internal resources. The public relations department may also get involved in improving the company's relations with its own employees by conducting attitude surveys, and instituting a regular program of communications.

Following is a *Typical Workday of a Public Relations Specialist* in a medium-size company:

8:30–9:30	Meets with Ruth Madden and Gene Fox of Harris Medical Center to plan company's sponsorship of road-running race, including schedule, route, publicity, awards, etc.
9:30–10:00	Prepares press release announcing company's backing of race; submits to area newspapers and radio stations

10:00–12:00	Meets with Terry Miller and Ann Ward of Communications Concepts to outline schedule for design and production of annual report
1:00–1:30	Prepares press releases announcing appointments of Howard Rogers and Patricia Frank to Director of Personnel and Director of Marketing, respectively; submits to local and national business editors
1:30–2:30	Reviews three requests for company to sponsor local causes, including charitable event, town's 200th birthday, and local hospice; prepares recommendation to Sam Burton, Director of Public Relations, for company sponsorship of town's birthday and for donation to hospice, along with recommended contribution; prepares letter to the one organization whose request was rejected
2:30–3:00	Returns phone calls from three local reporters seeking confirmation of company's plan to relocate its main manufacturing plant to a town 25 miles away
3:00–3:30	Prepares draft of article on company's new benefits package for publication in next issue of employee newsletter
3:30–5:00	Prepares speech on the need for corporate social responsibility to be delivered by Ross Warren, Chairman of the Board, to Lions Club meeting next month
5:00–6:00	Meeting with Sam Burton, Director of Public Relations, and Howard Rogers, Director of Personnel, to plan press conference next week formally announcing company's plans to relocate its main plant; reviews possible questions that could be raised and appropriate responses

Other typical duties of a public relations specialist include

- writing an annual report, if it is a publicly held company;
- representing the company at trade association meetings;
- representing the company at legislative hearings on issues affecting its business;
- serving on cultural and charitable organization boards and working on fund-raising programs;
- developing guidelines governing the conduct of senior management in their interactions with outside organizations; and
- monitoring company product programs and activities for their potential impact on the public and recommending communications programs to minimize negative effects.

10

Suggestions for Special Situations

COMMUNICATING EFFECTIVELY

All jobs can be classified in terms of the degree to which they involve working with things, people, and information. As a professional, your work is heavily oriented toward the people and information areas, which means that you have to do a lot of communicating: listening, talking, reading, and writing. While all these modes of communication are equally important, writing and speaking, because they are visible and audible activities, can be especially instrumental in contributing to your advancement within an organization—not to mention getting the job in the first place.

Commonly Made Errors in English

In my interactions with clients and other professionals I have repeatedly noticed a number of mistakes in the use of English. Since any of these could arise in a job interview and create a negative impression of one's communication ability, I would like to present them here. These common errors are

- Using the word "like" instead of "as," as, for example, in the expression "as I said." While the use of "like" in place of "as" may be widely accepted, it is, in the opinion of many well-educated people, an improper substitute, one that reflects a lower level of education and culture.
- Pronouncing "asterisk" as "asterick." There is no such word as "asterick."
- Using "verbally" to mean "orally." "Verbally" means through the use of words. Thus, whether a communication is written or spoken, it is done verbally. "Orally" means spoken.
- Using the contraction "there's" with a plural predicate. "There's" is a

contraction for "there is." Many people use expressions such as "There's a lot of people" or "There's a few reasons," which is incorrect, because "is" implies a singular—not a plural—predicate. The correct phrase to use when dealing with plural predicates is "There are."

- Using "pacific" instead of "specific." "Pacific" means peaceful. "Specific" refers to a particular instance or item.

Addressing Speech and Voice Problems

Earlier I stressed the importance of using a tone of voice and speech during the job-hunting process that enhance your candidacy. Once you get the job, the way you speak will influence your effectiveness with others in negotiating resources and commitments and, consequently, your promotional opportunities.

According to Sara R. Johnson, a speech pathologist, voice and speech problems fall into any of the following categories:

- the sound of the voice, e.g., too high- or too low-pitched; raspiness; hypernasality (sounding as though you are speaking through your nose);
- the clarity of speech, e.g., saying "w" when you mean "r";
- the processing of your language, i.e., your ability to present your thoughts so that they will be understood by others; and
- dysfluency, e.g., stuttering.

If you have a voice or speech problem, you should consult either an ear, nose, and throat specialist or a certified speech pathologist. If a physician determines that the problem is not medical, he or she will probably refer you to a speech pathologist. Should you first go to a speech pathologist, she or he will, depending on the type of problem, refer you to a physician to rule out any medical cause. If a physician determines that there is a physiological basis for your problem, the problem can sometimes be corrected surgically. For example, in the case of hypernasality (the creation of a sound that makes you appear to be speaking through your nose), the reason for the nasal sound may be that there is insufficient musculature to close off the nasal canal during oral speech. Surgery may be able to rectify this physiological problem, but after speaking that way for a number of years, speech therapy may be necessary to train one to speak differently.

I once had a woman client who was very presentable and intelligent, but whose voice had a raspy quality. Since I strongly believe in the advantage of using the telephone over the letter as an initial method of contact, I pointed out to her that the sound of her voice might make some people think she was unfriendly, since they would not be able to see her warm facial expressions in a telephone conversation. I suggested that she go to an ear, nose, and throat specialist to see if there was a physiological basis for the problem. She called me several months later and I did not recognize her voice—it was as soft as velvet. She told me that a physician had diagnosed her condition as nodules on her vocal cords. He removed them and the raspiness disappeared, enabling my client to convey a dramatically improved impression.

An accent is another example of a speech problem that can impede one's communication effectiveness, since many people tend to ascribe less intelligence to those who speak with certain kinds of accents. Distinctive regional accents may evoke this kind of reaction. Naturally, an accent is only a problem when the speaker is in an environment where most people speak differently. Fortunately, eliminating an accent is not difficult if you obtain the assistance of a speech professional.

Many companies, especially the larger ones, offer insurance plans that compensate employees either partially or fully for speech therapy. In some cases, therapy costs will be covered only if the speech or voice problem is physiologically based, or if an accident caused the problem. To find a Certified Speech Pathologist in your area, contact the American Speech and Hearing Association. (See Information Sources below.)

Anyone who has the money can spend thousands of dollars on the most appropriate clothing for a new job. But that money might as well be thrown in the garbage if the individual's communication skills aren't at least at a level consistent with the quality of his or her clothing. It may be harder to acquire good communication skills—but, unlike clothing, they never wear out and they never go out of style.

Information Sources

Toastmasters International, P.O. Box 10400, Santa Ana, CA 92711, 714/542–6793. This not-for-profit educational organization is devoted to the improvement and development of individual communication and leadership skills. There are more than 5,700 Toastmaster clubs and 120,000 members in the United States, Canada, and other countries. Members learn and practice techniques of effective public speaking and gain speaking experience related to specific career needs. Annual dues are nominal.

American Speech and Hearing Association, 10801 Rockville Pike, Rockville, MD 20852, 301/897–5700.

YOUR APPEARANCE

Some time ago I received a call from a young man who had just graduated from college with a major in journalism. He was disappointed with the results of his first professional job campaign in which he initiated contact with prospective employers; he wondered if I might be able to help him.

Whenever I get a call like this, I ask the person the same three questions:

1. How many prospective employers did you contact, by letter or telephone?
2. How many interviews resulted?
3. How many offers did you get?

I learn a great deal from the answers to these questions. If the answer to question number two is 10 percent or less of the answer to question number one, I immediately suspect that the individual's résumé and letter—or telephone contact—were weak. On the other hand, as the answer to number two rises to 20 percent and above *and* the answer to number three is zero or a very low percentage, then I start to suspect strongly that the person's interview presentation was at fault.*

The answers I got from this fellow were: 45 letters sent, 18 interviews, zero offers. In other words, he generated a 40 percent return rate on his mailings, and a 0 percent return on his personal appearances. Now, 40 percent is quite an unambiguous substantiation of the quality of the impression he made on paper. Although none of his contacts with these companies were in response to ads, I knew that 18 employers would not have granted him interviews just to be courteous; a good number of these had to be situations where a bona fide job was open, or about to be. So I told this fellow that based on the numbers he had given me, the only conclusion I could reach was that his zero-offer rate could be ascribed to how he conducted himself in the interview and/or his appearance. A long silence followed, after which he told me that he was very obese. I told him that it was now clear to me why his campaign was a failure. He was astonished when I told him that employers would hold his weight against him, but the fact is that many employers today are looking for physically fit candidates and will often exclude a person because of his or her weight.

Does this mean that a lot of competent people will fail at their job-hunting efforts merely because of this factor? Probably, so if people who are considerably overweight are in careers that entail working for others, they will enhance not only their chances of employment but also their opportunities for advancement by keeping their weight to an acceptable level.

There are a number of reputable weight-control companies that assist overweight people in losing weight in a sensible fashion, as opposed to the fad diets that so many people undertake. Check your local Yellow Pages under "Reducing and Weight Control" or similar heading.

Dress in a Manner Appropriate to Your Company and Position

All organizations have dress codes—written or unwritten—and while adhering to the code may not be a guarantee of success, not complying with it

---

*The individual's occupation and the economic climate in which the job hunt is being conducted will cause these threshold numbers to vary.

will almost always ensure that you will not be promoted above the level at which you were hired. If the dress code is formally communicated to employees, there is no doubt about its contents. When it is not, however, as is usually the case, the best way to determine the policy is to observe how each level in the organization dresses, and dress as though you are already in the next position on your career ladder. When you are considered for promotion, you will have reinforced your visual image as a successful candidate. If you have the technical and professional qualifications required for the job as well, you will come across as a strong candidate. But be careful not to dress better than your boss does—the watchword in business is to make your manager look good. Dressing in a fancier way than your boss does may make her or him feel threatened, which is certainly not conducive to your good relationship.

If you have an interview with a company and have no idea what its dress code is, you may be able to learn a lot by observing the employees as they arrive at or leave the offices, if the organization is in a facility of its own.

In a mobile society such as ours, if you shift your employment location from one geographical region to another, you may have to observe a different dress code. For example, West Coast professionals dress less formally than their counterparts on the East Coast. In isolated, rural areas people tend to dress less formally than in large urban areas.

Consider Getting Professional Assistance

Even when people know what the dress code is, they sometimes feel unsure about the colors and styles best for them. A whole industry has sprung up to satisfy the need to dress well on the job. You can draw on the following professionals to enhance your fashion know-how and image:

Image Consultants: These are people who critique your entire presentation, and make recommendations for improvements in all areas, e.g., speech, dress, posture.

Color Consultants: These are individuals who may be affiliated with any of a number of national companies that conduct group and private counseling on color selection for men and women.

(To find image and color consultants refer to "Image Consultants" and "Color Consultants" headings in your local Yellow Pages directory.)

Personal Shoppers: Many stores today offer their customers the services of a personal shopper who will assist them in putting together wardrobes suitable for their professional activities. These services are usually free, since they almost always result in large purchases by the customer. If your favorite store does not offer a formal personal shopping service, the store will probably be agreeable to providing it to you, since your use of it will translate into profits for them.

Information Sources

John T. Molloy, *John T. Molloy's New Dress For Success*. New York: Warner Books, 1988. Offers advice for men on selecting each component of their wardrobes, e.g., suits, shirts, accessories. One section is devoted to guidance on dressing for job interviews. The book also has a chapter on the differences in dress in about 20 regions of the country, which will be useful to men who do business with companies in these areas.

Carole Jackson and Kalia Lulow, *Color for Men*. New York: Ballantine Books, 1987. Helps the reader determine his most flattering suit style and fit. Also advises on how to select the most suitable colors, and how to build a business and casual wardrobe to reflect your personality; tips on hair styling and grooming are also included.

Carole Jackson, *Color Me Beautiful*. New York: Ballantine Books, 1985. This book guides women in analyzing their looks to determine the optimum color category. Using that as a basis, the author proceeds to show the reader how to select the most flattering clothing styles—including caveats on which to avoid—for their figures; also offers advice on makeup.

Janet Wallach, *Looks That Work: How to Match Your Wardrobe to Your Professional Profile & Create the Image That's Right for You*. New York: Viking, 1986. After discussing the psychology of clothing, the author explains how women in each of three types of jobs—corporate, communicator, creative—can build wardrobes that are consistent both with the requirements of their professional lives and their personal tastes.

IF YOUR RIGHTS AS AN APPLICANT WERE VIOLATED

Title VII of the Civil Rights Act of 1964 prohibits discrimination in employment on any of these grounds: race, color, sex, religion, or national origin. To enforce this law the Equal Employment Opportunity Commission was established in 1965. Since 1979, the commission has also been responsible for enforcing

- the Age Discrimination in Employment Act (ADEA), which protects workers between the ages of 40 and 70;
- the Equal Pay Act (EPA) of 1963, which protects women and men performing substantially equal work from pay discrimination based on sex; and

- Section 501 of the Rehabilitation Act of 1973, as amended, which prohibits discrimination on the basis of handicap.

In 1978, Title VII was amended to encompass the Pregnancy Discrimination Act, which requires employers to treat pregnancy and pregnancy-related medical conditions as they would any other medical disability with respect to all terms and conditions of employment, including employee health benefits. In 1981, the definition of discrimination under Title VII was expanded to include sexual harassment, i.e., where one's ability to obtain, retain, or advance in employment is linked to giving sexual favors.

Title VII applies to any of these types of organizations having 15 or more employees:

- private employers
- state and local governments
- educational institutions
- labor organizations

It is unlawful for an employer to discriminate with regard to the following:

- job advertisements
- recruitment
- testing
- hiring and firing
- compensation, assignment, or classification of employees
- transfer, promotion, layoff, or recall
- use of company facilities
- training and apprenticeship programs
- fringe benefits such as life and health insurance
- pay, retirement plans, and disability leave
- causing or attempting to cause a union to discriminate
- other terms and conditions of employment

It is unlawful for an employment agency to discriminate with regard to

- its own employees on the basis of race, color, religion, sex or national origin;
- receiving, classifying or referring applications for employment;
- job advertisements.

The types of remedies available under Title VII include reinstatement, hiring, reassignment, promotion, training, seniority rights, back pay, and other compensation and benefits.

In addition, many states have passed legislation similarly prohibiting the discriminatory practices I've enumerated, and have incorporated into the law certain remedies that may augment the federal law. For example, some states prohibit employment discrimination on the basis of marital status. In addition to providing specific remedies to address violations of the law, state laws may also enable plaintiffs' cases to be tried in a speedier fashion than those filed with the federal EEO Commission.

Despite the federal and state laws, discrimination on the cited illegal grounds is still rather widespread for several reasons:

- many people are unaware of their rights under the federal and state laws;
- many individuals victimized by discrimination do not want to undergo the strain of filing an EEO complaint and/or lawsuit and appearing in court;
- some employers are ignorant of the law, and some others might knowingly ignore it.

Naturally, if victims of employment discrimination fail to take action against it, those guilty of it will persist in their discrimination, and others will be victimized, too.

How to File a Discrimination Complaint

The process of filing a discrimination charge goes like this:

- You can telephone or mail your complaint to the Equal Employment Opportunity Commission.
- If you communicate your complaint by telephone, the Commission will mail you a copy of your oral complaint and ask you to sign it.
- The Commission will then conduct an investigation of your complaint. While it is considerably more advantageous to your case if you have witnesses to the discrimination, even if you do not you may still win— the Commission will investigate whether other applicants or employees were illegally discriminated against and, if so, may find that your claim is justified.
- The Commission will review your charge and hold a fact-finding conference at which you and the employer will discuss your allegations and, depending on the outcome of the conference, determine whether there is reasonable cause to believe discrimination has occurred.
- If the Commission investigation shows no reasonable cause, you and the employer will be notified of these findings, and you will be issued a "right-to-sue" letter, which permits you to take your case to court, if you choose.

Most charges filed with EEOC, even those where the Commission decides to sue, are conciliated or settled before trial. If, however, the EEOC finds that there is reasonable cause to believe that discrimination has occurred and yet is unable to conciliate your charge, the Commission will consider litigating your case and, if so, a lawsuit will be filed in federal district court.

There are time limitations on filing charges, which vary, depending on whether the charge is covered by the EEO law, the Age Discrimination in Employment Act, or the Equal Pay Act. To get detailed information on procedures for filing charges, call the EEOC's toll-free number: 1–800–USA-EEOC (202–634–7057 if you are hearing impaired), or write to them at: U.S. Equal Employment Opportunity Commission, 2401 E Street, NW, Washington, DC 20507.

Sexual Harassment

As I mentioned earlier, sexual harassment is considered a form of sex discrimination, and is covered by Title VII. There are many regional organizations that give advice on how to deal with sexual harassment, as well as offer educational programs to corporations on how they can prevent it. If you would like to get in touch with one of these organizations, a state agency that handles employment discrimination complaints may be able to help.

LOOKING FOR A JOB DURING A RECESSION

Recession. The very word sends chills up the spines of even the most seasoned and skillful professionals, for it's a period of layoffs and of frustrating—and often fruitless—job-hunting campaigns. Furthermore, the fact that this country has experienced six recessions in the past thirty years means that everyone in the job market will probably have to look for a job during a recession sometime. But there are some actions you can take that can enhance your prospects of getting a job during a recession.

Target Industries That Prosper During Recessions

One approach you can use is to concentrate your job-hunting efforts on companies in industries that benefit during recessionary periods, if your field is not industry-dependent. For example, one industry that is well known for prospering during a recession is leasing, since businesses must use their working capital during these slow periods to meet inventory and payroll requirements. Computers, as well as transportation and construction equipment, are most likely to be leased during recessions. To find leasing companies, use the *Standard Industrial Classification Manual* to find the SIC codes for leasing industries and then reference companies in those industries in the *Million*

Dollar Directory. (See page 82 for guidance on using the SIC code to research data on companies in a targeted industry.)

Other beneficiaries of the business sector's goal of reducing fixed costs during a recession are temporary employment and manpower services and business consulting services. The *Consultants and Consulting Organizations Directory* (see Appendix, page 281), available in many public libraries, contains information on consulting firms throughout the United States.

One of the most important objectives of any business organization is to increase market share and to protect it from eroding, since once it does, it's very difficult to reclaim the lost share. During a recession, businesses will often increase their advertising and promotional budgets, since generating the same number of sales in a tight economy will require that their brand names be displayed to more consumers. Therefore, end-user advertising and sales promotion departments might be good targets for job hunters. (I don't recommend the agency side of the business, since it's volatile even during nonrecessionary periods.)

Companies that publish books for the general public usually do not suffer during recessions—people can always justify the few dollars they spend on paperbacks, since they cut back on vacations and other luxury purchases. Similarly, the wine industry weathers a recession well; although consumers reduce their frequency of dining out, they tend to splurge a little more in preparing meals at home.

The Implications for How You Approach an Employer

Earlier I talked about the pros and cons of using go-betweens to obtain employment. During a recession it is even more important for you to initiate contact on your own, since employers are more reluctant to pay the agency and recruiter fees. The one exception to this is at the top-management level; even during tight economic times, companies usually do not lessen their use of recruiters to find executives—although that doesn't mean they would turn away a qualified applicant who initiated contact with them.

Another job-search strategy is to target organizations within your local area. It costs employers anywhere from $10,000 to $50,000 to move an employee and his or her family. Employers are very happy to avoid incurring this expense by finding a qualified individual who doesn't have to be moved.

Lastly, if applicable to your work, be sure to emphasize any cost-control accomplishments both on your résumé and in an interview.

More Resourcefulness Is Required During a Recession

If any generalization holds true in looking for employment during a recession, it is that those people who rely on advertisements and agencies and recruiters as their sole sources will probably be disappointed. During good economic periods initiating contact with prospective employers is highly advisable, but in a recession it is imperative. Studying business developments and thinking hard about what opportunities may be implied by them—as we did with *The Wall Street Journal* (page 90)—will be the most fruitful job-hunting method.

If you seriously apply the guidelines I have presented here, you will surely be better prepared to conduct a job search during an economic downturn.

IF YOU WERE FIRED OR LAID OFF

Whether through a layoff or an outright firing, losing your job is hard to face. But there are actions you can take that will minimize the impact, and help you find a better one in the shortest amount of time.

Understanding the Employer's Perspective

While there are numerous firings for fairly flimsy, usually political, reasons, the most understandable reason still accounts for the vast majority—namely, financial. Put yourself in the employer's position and imagine that sales may have fallen off in a business of your own, or that you had to make a decision about keeping a long-standing employee versus hiring someone with a skill you need to give you the competitive edge you must have to survive and grow. Do you think you might feel the pressure to terminate some employees, even though you like them personally? I believe that this is an important issue to address, because if you harbor ill will toward an employer who fired you, it's likely that your negative feelings will prevent you from launching an energetic, upbeat job campaign.

Severance Benefits

Many businesses have demonstrated their support of humane treatment for fired employees by providing very good termination benefits, including outplacement services, the cost of which can equal 10–15 percent of the employee's gross annual salary. The larger companies are well known for providing comprehensive outplacement assistance, but the service is by no means universally available. If you have been fired and your employer makes no mention of outplacement help being available at the company's expense, try to negotiate it, using as your argument the fact that it is a fairly common practice. If you have been employed at the company for a number of years, you can bolster your case by pointing to your contributions to the organization.

Many states have regulations governing procedures for firing employees, e.g., requiring employees to be offered the option of continuing their health insurance for a number of months. Contact your state Department of Labor and ask for a copy of the state's employment regulations.

Negotiating Employer Support for Your Job Hunt

Even if your job is terminated for reasons unrelated to your performance, prospective employers will usually believe that a company—especially a large one—that was satisfied with your performance would have found another job for you. Thus, whether you are fired because of dissatisfaction with your performance or through a layoff, always try to negotiate the company's support in allowing you to tell prospective employers that you are still working there. This imposes the responsibility on the company of providing you with telephone coverage, since some prospective employers may call you at the office. When people call you they should be told "She's at an off-site meeting" or "He's out of town for the day." You must call in for your messages daily, or have someone in the company call you with them. The key point to impress upon your employer is that anyone who could be the recipient of a call for you must be coached properly in handling your phone messages.

If your employer is not immediately agreeable to providing you with this service, explain that it is a very common practice in major companies. Even when employees are fired for poor performance, companies today appreciate the possibility that the situation resulted from a mismatch between the employee and the employer, as opposed to the employee being a bad egg.

If your employer agrees to provide you with telephone coverage, leave your office number when you call prospective employers. Saying you are on vacation as the reason for having them call you at home will not fool them.

Dealing in a Job Interview with Being Fired

If you were laid off from your job at a large organization and explain that to a prospective employer, he or she may wonder aloud why the organization could not find a place for you elsewhere in the organization. If you didn't accept offers in your former organization because it would have meant shifting your career focus, explain that to the interviewer. Another way of responding is to point to some significant differences between your former organization and the prospective employer, emphasizing that it's important that your next employer offer characteristics A, B, etc.—which you know the new employer to have and your former one not to have.

Nowadays being fired is not considered in as negative a light as it was in the past, probably because people have come to realize that there can be a wide range of reasons for firing an employee, few of which may have anything to do with an individual's ability to perform on the job. Partly as a result of this, many companies have a policy of limiting the information given to reference inquirers or investigators. If a prospective employer does know that you lost your job, your best strategy is to come across as confident and enthusiastic about finding a new and challenging opportunity. Above all, avoid sounding defensive or angry, since that will decrease your chances of beginning a new job soon.

When companies fire employees they often offer to provide them with excellent references to expedite their job search. If you are no longer with the company but have been able to negotiate an agreement with your employer that allows you to say that you are still employed, you should not use the company as a reference. Once a prospective employer hears that your former company is providing a reference, the suspicion arises that you were fired. Your best strategy is to give the impression that this is a confidential job hunt—offer to give prior employers only as references.

I once had a client who had worked for just one company during his fourteen-year career and had run into a political problem, resulting in his being eased out, but with the company offering to provide him with professional services to obtain a new job. In our initial discussion, he told me that his manager would give him an excellent reference. When I advised him against using it, he became very concerned about how a prospective employer would know what he was capable of doing if he could not give his current one as a reference. Well, a prospective employer was able to ascertain this man's capabilities during a three-hour interview, and he got an offer following that (his first) interview—although he gave not one professional reference.

Managing Stress—Managing Time

Some suggestions for dealing with the strain of being unemployed:

• Get into a regular routine of exercise, since that will make you feel better, and will help give you the energy you will need to come across as a vigorous candidate.

• Find out about local support groups for unemployed people sponsored by churches or civic organizations. These can be very helpful, both in giving you the emotional support you need to motivate yourself during your job hunt and in providing leads for possible jobs in other companies. If no groups of this kind exist, consider starting one—within a short time you will probably have more members than you can handle. If you are not the kind of person who is comfortable in a group but feel you need some support, consider short-term counseling by a psychologist or therapist.

• Get yourself a part-time, temporary job that will help reduce your worries over your financial situation, yet will allow you enough time to conduct your job hunt in an expeditious manner. If you are entitled to unemployment compensation, investigate with your state Department of Labor the implications for that benefit if you undertake limited employment.

• Negotiate an arrangement with a friend who owns a business, whereby you'll volunteer some time to assist him or her in dealing with vendors, proofreading reports, and answering telephones in exchange for word processing of your letters, use of the copying machine, etc. If your employer has agreed to provide you with telephone coverage until you obtain a job and to say that you are still employed by them, remember to give your old office number as a call-back number when you make phone calls from this location.

If there is a period of time when you are between jobs and your sole daytime activity is looking for one, make every effort to live as structured a day as when you had to report to work. Arise at the same time, and even if you are conducting your search from home, maintain a nine-to-five schedule.

Learn from the Experience

No one is going to tell you that being fired is a festive occasion. But as another instance of change in your life, it can be used as an opportunity— for example, you could explore new options that you would not have been willing to do before because you were in a "secure" position. And if one thing you learned from the experience is that being a loyal employee for fifteen or twenty-five years is no guarantee of job security, that isn't so bad—it's better to acknowledge the reality of the workplace and be prepared for it. This way, if it happens again, you will not be caught unaware and have to recover from the shock of learning the truth before you can begin a serious job-hunting effort.

Information Sources

Robert Coulson, *The Termination Handbook*. New York: Free Press, 1981. This book provides advice to employees who have been fired, including how to ensure that they get the various benefits (severance pay, unemployment insurance, vacation pay) they deserve. Employers are also given guidelines for terminating employees.

FOR TEACHERS, SOCIAL WORKERS, AND COUNSELORS SEEKING CAREER CHANGES

If you are a teacher, social worker, or counseling professional who has become dissatisfied with your work, you have probably been eyeing the business world as offering opportunities for an alternative career. I would like to assure you that despite the differences between the work you have been doing and the requirements of business careers, you have every reason to be optimistic about your chances of success in business. The communication and interpersonal skills that are mainstays of your profession are every bit as critical in the business world. Any intelligent person is capable of performing a great number of jobs in business satisfactorily, but those who *excel* at these tasks are those who have superior skills in human interaction—in negotiating resources from colleagues, communicating information, and motivating others.

Despite my optimism about your chances of success, the reality is that there are some people with hiring authority in companies who may not be as convinced of the transferability of your skills. And the significant differences between your present work environment and that of a business organization may require some adjustment on your part. Lastly, the large number of your colleagues who similarly seek business careers translates into stiff competition in realizing your goal. As such, I would like to offer some suggestions to make your transition as successful as possible.

Identifying Alternative Careers

The business function most akin to the work environments of teachers, social workers, and counselors is the human resources area. The training and development function (described in detail beginning on page 242) draws upon some of the same skills teachers use in their work. And with more and more employers offering some kind of counseling to their employees (see the discussion of Employee-Assistance Programs, beginning on page 58), social workers and counselors may find it relatively easy to move into the business environment. Lastly, the Affirmative Action/EEO and recruiting/manpower planning functions also draw upon counseling skills in researching and resolving employee grievances.

But if you are a teacher, social worker, or counselor, your sights should not be limited to these areas. You should consider all the fields described in Chapter 2, depending on your interests and capabilities, and, if you are willing to undertake formal study to prepare for a new career, many more fields will be open to you.

Targeting Prospective Employers

Regardless of the field you select, try to identify employers that are in the not-for-profit sector. For example, if you aim for a public relations career in a traditional consumer or industrial company, consider a two-step approach, with your first job being in a union, hospital, or trade association. Because these types of organizations are somewhat less competitive than business organizations, you'll experience less of a culture shock while getting your bearings in the new field.

Conducting Your Job Campaign

If you are a teacher, your inclination would probably be to wait until your summer vacation to launch a full-scale campaign. For this reason you should not, since your colleagues will likewise be planning summer job-hunting campaigns. One human resources executive told me that during the summer, executives in his company are contacted by many teachers who want to start business careers. While it may be less convenient for you to conduct a campaign during the school year, you may still have an hour or two after the school day to make phone calls (which should be conducted after hours anyway) and conduct your interviews . . . and have the distinct advantage of less competition.

Preparing Your Résumé

As a career changer, your résumé should be prepared in the functional format (see page 103) so that you can encourage the reader to think of you in terms other than teacher, social worker, or counselor. Here are some functional categories that may apply to the job you seek, along with suggestions for points to include:

Training and Development	If you use this heading, emphasize, if possible, the design of sophisticated audiovisual materials and development of curricula. Most important: describe any experience training other professionals, or any group of adults.
Administrative	Just about every job entails some administrative duties. The best ones to include are preparing reports, developing/administering budgets, writing grant requests, researching and evaluating vendors and suppliers, hiring and supervising people to provide support services for your organization.
Counseling	If you are a social worker or counselor seeking a counseling position within industry, emphasize your work with drug- and alcohol-dependent individuals and relocated families; also include any experience as group leader or facilitator.
Liaison	Examples of liaison responsibilities relevant to teachers, social workers, and counselors include representing your employer to professional groups and at conferences, and interactions with social service agencies.

Public Relations
Describe any experience in promoting your organization or school function—for example, establishing media contacts, writing press releases, planning and managing fund-raising events, negotiating the support of civic and business leaders.

The résumé presented on page 137 puts these guidelines into practice.

Conducting Yourself in an Interview

Be prepared to respond to questions regarding your ability to adapt to a business environment, which is quite different from your current one. A good way to address the issue is to draw parallels between the two environments. Here are some that may apply to your situation:

- Business positions often entail time-critical projects; you, as a teacher, social worker, or counselor, have curricula to present, a caseload to manage effectively, or crises to handle and are, therefore, highly skilled in time management.
- Business positions have a lot of paperwork, i.e., reports, proposals, budgets, etc.; you have paperwork, too—reports on students/clients; grant requests, proposals, budgets.
- Business positions often entail statistical analyses; in your job you may be required to perform statistical analyses of student populations or of client cases.

Explaining Why You Are Interested in a Business Career

As for how to explain your reasons for leaving: if you are like most people who leave your profession, you are attracted to the business world because of the higher financial rewards. Since the business sector is driven by the desire for money, this kind of response will be viewed as an acceptable reason for leaving. Explain that because you are a highly motivated, intelligent person, you would like to be rewarded for your efforts and believe that the business sector offers you that opportunity to a greater degree than your present job.

Many thousands of teachers, social workers, and counselors have switched to business careers in the past decade with considerable success, and this should provide you with the assurance that you, too, can make the transition. In fact, the executive you contact for a job may have similarly switched from your field, making the job of selling yourself that much easier.

11

Some Advice for Women, Minorities, and Those Over 50

FOR WOMEN

Women have made considerable gains in professional employment in the past decade, and have demonstrated to employers that they are just as capable as their male colleagues. However, as women, we may sometimes assume that the employer today views men and women candidates equally. I do not believe this to be true, and would like to offer some suggestions designed to offset some perceived liabilities of women on the part of employers.

Writing Your Résumé

A study was described in *Psychology Today** in which researchers mailed the résumés of two female M.B.A. students who had written their theses on job discrimination against women. The study concluded that when the résumés of these women did not include mention of the titles of their theses, the number of interviews generated was twice the number in cases where the thesis title was included. The obvious reason for this disparity is that employers may feel "gun-shy" when considering hiring a woman who vocalizes her support for women's rights, since that may imply that she would be a "walking lawsuit."

Because of this, if you wish to have the greatest chance of being accepted, do not include on your résumé mention of organizations that may imply that you are a militant feminist. On the other hand, if you are a militant feminist, you may feel that you don't want the job if you are not taken for the real person you are. That is your decision. It is my responsibility, however, to

---

*"Women's Lib: Love It—Quietly," *Psychology Today*, December 1985, p. 10.

provide you with this information, which will enable you to make an informed choice.

If an employer is considering a female candidate for a professional job who is thought to be married, he or she may assume—usually correctly—that her husband is also a professional whose employer may transfer him someday to another city. And, although nowadays there are men who follow their wives to jobs in new locations, the reverse is still much more common. Therefore, in considering a married woman applicant, an employer may be wary about investing a lot of time and money in someone he or she believes may leave in a couple of years. So, I recommend to my single and divorced female clients that they include a line of personal data, solely for the purpose of stating that they are single or divorced. I also suggest that they include several other items in this line—for example, "U.S. citizen, travel acceptable, excellent health"—to make the motivation for including it less obvious.

Another way to deal with this situation—and this applies regardless of whether you are married, single, or divorced—is to state on the résumé that you would consider relocation. The end of the profile section is a good place for this.

Getting the Interview Appointment

Despite the major strides made by women in professional positions in recent years, some male executives still harbor—consciously or subconsciously—a belief that women are not as effective in getting things done in organizations where people have to be fairly aggressive about negotiating for limited resources. Therefore, women seeking professional jobs in the business sector must project an image that will offset this impression, invalid as it might be. Initiating contact using the telephone will accomplish this objective, especially if you have to be pretty persistent about getting to speak to the person.

The Briefcase/Handbag Issue

I have noticed that many women use both a briefcase and handbag during the business day, and I recommend against it—both at the interview and once you are employed by the organization. First of all, it looks cumbersome; secondly, unless both your briefcase and handbag are hanging from your left hand or shoulder, you will find it awkward to shake hands with an interviewer.

Scents and Good Sense

A serious mistake made by women is wearing a strong scent to an interview. As a matter of fact, I recommend to my women clients that they wear no perfume either at the interview or on the job. If you have ever gotten a whiff of someone's perfume and wondered how she could have the poor taste to wear it, you might appreciate that someone could have the same reaction to yours. It is well known that humans have extremely diverse reactions to scents. Since you have no way of knowing what reaction an interviewer or colleague may have to yours, wouldn't it be a smart insurance policy not to wear any perfume, since as long as you bathe you can be sure that your unscented odor will not be unpleasant?

Clothing, Makeup, and Hair

Because the range of acceptability in women's clothing is much wider than in men's, there is much greater room for error and, in fact, I have seen a lot of mistakes made by women in this area. Just how you should dress for an interview and the job will depend largely on the type of industry you are in. For example, the fashion industry's dress code is much more flexible than the banking industry's. It is not my objective to prescribe how you should dress for business, but rather to call your attention to the importance of knowing how to dress. There are many books on the subject of women's dress in business. (See page 254 for suggestions.)

As with clothing, the fashion industry is more tolerant of a lot of makeup and elaborate hair styles. In other, more conservative work environments, however, women who wear a lot of makeup or who sport glamorous hair styles convey the message that they are more interested in looking glamorous than in doing the job. A study described in *Psychology Today* simulated a situation in which women candidates were evaluated for competence by personnel consultants.

> . . . personnel consultants judged businesswomen photographed under two different grooming conditions: one very feminine and made up, the other plainer and less sex-typed. The more feminine style included longer hair or hairstyles that concealed the face; soft sweaters, low necklines or ruffled blouses; dangling jewelry; and heavy makeup. In the other condition "candidates" wore tailored clothes with a jacket, subtle makeup, and either short hair or hair swept away from the face.*

The conclusions of the study were that

> . . . candidates groomed in a more feminine style were perceived to be less managerial; less intrinsically interested in work; less likely to be taken seriously by others; more illogical and overemotional in critical decision-making; less financially responsible; more helpless

---

*"The Eye of the Beholder," *Psychology Today,* December 1984, p. 50. Reprinted with permission from *Psychology Today* magazine. Copyright © 1984 (APA).

and dependent on the influence of others; sexier and more flirtatious in social relations; and less assertive, independent, and self-confident than those groomed in a less sex-typed style.*

If you are a woman you may resent the extent to which you must go to accommodate the perceptions of others. If this is the reality that characterizes the environment in which you want to succeed, it might be worth it to you to adjust your presentation. Remember, too, that you are not alone in having to consider the consequences of your appearance—in some organizations beards and mustaches are not tolerated, or white shirts are mandatory, creating a similar set of constraints for men.

In preparing for a job interview, you will naturally spend a lot of time thinking about how to present yourself, since you know that this will influence the outcome of an important event in your career. While your day-to-day job is not an interview per se, it is in the sense that you are *always* being evaluated . . . with important implications for your advancement. Therefore, the advice presented in this section should be observed throughout your employment.

FOR MINORITIES

By "minority," I mean those ethnic groups covered by the federal Affirmative Action program, i.e., individuals of black, Hispanic, Asian, Pacific Island, American Indian, and Alaskan native backgrounds. Here are some suggestions that members of these groups—and ethnic groups not covered by Affirmative Action—may want to use to enhance their job-hunting and on-the-job effectiveness.

Targeting Employers

An experiment† was conducted that entailed playing a tape of a meeting for participants while they were shown pictures of the people supposedly taking part in the discussion. The material on the tape did not change, but the composition of the all-male group did. In one of the situations, one member of the group was black; the rest were white. The other scenario had a mixed black-white group. When the experiment participants were asked to comment on the content of the discussion in the meeting with only one black man, they considerably exaggerated the importance of the black man's in-

---

*Ibid, p. 51.

†Shelley E. Taylor, "A Categorization Approach to Stereotyping." In *Cognitive Processes in Stereotyping and Intergroup Behavior,* David L. Hamilton, ed. (Hillsdale, NJ: Lawrence Erlbaum Associates, Inc., 1981).

volvement; when they were asked to comment on the content of the mixed meeting they did not single out any black participant's behavior as different from the rest of the group's. What this study tends to demonstrate is that when an individual is obviously very different from a group of which he or she is a member, observers of the individual's behavior tend to be influenced more by the individual's difference from the rest of the group than by his or her behavior.

If you are a member of a minority group, the implication of this study is that you should strive to identify organizations where members of your ethnic group are employed in numbers as large as possible. Thus you can increase the probability that both your effectiveness on the job and others' perceptions of your performance will not be overly influenced by something as irrelevant as your ethnic origin.

Since it would not be wise to question an interviewer about the organization's employment of members of your ethnic group, you must determine this information another way. During the interview process be especially observant as you walk through the hallways of the company en route to the interviewer's office. Make a point of asking to use the rest room, since the route may provide you with additional insight into the composition of the employee population. If the company is a manufacturing firm, you could ask for a plant tour. While you take mental notes about minority employees, you'll be racking up points as an interested candidate.

Still another approach you may be able to use to ensure that your ethnic group is adequately represented in an organization—and to enhance your chances of being considered for a job—is to target organizations that are known to be managed by members of your ethnic group. Many states compile lists of businesses owned by minority individuals, since many nonminority companies, in order to conform with government regulations, give a certain percentage of their business to minority-owned companies. You might find the management of these companies very receptive to considering you for employment. To find out if your state government can provide you with this information, refer to the *National Directory of State Agencies* (see Appendix, page 278), which is probably available in your local public library, and send an inquiry to your state's economic development commission. *The Minority Business Telephone Book* (see Information Sources following) lists 10,000 businesses owned by black, Hispanic, Asian, and native Americans, categorizing them by product or service category. Black job hunters could study a list of the 100 largest black-owned companies in the country, published annually by *Black Enterprise.* (See Information Sources following.) Also valuable is the magazine's monthly column detailing executive changes in the black business community. In Chapter 3 I discussed the opportunities resulting from executive changes.

A valuable reference book containing information on over 7,000 organizations and programs serving minority individuals is *Minority Organizations:*

A National Directory. (See Information Sources.) Corporations having EEO/ Affirmative Action Programs sometimes use this directory to recruit minority employees. Explore how you can become affiliated with any organizations that can provide you with exposure to the kind of employer you are seeking.

Preparing Your Résumé

Because many employers are interested in hiring qualified minority applicants, it would be helpful to your candidacy if the fact that you are a member of a minority group is obvious to anyone reading your résumé. For some minority applicants—for example, those of Hispanic or Asian ancestry—this is often communicated through their last names. For others, however, this is not the case. If your name does not imply that you are a member of a minority group, you could join a professional or community organization having a name that would immediately communicate that you are black, American Indian, or Eskimo, and list that organization under the heading "Memberships" on your résumé. A hypothetical example would be an organization called "Black Business and Professional Women's Caucus." Make sure that you do not list an organization whose title might imply that you might be too militant for an employer. To research organizations, refer to the *Encyclopedia of Associations*. (See Appendix, page 278.)

Communicating During an Interview and on the Job

I cannot overemphasize the importance of good communication skills, since a professional—as opposed to a blue-collar worker who rivets an airplane part—performs his or her job largely by receiving, processing, and communicating information and ideas. A study reported in *The New York Times** concluded that the English spoken by black Americans is becoming increasingly different from standard English. If you are black and you target employment in organizations primarily composed of whites, bear in mind that using language that is different from your co-workers' and supervisor's may make it hard for you to be understood, undermining your effectiveness. And while the study cited in the newspaper article dealt only with blacks' use of English, any member of a minority group—especially one whose native tongue is not English—who wants to be successful in an organization consisting mainly of U.S.-born Caucasians should be sensitive to the effect of his or her language. While pride in their heritage may make people cultivate or retain language differences, they sometimes do so at the expense of economic success.

But even being extremely analytical about one's speech may not be suffi-

---

*"Black and Standard English Held Diverging More," *The New York Times*, March 15, 1985, p. A14.

cient as a way of addressing this issue, since I know what I mean to say when I speak, but others don't. Therefore, my advice is that if you have any doubt about your speaking effectiveness, consult a licensed speech pathologist who will not only tell you whether your use of English should be improved, but can give you speaking exercises to attain a good level of communication. To find a speech pathologist in your area, consult your family physician or an ear, nose, and throat specialist, or contact the American Speech and Hearing Association. (See Information Sources following.)

There are also speech-improvement consultants who can be very effective in this area, and whose fees may be less than those of speech pathologists. However, since these are unlicensed practitioners, finding a competent one may be more difficult. If your local Yellow Pages has a listing for "Speech Improvement Consultants" or a similar category, you might call a few and try to obtain references of former clients.

Your Dress

Your dress is an important part of your total presentation on the job. Generally speaking, organizations peopled mainly by whites have fairly conservative dress codes. These are usually unwritten policies and are not communicated to each new employee, but since white employees have grown up with role models who themselves have had experience in these organizations, they are usually aware of these codes.

On the other hand, because minority individuals may come from environments with different customs, they sometimes dress in a manner inconsistent with the organization's dress code. While I certainly respect any minority individuals who decide to retain their form of dressing as a reflection of ethnic pride (and, in some instances, I know that their clothing may reflect religious beliefs), I must also point out that sometimes these individuals do so, unfortunately, at the expense of their advancement in white-dominated organizations.

If you are a member of a minority group and would like assistance in how to dress in a manner conducive to your success in a predominantly white organization, see below for some books offering advice on the subject.

Information Sources

American Speech and Hearing Association, 10801 Rockville Pike, Rockville, MD 20852, 301/897–5700.

Minority Organizations: A National Directory, Abbott, Langer & Associates, 548 First Street, Crete, IL 60417. Lists over 7,000 minority-group organizations and programs developed by other groups to serve minority-group members. Includes a geographical index.

Black Enterprise, 130 Fifth Avenue, New York, NY 10011, 212/242–8000. Publishes annual list of the 100 largest black-owned companies; also has monthly column on executive changes.

The Minority Business Telephone Book, 18 Hemlock Lane, Monroe, CT 06468, 203/268–1160. Lists 10,000 minority-owned businesses throughout the United States, categorizing them by product/service category.

FOR THOSE OVER 50

In a survey conducted by Yankelovich, Skelly, and White, 90 percent of 400 employers ranked workers over age 50 "high on attendance, punctuality, practical knowledge and experience, reliability, and emotional stability."* And while these workers might be a bit more inflexible in adapting to new technologies, their higher cost was justified, according to the survey respondents. Nevertheless, age discrimination in employment, which is illegal, does occur today. How much of it is based strictly on the financial implications of hiring older workers—i.e., higher salaries, medical expenses, and contributions to pension plans—is hard to say, but people over 50 do have a harder time finding employment. Therefore, let's consider some strategies you can use if you fall into this category:

Target Companies with Older Top Managers

There are many companies where the top executives are older. Some business directories—for example, the *Reference Book of Corporate Managements* (see Appendix, page 279)—provide the birth dates of executives. While it is no guarantee that you will be treated any better, the likelihood of your being considered a serious candidate by a company whose top executives' ages are, say, 58–63 is much greater than it would be in a company where the ages range from 37 to 42.

Target Organizations That Pride Themselves on Being Humanistic

Unions, educational institutions, and social service organizations, because of their activities and objectives, may be more sympathetic to the plight of older workers. While the pay may be considerably less in these types of organizations, many offer longer vacations than businesses do. In addition, if you're interested in studying for a second career, you should find the free

*"Life After Fifty," *Forbes,* April 28, 1986. Copyright © 1986 Forbes. Reprinted by permission.

tuition available to employees of many educational institutions an appealing benefit.

Explore Senior Personnel Agencies in Your Locality

Many cities have agencies, usually staffed by volunteers, who actively sell local companies on hiring older workers. They usually serve job hunters over 55. To find out if your area has one, contact your state's information bureau or your community's telephone counseling and referral service.

Consider Eliminating Some Dates from Your Résumé

If you are over 50, you might want to consider eliminating the date you graduated from college. In order for this to be effective, you must also eliminate the beginning date of your first job after college—as a matter of fact, you might consider eliminating your first two or three jobs after college. When I am dealing with a client over 50 I will usually summarize his or her several earliest positions in one paragraph, under a heading such as "Prior to 1966." Also, if you are responding to an advertisement or initiating contact with a prospective employer by mail, you could send a letter *only*—which would contain no dates at all. Naturally, in using these approaches, you may raise the suspicion in the reader's mind that you are an older worker. You must weigh the pros and cons of each of the three methods—including vs. not including all the dates on your résumé or sending a letter only—and make the decision for yourself.

While it is true that you will probably have to fill out an application form at any interview, which will request the starting and ending dates of your schooling and employment experiences, the fact that you will already have gotten the interview will be a plus.

Know Your Rights in Looking for Employment

As I explained in Chapter 6, it is discriminatory for an employer to ask your age prior to hiring you, but you can be asked that question for insurance purposes *after* you are hired. If you believe you have been discriminated against during the hiring process, find out how you can deal with it by reading pages 254–257.

Slant Your References and Recommendations to Address the Employer's Concern

Some employers may have a bona fide concern about the health of older applicants. You may be able to minimize this concern by advising your references to use such words as "energetic," "dynamic," "vigorous," and "fast-paced" to describe your work style. If you are using recommendation letters, these should similarly convey an impression of the energy and vitality with which you approach your job.

Consider Consulting Assignments

Even with these strategies, you may still find yourself being rejected for jobs. If so, consider forgoing the search for a job in an end-user company in favor of working for a consulting firm in your field. These organizations need to impress their clients with the skills of the people they assign to clients' projects and would probably be more receptive to you than an end-user company would. And, through exposure to the clients of the company for which you would be working, your work may impress a client sufficiently to elicit a job offer. To find consultants in your discipline, refer to the *Consultants* and Consulting Organizations Directory (see Appendix, page 281), available in many public libraries.

Information Sources

Forty-Plus Clubs

These are autonomous not-for-profit organizations located in many major cities. They are geared toward assisting people at a managerial level. Members receive guidance in all aspects of job hunting and can use the club's facilities as a base from which to conduct their campaigns. Fees are moderate when compared to many commercial services. Check your local telephone directory for a club in your area.

Appendix:
Reference Books Useful to
Job Hunters and Career Changers

Most of these books are rather expensive, but, fortunately, they are very likely to be in your public library or that of a university or college. You will find them to be great timesavers in conducting research. Other helpful books are listed under the "Information Sources" heading of the following sections: Marketing, Purchasing, Sales, Human Resources, Public Relations, Computers, Sports Marketing, Property Management, Employee-Assistance Programs, Meetings and Conventions.

FOR ALL JOB HUNTERS AND CAREER CHANGERS

Business Periodicals Index, H. W. Wilson Company, 950 University Avenue, Bronx, NY 10452. This index, published monthly except in August, enables the reader to use a company name or any one of many industry names and business-related topics to find pointers to relevant articles in numerous publications.

Directory of American Firms Operating in Foreign Countries, Uniworld Business Publications, Inc., 50 E. 42nd Street, New York, NY 10017. Published every two years; contains alphabetical listing of U.S. companies operating abroad. It also contains listings by country of American firms' operations, including address of parent firm and its local subsidiary, as well as information on the product or service involved.

Directory of Corporate Affiliations (Who Owns Whom), National Register Publishing Company, 3004 Glenview Road, Wilmette, IL 60091. This annual directory lists major companies, cross-referencing them according to their divisions, subsidiaries, affiliates, and parent companies. Information can be accessed through a geographical index as well as by SIC code.

Directory of Directories, Gale Research Company, Book Tower, Detroit, MI 48226. Over 9,600 directories are listed in this publication. Information can be located by category (sports, business, law and government, banking, etc.).

Directory of Foreign Firms Operating in the United States, Uniworld Business Publications, 50 E. 42nd Street, New York, NY 10017. This directory, which is published every three years, lists foreign firms operating in the U.S., grouped by country. It provides information on their American affiliates and on products/services.

Directory of Foreign Manufacturers in the United States, Business Publishing Division, Georgia State University, University Plaza, Atlanta, GA 30303. This is an annual directory which provides information on each company's U.S. manufacturing operation, parent company, products, and SIC code.

Encyclopedia of Associations, Gale Research Company, Book Tower, Detroit, MI 48226. Provides brief descriptions, including address, phone, and activities, of numerous types of associations, including trade and business, educational, cultural, social welfare, scientific, engineering and technical, hobby and vocational, labor, athletic and sports, and many others.

Europe's 15,000 Largest Companies, ELC International, Sinclair House, The Avenue, London W13 8NT, England. Published annually in English, German, and French. Includes industrial firms ranked by sales; trading/commerce firms ranked by sales; banks ranked by assets; other rankings of companies in selected industries.

Handbook of Dividend Achievers, Moody's Investor Service, 99 Church Street, New York, NY 10007. Highlights 400 companies that have increased their dividends consistently for more than ten years. Includes historical trends, current performance, and information on number of employees and shareholders.

Million Dollar Directory, Dun's Marketing Services, Three Century Drive, Parsippany, NJ 07054. This annual publication covers over 160,000 U.S. businesses (including privately owned) having net worth over $500,000, listing address/phone, sales volume, number of employees, SIC code, and officers. There are cross references geographically and by business classification.

National Directory of State Agencies, National Standards Association, Inc., 5161 River Road, Bethesda, MD 20816. Lists the contact person in each of 102 functions in each state. Provides the names of elected state officials. Also includes information about associations of state government officials.

The North American Online Directory, R. R. Bowker Co., 245 W. 17th St., New York, NY 10011. Job hunters with a computer and modem might be able to save a lot of time by accessing information on companies and industries through some of the data bases listed in this book. Information on business, scientific and many other types of data bases is provided, as are the names of computer services through which the data can be accessed. Many of these online access companies charge only for usage, with no minimum amount required.

Predicasts F&S Index United States Annual, Predicasts, 11001 Cedar Avenue, Cleveland, OH 44106. A two-volume index, this annual publication categorizes articles in over 750 publications according to industries and SIC codes, products, and companies. Interim updates are also published.

Principal International Businesses—The World Marketing Directory, Dun's Marketing Services, Three Century Drive, Parsippany, NJ 07054. Contains information on 55,000 major companies operating in 133 countries. They are organized by geographical location, industry classification, and alphabetically by name. There is a cross reference of SIC codes and an alphabetical index of product classifications.

Reference Book of Corporate Managements, Dun's Marketing Services, Three Century Drive, Parsippany, NJ 07054. An annual directory, this publication provides detailed biographical information on thousands of executives of leading public and private companies, including schools attended, former employers, and associated dates.

Standard & Poor's Industry Surveys, Standard & Poor's Corporation, 25 Broadway, New York, NY 10004. Analyses of current and long-term prospects for key industry categories are presented in this annual publication, with discussions of the trends and issues of the industries. Comparative analyses of the financial performance of major industry participants are also presented.

Standard & Poor's Outlook, Standard & Poor's Corporation, 25 Broadway, New York, NY 10004. Published annually, with weekly updates. Contains analyses of over 350 industries, reports changes in the preceding year, and evaluates implications for future business activities. Includes historical trends, recent performance data, and forecast tables.

Standard & Poor's Register of Corporations, Directors, and Executives, Standard & Poor's Corporation, 25 Broadway, New York, NY 10004. This three-volume directory is published annually and contains information on 45,000 U.S. corporations, including details on key executives. It has biographies of 70,000 corporate directors and executives and includes information on their memberships and other affiliations. Also provides an index to corporations by SIC and by corporate family groups.

Standard Industrial Classification Manual, Executive Office of the President, Office of Management and Budget, New Executive Office Building, Washington, DC 20503. Lists numerical codes for all industries. This book is invaluable to all job hunters because the SIC code can save a lot of time in using business reference books to find information about companies in selected industries.

Standard Rate & Data Service—Direct Mail List Rates And Data, Standard Rate and Data Service, Inc., 3004 Glenview Road, Wilmette, IL 60091. This book describes hundreds of mailing lists containing the names of businesses and executives in numerous industries. Purchasers of these lists can often select the names they want by a variety of criteria, including ZIP code, corporate level, etc.

Thomas Register of American Manufacturers and Thomas Register Catalog File, Thomas Publishing Co., 1 Penn Plaza, New York, NY 10119. A 21-volume annual directory of manufacturers. Includes company profiles, locations of branch offices, financial ratings, top management, brand names. Information is arranged alphabetically by products and services and by company name.

Ulrich's International Periodicals Directory, R. R. Bowker Co., 245 W. 17th St., New York, NY 10011. This annual publication lists periodicals by subject, e.g., business and economics, education, energy. It also has a section detailing periodicals available through on-line computer access and the vendors offering this service.

U.S. Industrial Outlook, U.S. Department of Commerce/International Trade Administration, Main Commerce Building, Washington, DC 20230. Provides information on 350 industries, e.g., recent trends, the outlook for the year, and the industry's long-term prospects.

Wall Street Journal Index, Dow Jones Company, 200 Liberty Street, New York, NY 10281. This annual index categorizes *The Wall Street Journal* articles by pertinent business or general subject and by company name. It provides a synopsis of the subject and a pointer to the date and page of the publication in which the article appeared.

Ward's Business Directory, Information Access Company, 11 Davis Drive, Belmont, CA 94002. This directory consists of three volumes: the first provides sales volume, market share and other data on 45,000 private U.S. companies and selected public companies having annual sales of at least $11 million; the second contains similar information about 40,000 private companies with sales ranging from $1 million to $10.5 million; the third volume lists private and public U.S. companies by SIC code.

FOR PRACTITIONERS IN SPECIFIC FIELDS
AND INDUSTRIES

Accounting Firms and Practitioners, American Institute of CPAs, 1211 Avenue of the Americas, New York, NY 10036. Lists individuals, accounting firms, and professional corporations whose CPA partners or shareholders are all members of the American Institute of CPAs. Firms and practitioners are cross-referenced by geographic location.

Audiovideo Marketplace, R. R. Bowker Co., 245 W. 17th Street, New York, NY 10011. An annual directory, this includes over 4,000 businesses providing various audiovisual services—production, film/TV, awards/festivals, associations. Information on company executives, products/services, and locations is provided.

Bradford's Directory of Marketing Research Agencies and Management Consultants in the United States and the World, Bradford Directory of Marketing Research Agencies, P. O. Box 276, Fairfax, VA 22030. Contains names and addresses of 900 marketing research agencies and management consultants in the United States, Canada, and abroad, with details on types of services (e.g., surveys, public opinion research, store audits) provided.

Consultants and Consulting Organizations Directory, Gale Research Company, Book Tower, Detroit, MI 48226. Companies are listed by geographical location. One can locate companies according to the fields in which they consult, as well as by key personnel.

Directory of American Research and Technology, R. R. Bowker Co., 245 W. 17th Street, New York, NY 10011. This directory lists over 6,000 parent organizations, along with their 4,900 + subsidiaries. It provides detailed information on type of laboratory, key executives, size of staff, and scientific discipline.

Directory of Management Consultants, Consultants News, Templeton Road, Fitzwilliam, NH 03447. This is a biannual publication listing over 800 companies. The directory indexes these companies by types of services offered, industries serviced, location, and key executives.

Dun's Guide to Healthcare Companies, Dun's Marketing Services, Three Century Drive, Parsippany, NJ 07054. Includes over 10,000 companies in the following businesses: pharmaceutical medications, diagnostic equipment, dental equipment, syringes, optical instruments, health and disability insurance. Information provided includes address/phone, description of business, SIC code, list of products and brand names, and key executives.

Literary Market Place, R. R. Bowker Co., 245 W. 17th Street, New York, NY 10011. This annual directory lists book publishers by geographical location and fields (e.g., cassettes, reference books); it also lists book producers, companies selling services and supplies to the publishing industry, employment agencies specializing in placing book publishing personnel, professional associations for the field, etc.

Polk's Bank Directory, R. L. Polk & Co., 2001 Elm Hill Pike, Nashville, TN 37210. The North American edition of this directory, published semiannually, provides information on state banking board members, examiners, and bank-related associations. The directory lists banks alphabetically, including names of key personnel, statement of bank financial condition, and details on branches. The International edition of the directory, published annually, provides similar information about foreign banking officials and organizations.

Rand McNally Bankers Directory, Rand McNally, Box 7600, Chicago, IL 60680. Published every six months, this directory lists every chartered U.S. bank, including principal location, branch information, classification of assets, and information on key executives. It also includes an international section with information on banks involved in foreign exchange or foreign trade.

Sheldon's Retail Directory of the United States and Canada, and Phelon's Resident Buyers and Merchandise Brokers, Phelon, Sheldon & Marsar, Inc., 15 Industrial Avenue, Fairview, NJ 07022. This is an annual directory covering over 3,100 chain, independent, department, junior department, and specialty stores. The reader can locate key executives in these functions by U.S. states and cities, and Canadian provinces and cities.

Standard & Poor's Security Dealers of North America, Standard & Poor's Corporation, 25 Broadway, New York, NY 10004. Provides information on investment firms, including type of business, location, key executives, and stock exchanges.

Television and Cable Factbook, Warren Publishing, Inc., 2115 Ward Court, NW, Washington, DC 20037. This annual publication covers commercial and noncommercial television stations and networks, providing information on location, owners, key personnel. It also lists cable systems and vendors/suppliers to the industry.

Working Press of the Nation, National Research Bureau, 310 South Michigan Avenue, Chicago, IL 60604. This annual directory contains five volumes: *Newspaper, Magazine, TV and Radio, Feature Writers and Photographers,* and *Internal Publications.* The last volume should be especially useful to job hunters targeting corporate public relations positions.

Index

Ability. *See* Capabilities
Academic degrees, 8, 38
  lack of, 174–75
  M.B.A., 16, 18
Accomplishments
  in cover letter, 143
  importance of quantifying, 114–17
  lack of substantial, 175–76
  in résumé, 112–13, 120–21, 167–68
Accounting. *See* Finance/accounting
  functional area
Administrative functional area, 206–7
  see also Management
Advertisements
  blind/bogus, 78–79
  responding to, 77–79, 80, 97, 140, 258, 274
Advertising (defined), 225
Advertising agencies, 54
Advertising and sales promotion function, 16, 18, 221, 225–28, 258
  career path, 24–25
  job strategies, 23–24
  responsibilities, 22–23
Aesthetics (résumé), 99, 144, 149
Affirmative Action, 269
Affirmative Action/Equal Employment Opportunity function, 237, 263, 271
Age discrimination, 125, 182, 273, 274
Age Discrimination in Employment Act (ADEA), 254, 257
Aggressiveness, 79, 163, 267

Alcoholism, 58–59
American Marketing Association, 20
American Society of Association Executives, 61
American Speech and Hearing Association, 251
Annual reports, 73, 86, 248
Appearance, 5, 251–54
  in interview, 184
  of women applicants, 268–69
Application form(s), 98, 185, 274
Appropriation request(s), 220–21
Aptitude tests, 13–14, 50
Aptitudes, 67
Assertiveness, 182
Attitude, positive, 81, 194

Benefits, 181, 199
  organization size and, 212–13
  severance, 73, 259–60
Benefits and compensation administration function, 237
Body Language (Fast), 176–77
Briefcase(s), 165, 267
Buegler, Jerry, 171
Business associations, 95–96
Business consulting services, 258
Business news
  and job opportunities, 90–95
  about targeted companies, 84–87
Business organizations, 10, 40
  functions of, 3, 15
  see also Companies; Organizations